BRINGING
THE ECONOMY
HOME
FROM THE MARKET

BRINGING
THE ECONOMY
HOME
FROM THE MARKET

Ross V.G. Dobson

BLACK
ROSE
BOOKS

Montréal/New York
London

BLACK ROSE BOOKS No. v186
Hardcover ISBN 1-895431-51-4
Paperback ISBN 1-895431-50-6

Library of Congress No. 92-72629

Canadian Cataloguing in Publication Data
Dobson, Ross V.G.
Bringing the economy home from the market

Includes index
ISBN: 1-895431-51-4 (bound) —
ISBN: 1-895431-50-6 (pbk.)

1. Community development. 2. Social action.
I. Title.

HN110.z9C6 1992 338.9 C92-090360-6

Cover Illustration: Michel Granger

Mailing Address

BLACK ROSE BOOKS
C.P. 1258
Succ. Place du Parc
Montréal, Québec
H2W 2R3 Canada

BLACK ROSE BOOKS
340 Nagel Drive
Cheektowaga, New York
14225 USA

Printed in Canada

A publication of the Institute of Policy Alternatives of Montréal
(IPAM)

Contents

DEDICATION

The Second World War killed one of my two older brothers, in North Africa in 1942. We received the telegram on the Christmas morning when I was eight years old. I answered the door. Forty-eight years later I can still see the telegram boy's grey uniform and high shiny black leather bicycle spats against the red brick wall of our front porch, and I can still recite from memory the telegram my father took from me. I can still hear and see my black-sheep auntie, "the divorced one," out in the lane shaking her fist at Heaven and cursing God.

An R.C.A.F. Sergeant Pilot, my brother is the only Canadian buried in the British War Cemetery at Beja in Tunis, Tunisia. He was 20 years old.

After the war, when I reached my curious early teens, I wondered why such things happen, and what I should study to find out. My father said "economics," but I never did formally study "the dismal science." Perhaps something in me felt that if economics could do such things, I wanted nothing to do with it.

When I did finally go to university I followed my interests and studied classics, philosophy, english literature, aesthetics, film, and city planning, all of which have led me by other avenues now to answer my adolescent question, at least to my own satisfaction.

And, I believe, to what would have been the immense satisfaction and pride of my brothers, Wally and Bill (who survived the North Atlantic war to die in his early forties), and also, to the pride of those others — my parents, Walter and Doris, my grandmother Eliza, "who was a Harriman," and my Aunt Bea, all gone now — who wept in our living room on Christmas morning, 1942.

PREFACE

In The Mid-1930s, I was a late addition — a third son — to a family just coming out of the Great Depression. We lived in what was at that time a working-class rental neighbourhood in a city of nearly 100,000 — London East in London, Ontario. The neighbourhood was predominantly British: English, Irish, Scots, and Welsh. After thirty-three years in Manitoba, with its more diverse ethnic mix, the names of those neighbours now seem exotic. Moon, Golightly, Hexter, Stothers, Dunleavey, Brighton, Ogg, Ford, Yelf: most of them now seem to me almost like icons and incantations in some Celtic mystery.

It was a tight little neighbourhood. It was a community. The relations of the convivial production of home and community life were not so fully *privatized* as they are in Suburbia, 1990. From my bedroom window, I used to observe the work and the gossip that went on in the summer sunshine at quilting bees in the driveway between 86 and 88 Smith Street. If my mother needed help with housecleaning, it came from the other women of the neighbourhood, not from Molly-Maid. These people had survived the Depression together. They gave support to one another, and not merely house and yard work and emotional support either, they were present at all the gateways of one another's lives.

My mother was delivered of me at home with the help of Mrs. Yelf, who was a nurse but who was, in this, simply a neighbour. When my father came home from work that afternoon there was another mouth to feed. But he held me on the day I was born, and so did my grandfather, grandmother, aunt, brothers — and neighbours. By contrast, my own children were born in technocratic medical factories, their mothers sedated by chemicals, and I observed them at first only through glass. Their grandparents lived a thousand miles away, and our neighbours were, although not quite strangers, not intimate members of our private lives.

The community I grew up in had a different physical as well as emotional shape to it. At the top of our three-block street was a major urban thoroughfare, Hamilton Road, with substantial homes and bus service, big brick churches and schools, and stores and shops, restaurants and movie theatres a few blocks in either direction at the major intersections. Downtown was a fifteen-minute bus ride away. I was thoroughly urban, by environment, upbringing, and education. But at the foot of our street, three blocks away, was wild marsh, meadow, bush and farmland along the river — hundreds of acres of it.

Right at the bottom of our street, not fifty feet from the pavement, there ran a living spring you could drink from, fields of goldenrod and bullrushes, and a dense bush where we played run-sheep-run and cowboys-and-Indians, and had secret dens. There was also a producing farm, as well as edible fish in the river. A block away was a bakery you could visit to watch the bakers rolling dough into baked bread that was delivered from door to door. A few blocks farther was a ceramics works that made flower pots, and I could see them molten red in the kiln. Right at the top of the street, in a small, concrete-block building, a mysterious process produced cottage cheese in a long little pool of pungent curds and whey, that the cheesemaker sometimes let me dip from.

I can now only recall that very urban but partly rural space, that vestige of a less specialized and more vital, complex and complete living community, for I cannot visit it any more — it has vanished. And I can now recognize that community life of mutual support created by my parents and their friends only by deduction, for as I grew up into the 1940s and World War Two, economic times had already improved, and the solid neighbourhood on Smith Street off the Hamilton Road was breaking up, and life was becoming a more private thing. I deduce its former communion only from dim memories of conversations at increasingly rare parties and reminiscent encounters between my parents and their former circle of friends, even then dispersing.

I think of that community as I read art philosopher R.G. Collingwood's casual comment that the British tribal consciousness was only finally rendered a mere shadow — as art, entertainment and soccer football — of what it had been as a vital personal, community and religious ethos, by the Education Act of 1870 — only sixty-four years before my birth.

It is perhaps within that shadow of shadows, and with these memories of memories that I approach the issues of Community Economic Development. Nevertheless, I believe I have in that shadowy memory firm ground to stand upon in the discipline. I acknowledge a debt to those who, like my parents, made their communities living places out of the substance of their own lives. I hope I can help to find new ways to do that now for us all, as we create the necessarily new and different future together. I hope we can do it for its own good reasons, and not only if the times be hard.

Ross Dobson
Winnipeg, Manitoba
September, 1992

ACKNOWLEDGEMENTS

I wish to thank most profoundly the two hundred or so Winnipeggers who have over five years joined and taken part in the Winnipeg LETSystem, demonstrating, proving and disproving, by their participation in and rejections of our local LETSystem, various theories and ideas about the possibilities of a non-monetary local economics and a very special kind of Community Economic Development.

I wish to thank especially those who have helped in its development and direction over many discussions, such as Laura Anne Holden and Bryan Hammond, early Directors of Community Circle, Janine Gibson who became Treasurer, Ruth Fletcher who became President, and later members Robin Faye, Jason Loughead, Lydia Giles and Marion Chyzzy who have done invaluable telephone research for the organization which I also used in formal study of the LETSystem.

And I wish to thank my partner, Roberta Simpson, for hours of proof-reading, spell-checking and constructive criticism, and also for her generous support—material, emotional and intellectual — for what often must have seemed to be a hare-brained project.

I also wish to acknowledge and remember my late friend and professor, Kent Gerecke, for his abiding belief in the importance of the LETSystem to the birth of a new economics, and for his guidance and support. I met Kent ten years ago as a co-worker in city politics. Because of him I entered the Master's Program in City Planning at the University of Manitoba, the thesis for which forms the basis for this book, and from which I have now embarked on a further study of how we might develop sustainability based on the greening of our cities. Kent became my teacher, my advisor, my mentor and my friend, and he afforded me—and many another of his students—the invaluable opportunity for publication in *City Magazine,* of which he was a co-founder and editor.

While also conducting a parallel exercise in radical magazine publishing, pamphleteering, civic activism and environmental politics—in which he involved many of his friends and associates—Kent piloted me to my MCP degree. When I got it, he said "Hello colleague," welcoming me as a professional equal. He believed in my professional competence and, because he did, so could I. He died in May 1992, shortly after this text was accepted for publication, tragically aborting the completion of his own book, which would have been a definitive statement on the political history of Canadian cities.

In the pompous words of my thesis dedication I called Kent an "analeptic" teacher, "analeptic" meaning something curative, that acts against disease. Kent not only taught, he mended and he cured. He struggled against disease, those of his own body and soul, and also against the diseases of elitism, of arrogant disempowering professionalism, bureaucratic formality, the loss of responsible, effective citizenship from our civic life, and the growing corporate power in our cities — a deliberate agenda according to which we are to become workers, consumers and taxpayers in our own cities, but not true citizens.

Kent struggled against these diseases, and the disease of social and environmental exploitation and degradation — and he taught others to do so and how to do so. He cared so much — and he was so fierce and passionate in his caring. He taught us who already cared how to care better, how to care more, how to care whole.

As a teacher, Kent taught by example not lecture — which is probably what the word "professor" is supposed to mean. He lived what he taught. As an advisor he always had a wise and considered answer to every question, and it usually showed the way to finding the answer within oneself. A true educator — he led our own knowledge and competence out from our own hidden resources.

Kent Gerecke was the friend one gets only once or twice in a lifetime. After his death, I realized that — although two years my junior — he had begun to fill the void left by the long loss of my older brothers. More than a friend, more than a colleague, more than a brother, he was all of those together. We could *think* together. We had thought to do so much together, to change the city we live in, and the world we live in, through examining and defining the ecology of community. Such was Kent's gift that I believed we could do it, and would do it. And the work would not have been separate from the joy.

PART ONE

Money and Community

Chapter One

COMMUNITY, WEALTH AND POWER
The Context of Our Economic Development

Concerning Development

Both Community Development and Local Economic Development, as disciplines within the lexicon of urban planning, can be described as having local well-being as a goal. I submit, however, that the relations of our present economics, mediated by money as we know it, are fundamentally inimical to both. I believe that our economic system — facilitated by money — destroys community.

The rational economic man of Adam Smith's economics is not a communitarian co-operator, he is an individualistic competitor. He is the hero and common man alike of a system which glorifies him as the be-all and end-all of human existence. But the self-interested acquisitiveness of the system in which he functions is not congruent with the social and cultural development goals of Community Development. Also, for reasons that are structural within our economic system and necessary to it, I believe that the attempt to enhance local wealth and productivity through Local Economic Development cannot achieve either local wealth or local productivity in the long run, functioning within that economic system. If these beliefs are justifiable then, within our present general economic model, only an imperfect and temporary Local Economic Development can ever be achieved, and Community Economic Development cannot be achieved at all. A different model is required.

It seems to me that one possible way to describe *community* development is that it seeks to transfer the unified self-consciousness of the *family* — its sense of unity, uniqueness, identity — to the larger *community*. That would necessarily involve first identifying, defining, or creating a community, and then engendering the functioning of something like a *family* ethic and morality in its relations. Recognizing, then, that those relations should also include internal, self-generated and self-realized *economic* relations of production, exchange and consumption moves community development to include the economic, and hence to become Community Economic Development, as distinct from both Community Development and Local Economic Development. It *combines the goals of each* of them, which suggests the purpose of the new model — recreating a living community which is self-replicating, self-reliant and semi-autonomous, at least in basic needs satisfaction. It is immediately evident that this model is diametrically *opposite* to the *world market economy* we now inhabit and seek to enlarge.

This concept of carrying out the cultural, social and economic development of communities as a *single unified project* is strongly suggested — and so is the shape of the alternative model — by a comment of planning philosopher and writer John Friedmann, if we replace his use of the word *household* with the word *community* in the following passage from *Planning in the Public Domain:*

> To gain their autonomy and to transform themselves into politically active, producing units, [communities] must selectively de-link from the system that keeps them in servitude. Their allocation of time to the exchange economy must be reduced so that resources can be gained for other activities. [Communities] must learn to be more self-reliant in the production of life and do for themselves what they used to obtain from the market.[1]

Applying to communities Friedmann's formula for the autonomy of the family immediately suggests a number of things. Most startling among them is the notion of ceasing to rely on *the market* — meaning the national and world economy we are now being exhorted to plunge more deeply into — and providing internally, within our smaller economic units, what is now usually obtained externally. In other words, he suggests that we should adopt the model of *community economic development.* That short passage also suggests a defining *character* for the community, which is that it must be largely self-reliant economically. This excerpt suggests a definition of what *community* has to become in our society: *a politically active, producing unit* — which, of course, also adds the dimension of *political* as well as *economic* autonomy. While this is not a political tract, it is, I believe, self-evident that the economic necessarily engenders the political.

There are three notions in the definition of community derived from Friedmann. The least contentious of them is *unit,* which is fundamental to the word *community* itself. But even here, questions of the degree, complexity and completeness of that unity arise. We tend to see community today in any commonality of purpose, activity, or even mere interest. Professional, social, or even temporary commonalities like school, workplace or lodge, are called *communities*. It escapes our notice that this use of the word is originally metaphorical, and that substituting the metaphorical use for the original use is one process of the change — some might say degradation — of language. Such commonalities are not true *communities*, they are but aggregations or associations. *Community* is something else.

It is easy to relate the term "politically active" to a more complete notion of *community*. In doing so, we start to journey back to the original meaning of *community*. But the word *political* needs some unravelling. *Politically active community* could describe, in present usage, the collective action of a union or professional association or a policy pressure group. What constitutes *political* varies in definition from our everyday personal acts to partisan electoral activity. The *polis* part of *political*, however, points us in the right direction. *Political* originally described the collective activity of the *polis* or city-state as distinct from the strictly private activity of the family. It referred, originally, to all the activity that took place beyond one's own doorstep — the all-inclusive social, trade and legal life of the *polity*, as well as its governance.

"Producing," however, I find to be the essential and operative word in the definition borrowed from Friedmann because, of all the relations of the family and of the primitive city-state, that most *debased* by modern practice is *production*. *De-based* is the right word here. Production has literally been removed from its original base, nested in family or community, and re-located, baseless, as the basis for a ubiquitous and calamitous system that now knows no home-base, but is rooted in nothing but itself. Our economic system has come en-rooted from the original limitations of local resource availability and the immediate consequences of exceeding that local capacity — local resource depletion. It has come en-rooted from what used to be its social and ecological limitations — the ethic (or aesthetic) that either production supported its participants, and the relations of production respected and were responsible to both those constituents and the source of productivity, or it ceased.

Only an economic venture whose decisions are made outside the community and independently of the community webs which support it is capable of abandoning its community, or of destroying its supporting ecosystem with impunity. World-wide in scope, our economic system can now destroy both the resources and the people of any locality, and skip on to new horizons of environmental and social exploitation, without its prime operators themselves suffering loss — indeed, usually experiencing profit, which is both their primary purpose, and the purpose for which the economic system itself is designed.

The national and world scope of our economic system has resulted in our dis-engagement from the capacity we once had to look after ourselves and, in doing so, also take care that the ecosystems which once supported us are not exploited beyond their capacity. And that *disengagement* has resulted in the loss of both those capacities. That has resulted in our *disempowerment*. We no longer produce what we consume, nor, for the most part, do we consume what we produce. And, while we may be essential cogs in the grand wheel of far-flung industrial production, distribution, exchange and consumption, we are no longer very influential in its course, despite our so-called "money vote." We are, instead, most likely to be helpless, dangling appendages in the fundamental economy of our own basic material existence, coerced by the material bounty imported from distant places, which we believe we now "need," and also by the need to maintain participation in the money economy controlled by others — in order to maintain that bountiful flow — by increasingly degrading our own environments for profit.

Adam Smith, in *The Wealth of Nations,* predicates our modern economics — the exchange economy Friedmann speaks of — upon the concept of the *division of labour.* Smith's *rational economic man* maintains his material life by means of doing the one thing he does best and filling his other needs through the *exchange* of products which have been produced, more efficiently, by means of other compartmentalized, specialized production by other people. Smith's economics discounts as *inefficient* the production relations of the self-reliant family, city-state or primitive community, which produces internally most of what the unit needs. He ignores the concomitant values of familial and community solidarity — including the autonomous political — as irrelevant externalities. Further, he discounts the *communitarian* or *family ethic* of the common good and of co-operation, in favour of our now-familiar one of self-interested competition — reducing the complex motivations of social inter-action to only one — material self-interest. He applies the 18th-century *rational scientific* method of the Enlightenment — reduction and specialization — to the whole complex of society.

> ...Man has almost constant occasion for the help of his brethren, and it is in vain for him to expect it from their benevolence only. He will be more likely to prevail if he

can interest their self-love in his favour, and show them that it is for their own advantage to do for him what he requires of them.[2]

The result of becoming the *rational, economic men* of the market place has been the *reduction and specialization* of our social and personal lives — socially, we are reduced, by the primacy of market-place economics, from *politically active, producing communities* to aggregations and conurbations of *full-time workers and consumers.* Our general participation in the full life of our communities has been curtailed. We do not have the time any more to be citizens. And to those who would point out that the "citizen" of the classical City-State was to be found only in the leisured upper class, I would answer that what we call "primitive" societies, such as hunter-gatherers, typically spent about twenty hours a week in activities to keep body and soul together, leaving the rest for the "political" activity of their societies. Even agrarian peasant societies, before the industrial age, spent much more time in communal social and normative pursuits than we can afford. The annual vacation was originally a *limit* to the free time the first factory workers had been accustomed to as self-sufficient peasants. The industrial revolution may have increased our productivity as specialized factory "hands," but it reduced our functions as socially, politically *and materially* productive beings in society.

Physical isolation originally defined a community. I think, however, that isolation merely made the self-production that was typical an unremarkable characteristic rather than the essential element of community that it has always been. As a result of the research behind this book, I have come to believe that *production for its own use* is probably the *essential* defining characteristic of a true community. A definition relying on the relations of production, exchange and consumption is, in our geographically homogenized world, probably more useful today than one of geographical isolation. That is to say, we no longer need to isolate ourselves to create utopian communities. We can do it right from where we already live, *merely by acting differently in our producing and consuming lives.* That is to say, we can move to Utopia by staying still and altering our economic behaviour: by disengaging our work and our need from the national-international economic structure that is bedevilling us, and re-connecting them directly. We must learn to spend our work first for our own needs.

If that is so, and if it is the holistic and co-operative *family* ethic and morality that, following Friedmann, we seek to transfer to the larger *community* to provide a matrix which will support our efforts to re-direct our work to our own self-reliance, then combining the family ethic with the need for self-production and locally-sourced consumption is our direct route to an attainable Utopia.

Friedmann's definition is in a real sense the opposite of Smith's anti-benevolence sentiment, and certainly the opposite of the market morality which has become our general social morality. Yet, I find it un-necessary to deny either Adam Smith's *rational economic man,* or the so-called efficiencies of the division of labour, or even the elite specializations of the tool we know as *capital* to which it leads. Nor is it necessary to enter and take sides in the debate between the believers in competitive social Darwinism that Smith's philosophy of economics encouraged, and those — Darwinism's critics and opposites, like the anarchist prince and philosopher, Peter Kropotkin — who declare the paramountcy of co-operation in both animal and human affairs.

The arguments about production relations — that *rational economic man* can interest others in his welfare only through engaging their own self-interest and that *unspoiled natural man* is naturally co-operative — ultimately conflate. Smith's man is securing co-operation through self-interest and Kropotkin's man is securing self-interest through co-operation. I am as sure that there were workers in primitive society who specialized as I am that business proceeds through co-operation as much as by competition. The dichotomy is illusory, or at best, only one of emphasis, style and choice. It is ultimately an article of *faith* — a mat-ter of religion, not economics; a matter of emotion, not reason, as Lewis Lapham has pointed out, humorously, in his very serious book, *Money and Class in America: Notes and Comments on the Civil Religion.*[3]

It is not that the theory that division of labour and the efficiencies and comparative advantage that accrue from specialization is wrong. It is just that their extremist application, as *sufficient* to define humankind, is misplaced fervour. The market place is not the whole of human exist-ence, and its morality is not universally appropriate. The belief in the *sufficiency* of the market as the arbiter of human affairs is quite unjus-tified — even gainsaid — by economic history since the 14th Century, as well as by Kropotkin.

> Man is not a being whose exclusive purpose in life is eating, drinking, and providing shelter for himself. As soon as his material wants are satisfied, other needs, which generally speaking, may be described as of an ar-tistic nature, will thrust themselves forward.[4]

Quite simply, neither rational man nor economic man is the whole of either mankind or humankind, and continuing to claim that a reduction to rational economics defines humankind is the universal sin of modern reductionism of both the Left and Right that has led to both social and environmental degradation. Yet, while economics is not the totality of life of either individuals or communities, it is foundational. Its tenets are of immense and definitive consequence. A society's *economics* is what gives that society its *form*. The existential realities of its members daily necessities of life *in-form* everything within that society.

To build the whole of society upon Smith's *reduced* foundation, as we have done, is to build a society with such structural flaws that it does not work for all that are in it. To build society on the market place leaves out all those who are not in the market, for any of a number of reasons, most pressing of which may be their lack of money and, therefore, their lack of capacity to demand *anything* in the marketplace, irrespective of their *needs*. To structure a whole society upon the morality and disciplines of the market place and its twin requirements that those who are in it generate *money* from its operations and that participation in the market with that money is the *only and absolute pre-requisite to living*, is to build a society that is destroying itself and the world it inhabits. We observe that destruction daily. Yet, I insist, it is not destruction as a deliberate *choice*, but destruction that flows from the magnification of the market-money system's foundational flaw of *reductionism*.

Never has the need for Community Economic Development *in the alternate model described herein* been greater. Never have we so specifically needed the holistic re-development — re-structuring, actually — of *community* and *economics* together, for we must not only rebuild an economics that is more appropriately effective and less destructively affective, we must rebuild the institutions of society and culture within which that economics can have play. We must do both together, and we must do that *outside* of the present socio-economic model, since it is our present economic model — and how it has structured our society — which is the problem. If economics *informs* our social structure and its institutions, then, in order to re-create *community* — or communities — we must re-create the *local economics* that once supported community life.

We think of our society as being based upon the freedoms of the individual. And the truly successful market man has, with his wealth, considerable freedom in our society. But the vision of man, the individual, captain of his soul and supreme in nature because of his wit, is a fallacy of the Enlightenment — what used to be called the Age of

Reason — a creation of the 18th Century in which Adam Smith lived and wrote. The 19th Century *celebrated* the individual. The individual was the creative genius of art and the rugged individualist of industry — Lautrec and Tom Swift. But we did not evolve as individuals or as individualists, we evolved as cultures and societies. We evolved as members of collectivities, and members of collectivities, no matter how un-naturally structured they may be, is what we still are — even as rational economic beings.

There is a socially important corollary to this. If we don't belong, we lose ourselves, and we tend to destroy ourselves and everything around us. Alternatively, if we don't belong positively, we will belong negatively. We *will* form ourselves into collectivities — we evolved as *communities,* and that is the minimal natural human unit of society for any purpose. The only question is whether our collectivities are productive communities or destructive conglomerations exhibiting all sorts of social pathologies.

To understand the *community* rather than the *individual* as the basic unit of production and consumption begs the question of *rational economic man versus natural co-operative man.* Positing *community* as the basic economic and social unit of humanity, and defining the minimum healthy and sustainable goal of the relations of production as *self-reliance in basic needs within a community,* we find the historically "natural" social and economic state of humanity. That given, we might then find individual division of labour functioning within the holistic co-operation of the community, or even specialized production by several communities within a regional grouping of communities. We might find, within such holistic units, the common good organized through Smith's mutuality of private self-interest or Kropotkin's natural co-operation of collective man. *Competition* in production — the building of a better mousetrap — might (and probably should) exist right alongside the *complementation* found in primitive barter societies, in which, if you build an effective mousetrap, I choose to make fish nets. The *nature* of the *relations* of production are less important than the *fact* of *internal* production and consumption for *need,* however facilitated, and the locus of that activity within the *community* as the primary economic unit.

Such a concept does, of course, run counter to the construct that has been elaborated upon Adam Smith's reductionist view of man — the integrated world economy, whose basic unit is the individual worker and consumer, *reduced out* from his community, although usually addressed in the mass and plugged in, in isolation and alienation, to a world-wide system that transcends community. Community Economic Development in the different model suggested by Friedmann's comment, is, I think, of critical importance. It is important in part because our 20th-century apotheosis of the division of labour and trade for comparative advantage in the mass-individual world has acted universally and historically to destroy *community*, our home and cradle, by destroying its essential relations, ethic and morality. It is also important to simply rescue holistic humankind — and the ecosystems which must support it — from the irrational results of rational economics.

As Friedmann points out, a necessary pre-condition of that rescue is *de-linking* from the present exchange or market economy. Describing that destruction is what the first part of this book is about. The second part describes an alternative economic model that can facilitate that de-linking. The third is a handbook about developing that alternative economic model in and through a novel "boot-strapping" system for Community Economic Development.

Sustainability

Sustainable Development is *the* current buzz-word, but it means little if it is not grounded in the concept of *sustainability*. Sustainability is a biological concept having to do with maintaining the natural cycles of the biosphere and with perpetuating their continual productivity in order to maintain them and the cycles of life that they support. The bio-sphere cycle is a loop of continuous and simultaneous growth, harvest, decay and regeneration, however long, that must be able to sustain itself, and do whatever growing is required of it, using only the regular ration of energy that comes directly from the sun or the recent sun energy stored in living or newly-dead things.

Instead of living off that regular *renewable* energy ration, available to us largely only second-hand through plant and animal life and hydro-electrical generation, we have come to rely upon fossil sun ener-gy stored in the earth in the residue of living things from our remote past. And nuclear power relies upon an even older fossil source, the energy which binds matter itself. It is not a qualitative improvement toward sustainability over other fossil fuels — it merely promises to stave off the end of fossil fuels by permitting us to eat the earth itself. Living off our *current income,* rather than our *stored capital,* of coal, oil or uranium, is a very nice balancing trick which we must re-learn for our-selves, since the mining of past sun-energy has a finite limit which we will inevitably reach, and are now reaching within the near future, and within the limitations of foreseeable scientific invention.

The market-money system not only leaves out all those who cannot participate because they have no money, it also leaves out all of that which cannot be expressed as money demand in the market, such as the basic essential health of the ecosystems which support us, and whose ecological realities dictate the form which our economic and social life must take. Not only does our economy not work in social terms, it does not work in ecological terms. In both our social and ecological systems, our economic relations tend to be positive feedback loops pushing those systems recklessly to overload and collapse. Our economic structure and its institutional practices are predicated on the assumption that the world's eco-systems are an irreducible constant. Their limitations and fragility are not factored into the economic equations we work with. We act as if their capacity to continue providing resources were infinite — resource economists will tell you that they are, that the magic of price mechanisms will call out an infinite resource supply — which is patent mysticism. The same economic equations assume that the same eco-systems also have an infinite capacity to absorb and process waste — even waste that is no longer material in any useable or processable form, and even waste that is toxic — which is an even more dangerous fantasy. Our economic equations ignore the *necessity* that any living community — *all living, biotic communities of any kind whatsoever* — must remain in ecological equilibrium within an eco-system which supports both its biotic and economic health in a state of homeostatic sustainability, or it will cease to be a living community.

Our necessary task is not only the development of *community*, but the *development of sustainability*. In that context, the necessary context of our lives, what must we mean by words like *wealth* and *development* and *growth?*

Wealth, Development and Growth

Humankind is so widespread because our life-form has the capacity to fit itself into a vast selection of niches in the biosphere. We can do that because our large brain permitted our subsequent evolutionary adaptations to be principally cultural, social and technological rather than merely physiological, and we learned to manipulate the regeneration of some of those bio-cycles artificially. We developed *adaptive technologies*. We learned agriculture to replace hunting and gathering. We learned about selective plant and animal breeding. We learned to manipulate our environment, and protect ourselves from elements in it that could destroy us.

At about the same time we also figured out how to dominate our neighbours, so that when a particular human population depleted the eco-system which supported it, they could move elsewhere and help themselves to what was next door, by force if necessary. That was accomplished through population growth, superiority in numbers of both strong young men and the females to breed them. It was advantageous for a society to grow in population, even at the cost of short-term over-use of its own ecosystem, if that gave it the *temporary power* to plunder its neighbour's ecosystem and eliminate or enslave the neighbours while doing so. We found a reason to un-balance nature and a means to short-circuit the negative feedback mechanisms that kept our original populations in homeostasis — dynamic balance — within the carrying capacity of their ecosystems. Our cultural change to domination was a positive feedback that accelerated change and created a new, but more precarious, homeostasis — what we might call progress — which was, however, systemically *maladaptive*, in that it tended — as the history of ancient empires attests — towards ecosystem destruction and, with that, the destruction of human populations in both physical and cultural terms.

So grew up kings, cities and empires, grounded in the concept of population growth and centrally administered *power* as icons of progress. With them grew up our ideas about what *wealth* is — that it is not merely having, *but consuming or using, more than you need,* as an expression of your real or potential *power.* Initially, and relatively harmlessly, that meant giving material goods away, with prestige (a kind of power) accruing to he who had most to get rid of. Within a group, such adaptations result in a relatively equal sharing of production, and enhanced survival for all. In a tribal context, anyone's excess production, in the absence of good storage technology, was stored in the belly of his friends, and reciprocated from their later industry or good fortune. There was no incentive to over-produce. Excess production led directly to more leisure, since production was geared to the survival level of the lean years.

But when the excess production of a series of good years could be used to produce more people, who could then be used to plunder the neighbours in the inevitable poor crop years — so the neighbours died instead of the home group — excess production and a surfeit of goods became associated with absolute *power,* and excess production as a hedge against disaster gave way to the excess production necessary to *growth,* and the *requirement* of *maintaining* dominating *power.* A larger-than-natural lifestyle became necessary and normal, a temporary embarrassment of *excess* became a permanently necessary wealth, and from dominant chiefs, big-men and kings we moved to dominant societies — empires, mandated to grow and continue growing. Maladaptation became a social and cultural norm. We enshrined non-sustainability as a necessity — the world's most dangerous oxymoron.

Most of the economic development that we still reward lies in this context of *excess* translated into outward-directed *power.* We admire the successful, *developed* units in our world, not recognizing their ultimate non-viability, and seek to become either as *fully developed* as them, or at least, *developed fully* within their powerful economic shadow. *Local* economic development — as must any growth, economic or biological — can be maintained within this system only by some application of *power,* some use of *energy,* some exploitation of *advantage* within a boundary-transcending context, and it must be maintained competitively against other aggressive localities and with relation to any centrality that the locality relates to. In this context, lacking *power* of our own — and that must be the case or development would not be requiring special effort — we typically court the attention, grace and favour of some *external* economic power and call that Local Economic Development. Or we seek as development what amounts to the same thing, access to external *money wealth,* the abstraction of real wealth *extracted* — wealth *re-located* from one place to another, and standing in now for an excess of power-bestowing goods.

Wealth being *extracted* and *alienated* from one place to another through the liquidity of *money* is the modern version of plundering your neighbour to support yourself. One place's development is another's diminishment. The enforced creation of local economic excess by transfers from one place to another, or by the transfer of extracted wealth represented by money, is ultimately not development. It is a win-lose game, ultimately not sustainable. It is simply a temporary and local distortion in the general pattern of human economic use of the biosphere. The expansion of empires — the local economic development of Uruk, for example, or of Rome — could not continue once insurmountable barriers were reached. Once there were no more exploitable neighbours and the final accessible ecosystem had been ravaged — leaving behind, progressively, a bleached-out Mesopotamia, a desertified Sahara, and a de-forested Mediterranean basin — decline was as rapid as it was inevitable. Just so, we cannot continue to put a premium on extraction to *excess* — our definition of *wealth* —

and legitimize that as *growth*. Nor can we continue to legitimize as *progress*, any kind of *growth*, itself an excess that can neither be legitimate in a populated world nor continue in a finite world. The practices of over-production, over-consumption and over-growth cease at some point to be survival mechanisms and then act to destroy very quickly the cultures that permit them. They are maladaptive. In our modern world, *development*, which is still being carried out in this aggrandizing context of power and conspicuous consumption (the market's necessary engine), is obviously, fundamentally not sustainable. Having crossed all the barriers to continued plunder, and having created a production and consumption system that now encompasses the entire earth, world-wide over-production — the system that demands continual productivity for its very survival — must come to an end, or else we will.

Excess can never be more than a temporary and fortuitous part of the balanced life of any bio-cycle. There is no short-term perpetual motion machine, no process on earth which produces more energy than it consumes. Fortuitous periods of over-production cannot be permitted to go on producing population explosions, the pattern of the past, unless we accept as legitimate what that entails. Our excess populations now have nowhere else to go except to where there is already full population. The powerful are becoming arbiters of genocide.

We are at, or in sight of, the finite carrying capacity of the earth. At the human scales of physical resources and of our time and science, the sources of energy necessary for our life are recognizably finite, and humanity itself is now in excess — certainly not sustainable in our present modes of production and consumption and our present uses of economic, political and military *power* to maintain them.

Wealth as forced or maintained excess production is not sustainable. In the context of *sustainability*, wealth has to mean *adequacy* rather than *excess* — what it meant in the beginning of our sojourn on earth. But now, rather than simply enjoying the illusory advantages of a maladaptive cultural practice which made its ignorant practitioners the temporary survivors in an evolutionary shake-down that is not over yet, we must consciously and rationally adopt the difficult task of finding and maintaining the balance of production and consumption at which our lives, and the life of each of our portions of the biosphere, can proceed comfortably without overtaxing either itself or other segments of the whole biosphere. If we do not, the shake-down will evolve us right out of existence.

Power and Distribution

With the combination of dominating nature and each other and extracting excessively from both, and having developed the capacity to create distortions in the general pattern of human economic use of the biosphere, it is our conceit to believe that we have established power over our environment, our own kind, our selves, and what we consider to be our destiny. With our science and technologies, including our economics and other cultural technologies, we imagine that we have broken out of the necessarily limited cycles of the biosphere into a *Starship Enterprise* kind of existence, free from constraints that might arise from our grounding in the natural world. One degree below that, we are now trying to convince ourselves that, with our combination of scientific and monetary power, we can — we must — begin to manage the total biosphere of the whole earth. That is the theory that underlies the Brundtland Report.[5]

The Brundtland Report is an expression of Keynesian re-distributive economic theory from the 1930s, when the economist Lord Keynes "felt moved to speculate on the 'economic possibilities for our grandchildren' and concluded that the day might not be all that far off when everybody would be rich."[6] With the usual development ethic fundamentally unaltered, the Brundtland Report seems to maintain that all the societies of the earth can be raised to something like the higher Western standard of living within the context of our present economic system, tempered, merely, through local economic development of Third-World countries coupled with a comfortable modification of our present Western tendencies to excess.[7] Local Economic Development is yet another version of Keynes' *universal wealth* syndrome: the belief that all can share in the *development* fostered by *growth*.

In a finite world, neither growth nor development so postulated can, of itself, be a realistic agenda for the new century. It is not a sustainable possibility.

The True Power Struggle

It is my belief that our present economic system, that which is based in the power, represented by money, which we glorify as *wealth*, and which is the power to create distortions in the web of human economic use of the biosphere and of social life, is ultimately destructive of our society. Our present system is certainly destructive of those things we want to preserve through Community Economic Development. Those are our non-economic relations of support and co-operation, our consciousness of relationship to one another and to place, and the desire to preserve and enhance both one another and place which flows from that. These are the adaptive social artifacts that will preserve community, and, through preserving or restoring community, will ultimately preserve our society. Our present system destroys these things because in it is embedded the concept of abstract, alienated, objective, coercive power — power abstracted from the real wealth of the biosphere which gave it its genesis; power alienated from the ameliorating influence of subservience to the balanced laws of the biosphere; power objectified and turned against that which enabled it; power used not to support life but to subvert and coerce life; power that is a positive feedback mechanism creating only more power, all of which pushes us ultimately to the over-consumption that will bring us to collapse. And the supreme representation of this extracted and alienated wealth, the distillation of not only valuable commodities but the distillation of this thrice-cursed power, is *money*.

Power is bestowed by the possession of excess commodities and the capacity to command services by rewarding those services with the bestowal of desired commodities. Money is the distillation of that power in a highly efficient form. The great contention in our world in the next century is going to be between those who believe we can manage the whole earth, massively, by using this mode of economic power *over* resources and *over* people, and those who believe we can manage the earth properly — make sense of it — only minimally, one small piece at a time, and in the different ethical mode of sharing in its life-cycles, using the subtle power of *knowledge* to enhance and solidify our place within the life-cycles rather than to try to escape from them. The contention will be between those who believe we can maintain our present levels of exploitation of one another and of our ecosystems with legal and economic rules *enforcing* environmental, social and economic sustainability in a context of hoped-for, power-oriented technological advancement, and those who believe we can effectively exercise power only by sharing it, by *co-operating* among one another and with the natural biosphere, and keeping our demands from out-stripping our technological capabilities while directing those capabilities to developing sustainable, subtle rather than powerful, technologies. It will be between those who exercise power over nature and people, and those who seek to exercise power with other people and with nature.

Those who believe that we can keep the whole in balance only by co-operatively addressing the parts can be called *bio-regionalists*. They favour local autonomy at the level of a naturally logical biotic and social regime, and a variety of management methods applied within that regional regime, especially direct, hands-on personal effort and responsibility, to limit their draw-down of resources to the particular ecosystem they inhabit. As *ecosystem* people, they can immediately notice ill effects in the environment of their ecosystems and, feeling them, act to correct them. Responsibility, in their lexicon, includes — especially — a view of nature as co-equal with humanity. It must necessarily also entail an egalitarian view of humanity as co-equal with itself, which entails a humanitarian social ethic constrained only by the limitations of bio-regional carrying capacity. Their guiding ethic is that of sharing. Their contention is with the *centralists,* the world-class power lobby, who operate in a more remote and detached mode. The centralists usually mediate their effort through the investment of money, which carries with it an ethic of competition, excessive, unending growth, and the commodification of *power.* Such people will continue to draw upon the resources of the entire world — the whole *biosphere* — to sustain themselves. As *biosphere people,* they do not necessarily feel the results of their excess impact on the environment. They are insulated from much of their impact, and do not , cannot act — in many cases, will not act — to correct them. These, and unfortunately they include all of us in the so-called "developed" world, are the exploiters destroying peoples and the earth.

The coming struggle will be to fix where the autonomy (which is to say, the power) lies, how it should be used — indeed, what it is for. It will be a struggle between styles of engagement — co-operative, direct and subjective or competitive, remote and objective. It will also be a struggle between concepts of the proper source of the resources that support us — from within our own ecosystems, where we can act quickly to keep our support systems in equilibrium, or from beyond our ecosystem, from the whole biosphere, where sustainable systems can be subverted by unrecognized positive feedback mechanisms tending to push our life-support systems beyond capacity.

This is a struggle in Western society between the world of the urban mall, with its TV-commercial muscle-car images of the veiled threat of *power barely leashed,* contained in a midnight blue, smoke-hazed and *artificial* world, and the bucolic image of *natural* nurturing forest and life-supporting grassy farmlands. It is being played out now in the struggle for control of the food supply between petro-chemical industrial agriculture (with its TV-ad images of macho chemical weed destruction) and the small-scale life-supporting practices of organic farmers who seek to work with and within their own local ecosystems, rather than subvert them, or see them — or those of others — subverted in some attempt to exploit the whole biosphere. It seems to me, however, to be a mistake to call it a struggle between *capitalism* and *socialism*, although it is that. They are only symptoms, not causes, of our malaise. It is a struggle against *coercive power*, whether that be monetary, military, social or political. It is a struggle, therefore, against the collectivism of centralist social democracy as well as the Leftist tyranny of the majority just as much as it is a struggle against the centralist money-power of the undemocratic capitalist Right.

The old East-West, Right-Left contest is, in fact, passé, if it ever was a real one for most of the earth's people. In the context of *sustainability,* the contest has always been between centralized power and the separate, free and anarchic societies (and economies) of pre-monetary, pre-industrial primitive tribes and peasant villages. It has always been a struggle between the autonomous and self-sufficient *communities* of our world and the aggrandizement and control of centralist empires — military, political and economic. It has been a struggle between self-sufficient local societies in which production and consumption was a closed and self-managed, all-inclusive, all-supportive, circuit — which the industrial revolution overturned for both East and West — and those who wanted to *grow.* It is the old struggle between the village and the city.

This is a point made by Alvin Toffler in *The Third Wave.*[8] What we call Local Economic Development is clearly on the centralist side of that struggle, legitimizing centralization, and what we call Community Economic Development is clearly on the other, re-empowering local communities. We must be clearly aware of the difference.

Chapter Two

TO MARKET, TO MARKET
The Hidden Structure of Our Economy

Theory and Reality

The late French historian, Fernand Braudel, in his book *Civilization and Capitalism, 15th to 18th Century,*[1] examines the functioning of The Economy during this four-hundred year period of development, from roughly 1400 to 1800.

> The more research I did, the more disconcerted I became by the direct observation of so-called economic realities between the fifteenth and the eighteenth centuries ... because they did not seem to fit, or even flatly contradicted the classical and traditional theories of what was supposed to have happened. According to the textbooks, the development of pre-industrial Europe consisted of its gradual progress towards the rational world of the market, the firm, and capitalist investment, until the coming of the Industrial Revolution ...[2]

Braudel found that there had been no inevitable, rational progression toward the modern European industrial economy. He found that what has been characterized as the evolutionary march of progress toward a unitary economic enlightenment has been principally retroactive, self-serving, propagandist invention. "In fact, observed reality before the nineteenth century is much more complicated."[3]

Braudel found that there was never only one economy but always several, and that we live now not in one economy, but in at least three connected but distinct economies — the market economy, the capital economy that grew out of it, and what he calls ordinary material life. It is principally what is called the "market" economy, which developed after the Crusades out of what had always been world-wide free trade, that the founders of economics wrote about because it was the most evident, quantifiable and recordable. Because of their exclusivity — their reductionism — it is only this large and easily seen stream that we refer to as The Economy, what we mean now when we use the phrase, and wherein we habitually seek development. It is, however, merely the most evident of the three levels of economic activity which Braudel claims function to drive our world:

> ... the mechanisms of production and exchange linked to rural networks, to small shops and workshops, to banks, exchanges, fairs and (of course) markets. It was on these 'transparent' visible realities, and in the easily observed processes that took place within them that the language of economic science was originally founded. And as a result it was from the start confined within this privileged area, to the exclusion of any other.[4]

The Market Economy

This once exotic "market" economy is, generally speaking, the "money" economy that we now believe we live by, day to day. This "market" economy did not invent money, but it certainly created, developed and proliferated money as we know it, by which I mean, in this book, that which the eminent economist John Kenneth Galbraith means by money: "... what is commonly offered or received for the purchase or sale of goods and services ...."[5] It is important to emphasize "commonly" in that definition, for there are uncommon moneys, and classical economists argue a much broader *general* definition of money, which Galbraith leaves room for in the above quotation, but that we will get to later.

That *common* money, *money as we know it* — which I also herein call *commodity money* — was a new kind of wealth quite different from the old wealth based on land and the productivity of land when worked by people, and on the power to command armed force and therefore possession of the land and its people together with the fruits of their productivity. This new kind of wealth was an *abstraction* of *real* value. As such, convenient and highly *liquid*, it facilitated the world market's functioning and accelerated market growth because of its ease of transfer and exchange. The new wealth, *money wealth*, translated *real, concrete* value into a universally interchangeable *abstract symbol* of value. But it was an abstract symbol which did not remain merely symbolic. Because it was readily convertible into valuable real goods, and became the medium in which real goods and services were evaluated, it eventually became accepted as *value that was itself real,* and itself took on the characteristics — derived from the marketplace — of the commodities that it at first merely represented.

Money is now a *symbol* that has itself been *reified* and *commodified.* As an artificial thing of value in its own right, it has built some knotty problems into the foundation of our economics, which we will get to in due course. But, viewed as a concrete commodity in its own right, *money as we know it* also developed characteristics that facilitated the growth of a separate economy parallel to, but distinct from, the "market" economy. These characteristics were the exclusivity (the monopoly or oligopoly) of money creation, the limitation of money supply, and *interest* — which is an *artificial simulation* of organic growth. The parallel but separate economy was the economy of *capitalism.*

The Capital Economy

The world "market-money" economy provided the new kind of *money wealth,* or *capital,* that permitted the development of the "capital" economy. The "capital" economy grew out of the upper reaches of the "market-money" economy as a controlling reaction to its free-wheeling and anarchic tendencies. We tend to conflate the "capital" and "market" economies and think of them as one, but Braudel claims they are quite different and distinct.

> Looking up ... from the vast plain of the market economy, one finds that active social hierarchies were constructed on top of it; they could manipulate exchange to their advantage and disturb the desired order.... To me, this ... shadowy zone, hovering above the sunlit world of the market economy and constituting its upper limit ... represents the favoured domain of capitalism....[6]

Braudel finds the "capital" economy distinguishable from the "market" economy in a number of ways that traditional economists overlook or try to explain within the bounds of a single system. He claims that there is no need to explain these differences as contradictions within a single system. There are a number of closely linked but distinct systems at work here which are different in character, function, and ends.

"Capital" is the *concentration* of abstract value (as *commodified money wealth*) translated from *real* value in and by the "market" economy, and *capitalism* feeds itself according to the classical Marxist theories of the alienation of labour.[7] In this context, these should be understood more broadly as the alienation of *value added,* which is value created by the interaction of people and resources (a little broader than Marxist *theory of labour,* but essentially similar) and made available for alienation through the value-abstraction process of modern money functioning in the "market" economy. The world-wide "market" economy turns real value into a *liquid abstraction* and facilitates its *flow,* and the "capital" economy diverts that flow from free circulation, alienates that value from the "market" economy, and concentrates it as a *head* (the Latin root is *caput*) of economic, market, social and political *power.* That power is subsequently used to control and manipulate the "market" economy that it originally came from.

The participants in the "capital" economy were able to turn the free market rules on their head and subvert the free-wheeling democracy of the market. The alienation of value runs counter to the need for the market to balance give and take. The central concentration of value taken out of the market runs counter to the market's need for money to *circulate* continuously and naturally, and for cash to *flow* freely. The use of that concentrated money power to manipulate the market runs counter to the need for the market to regulate itself according to supposedly free market laws.

What permitted this overturning of the so-called *market rules* was, in the first instance, money's flexibility — the flexibility derived from the liquidity of *value abstracted* rather than value that has remained *value realized. Real value* is likely to be in some concrete, natural, actual form that is physically more difficult both to alienate and to centralize than money is. Even crude and primitive money was easier to shift than grain, cattle, or trade goods. Gold was easier and more convenient than any of those, paper money easier than gold, and modern *monies of account* (mere ledger entries) were easier than paper money. Now it's an electronic snap and it can all be done instantly.

Added to the ease with which money could transfer value, the limitation, by law, of who could print money, the close control of who could *create* money (and how) and, through that limiting mechanism, the limitation of its *supply,* permitted the participants in the capital economy to develop the necessary control mechanisms. Those already in positions of authority were able to reserve to themselves the right of money creation *by fiat,* yet the institution of interest made it generally possible for those who already had the power conferred by money to create more money — and more power — by means of it, and in exactly the proportion that they already possessed. A nicer balancing and distribution of power among the already powerful — those at the top and their challengers — could never have been devised. It was not, of course, devised, it evolved. That is to say, this new mechanism of power developed in a manner and into a shape that the realities of the real world pressed it to.

Relying on the liquidity of value abstracted, or *money*, and the ease of shifting it about, and upon the nicely developed mechanisms of economic control which the money system also permitted, the "capital" economy has the capacity to shift its focus and involvement quickly, easily and effectively to whatever economic activity is most profitable, anywhere, anytime. So the capital economy, now and historically, might at one time concentrate on the marketing of goods, discovering or creating the resources and markets for trade through exploration, conquest and empire development; at another time it might concentrate on land control, development, manipulation and resource extraction; at yet another on manufacturing and industry, or yet again, as seems to be the case today, in real estate *development* and on *money farming*.

Real estate development is the essentially empty process of creating new money by means of the artificial inflation of real estate values. Money farming is the equally empty making of money directly from money, long castigated as the sin of *usury*, probably because it has always been, in *real* terms, essentially non-productive. Now we can see that it is even worse: inflating the amount of the artificial sign, the symbol, of value, mandates and drives the production of real goods and services — the realization of resources to catch up to and match the proliferation of the symbolic representation. The tragedy of resource depletion driven by that profit motive — and that includes both social and environmental degradation — is our primary world crisis. Problems of the *money* system are becoming evident.

Ordinary Material Life

Beneath the easily recognized "market" economy, says Braudel, is the everyday functioning, the ordinary material activities, of the peasant or aboriginal village or tribe — or of modern individuals, families and groups — just getting along from day to day. It is the home-built, local economy "of the country..."

> ... another, shadowy zone, often hard to see for lack of adequate historical documents, lying underneath the

market economy: this is that elementary basic activity which went on everywhere and the volume of which is truly fantastic ... a layer covering the earth.[8]

This has actually been the vital and functioning economy of most of humanity throughout most of human history. I call it the "root" economy. Alvin Toffler describes something similar in what he calls "prosumer" economies.

> ... Most people [had always] consumed what they them-selves produced. They were neither producers nor con-sumers in the usual sense. They were instead what might be called 'prosumers.'
> ... We went from an agricultural society based on 'production for use' — an economy of prosumers ... to an industrial society based on 'production for exchange'.[9]

Braudel says the development of the "market" economy changed everything.

> On the one hand, peasants lived in their villages in an al-most autonomous way [and] on the other hand, a market-oriented economy and an expanding capitalism began to spread out, gradually creating the very world in which we live.... Thus we have two universes, two ways of life foreign to each other, yet whose respective wholes explain one another.[10]

George McRobie prefigures Braudel and Toffler in discerning this dichotomy.

> There are always two systems by which we support our-selves — the 'self-care' system and the market system; the latter requires us to earn money in order to buy goods and services produced by others. The self-care system has declined to near-vanishing point, and the result is a great deal of waste and expense, and a loss of independence for the family and the community.[11]

Braudel's claim is that this economy of *ordinary material life* has not entirely vanished but is still present inside, alongside, integrally with and in spite of the "market-money" and "capital" economies that economists are able to discern.

> This triple division is ... controversial.... But in the end I accepted that the market economy had ... been a restrictive order, and that like all restrictive orders ... it had created an opposition, counter forces, both above and below itself.
>
> What I find most encouraging is that the same schema can be used to show easily and clearly the articulations of present-day societies.[12]
>
> Today, just as in the eighteenth century, there is quite a sizeable lower floor, a sort of bargain basement, below the other two storeys; some economists estimate it at about 30% to 40% of economic activity in the industrialized countries. This surprisingly large figure, for which estimates have but recently appeared, is made up of all the activities outside the market and State controls — fraud, barter of goods and services, moonlighting, [and] housework, that domestic economy which Thomas Aquinas regarded as the *economia pura* and which still of course exists today ... and our statistics, which do not find room anywhere for the 'basement' of the economy, give us only an incomplete picture.[13]

We are beginning to understand that lack. But there does not seem to be anywhere a deep appreciation of Braudel's further suggestion that the informal and underground economies of today *still support the whole economic structure* in necessary and material ways, nor are there studies to discover the extent to which this idea is true, and what its significance might be. Braudel's findings are controversial probably because they cannot be easily studied by orthodox economic theory. This is not, however, reason to discount them. A moment's thought will reveal that the economics of *ordinary material life* are, everywhere and always, *necessary* to the "market" and "capital" economies, even if only to the extent that family and friends support one another between jobs, which is to say, in the gaps the formal economy does not concern itself with.

In *informal* economies, people typically help one another outside the formal "market" economy, trading goods and services back and forth, co-operating on construction projects, for example, or sharing garden produce, or just helping one another to survive. This is usually accomplished, however, without any currency, or with only casual and often imperfect reciprocity if currency is used. The *underground* economy is also hard to quantify. In *underground* economies, people exchange goods and services, also outside the formal "market" economy, usually duplicating its reciprocity quite carefully, although in such a way as to deliberately defy *official* accounting. Barter flourishes among welfare recipients, for example, in every *socially advanced* economy, in spite of income controls, and welfare officials tell me that they generally ignore it because it cannot be policed. A very local economy of garage and rummage sales and flea markets keeps the poor in otherwise expensive "pre-owned" necessities, and tax laws are rarely honoured — again because such activity cannot be policed.

The principal characteristic I would suggest to encapsulate a practical conceptualization of the "root" economy is that its internal reciprocal trade or barter of real goods and services is accomplished principally by *direct and unmediated exchange* that does *not* make extensive use of our modern, *commodity money.* I think this can be derived from Braudel's analysis and Toffler's *prosumer* concept and by encompassing the *informal* and *underground* economies. This cashless commerce may be of primary production, as from our gardens or the direct services we do for one another, or of secondary production, as of used goods. I suggest that this commerce — these familial, informal and underground economies — are, indeed, the modern version of Braudel's primitive *ordinary material life.* The connection can be seen as direct in at least the *invisible work* of home, house and family, although other aspects of it are, like the modern "capital" economy, *reactions* to the "market" economy. Money creeps into all of these modern "root" economies, but that is merely an artifact of our times and of our ubiquitous internalized money consciousness. We should not be misled as to their essential character by the mere presence of money, more or less, within them. They are, essentially, non-monetary economies.

Chapter Three

AND YOU'RE THE FAT PIG
The Effects of the World Market Economy on
People, Peoples and Community

The Perversions of Money

We have been so conditioned to link the concepts *economy* and *money* that most of us can hardly conceive of them separately. The economy is not a matter of money at all. It consists of the goods and services that support us, how we transform our resources into those goods and services, and how we share the resources, goods and services around. Money is just a tool that helps us facilitate the transformation and accomplish and measure the sharing, or distribution. Many of our economic problems arise because we commonly mistake the tool for the engine and think of economics — and wealth and poverty — as a matter of money rather than money as a mere symbol or measure of wealth and economic activity.

Placed at the centre of economic, and therefore of social and political life, the necessary *ethic* appertaining to the acquisition and use of money pervades society wherever money goes. Since we facilitate almost every aspect of our daily lives, and even of family life, using that really very new creation of the "market" economy, *abstract commodity money,* we see everything now primarily from the perspective of the "money" or "market" economy. Our general *morality* is driven by the *ethics* necessarily associated with money, and we function with market values even when and where it is not appropriate. We accept uncritically the belief that *the market* and its operations are sufficient to both explain and define our society, and that its ethics and morals are sufficient and appropriate to justify and inform our behaviour. On the contrary, they are not.

We are overtly taught, and pay lip-service to, the ethic and morality of family, of neighbourliness and of community, and the depth and variety of life and living. But in practice, in the two hundred-odd years since Adam Smith posited *rational economic man,* we have all internalized and generalized the rational economists' sin of reductionism, of personal gain as the true meaning of life, and we have adopted generally the morals of money. In that time we have also learned to accord much honour to the work of production — or supply — and to respect the rights of consumption — or demand — as functions driven by the ethic of gain alone, and expressed only through the mediation of money. We accord neither honour nor respect to *need*, except as the market demand for our charity.

Among half a millennium of moralists insisting otherwise, Michael Ignatieff in his small book *The Needs of Strangers* makes the point succinctly, and within the bounds of rational economic discourse.

> The political arguments between right and left ... assume that what [we] need is income, food, clothing, shelter and medical care ... What almost never gets asked is whether [we] might need something more than the means of mere survival ....
>
> It is because fraternity, love, belonging, dignity and respect cannot be specified as rights that we ought to specify them as needs ....
>
> The [language] our society lives by — a language of rights — [however] has no terms for those dimensions of the human good which require acts of virtue unspecifiable as a legal or civil obligation.[1]

One could add, "or as an economic transaction." What would you think, for example, of a parent who refused to feed a child who had not performed assigned household chores? The familial relationship apart, that would be a reasonable act in a "market" economy — no performance, no reward, no work, no right to demand. But the familial relationship is not apart. Withholding essential sustenance for non-performance is not reasonable within the economy of the family. It is not even legal. Nor is the provision of sustenance properly explainable within the family as an act of *charity*. The nurturing of the young is not a *rational economic* act at all.

The best you can do to rationalize such necessary, and necessarily irrational, *uneconomic* behaviour in our modern *rational economic* society is to claim that sustenance is the child's *right* as a member of the family, matched by the parent's obligation. Both are supported as such in our law. Our proper *family* morality, however, merely accepts the reality, the actuality, the necessity, of the *sustaining relationship*. It simply *is*, tacit, implicit, endemic, a part of the definition of what a *family* is, and the language of *rights* does not even properly enter the question. Plainly, market values do not belong here. Yet, in nurturing children, there is clearly activity of an economic nature going on, and an economic outcome to be anticipated, if nothing else than the continuance of the family as an economic unit. Perhaps some new economic theory needs to be elaborated.

The set of economic relations that is true, even today, for our families used to be true for *community*. That nurturing and mutual caring, and the institutions in which those have their being and can flourish, are what we need to re-construct at the level of *community*, to properly effect Community Economic Development. They are what we need to consciously, deliberately *re*-establish in our economic relations of production, exchange and consumption, even if, as is probable, we have to define them with a rational, or even an economic, vocabulary. We cannot do it as a moral exercise. Our morality, even supported by fulminations of thunder and lightning, has never withstood the seduction of money. We must restore those more ethical economic relations structurally. It will be simple to do so, but very difficult, because those relations are, specifically, part and parcel of the necessary *irrationality* that the *money system* destroyed.

Money and Power

No matter what the apparent current interests of the "capital" economy are that occasionally make it seem to be several different economies, Braudel says it remains essentially distinct from the "market" economy and always stays essentially the same. It has always been in the hands of relatively few people, although they change in identity. It has always been centralized. And its primary purpose has always been the further accumulation and concentration of capital, which is to say, *money wealth*, out of the market economy and into the capital economy.

It is true that many good purposes have been achieved by the use of the power of money concentrated as *capital*. But any study of colonial and market expansion shows that the power of capital used in market, industrial, developmental, social, political and military adventuring, and at play in every form of manipulation, coercion, domination and control — justified for a large variety of reasons — has facilitated the expansion of trade, markets and profits. The market itself soon became simply the tool for achieving the abstraction, alienation, accumulation and concentration of more *abstract commodity money* as *capital*. *Real* productivity, the creation of goods and services of real value, has always been secondary in the "capital" economy, a *means* to the end of accumulating abstract money wealth and the useful, liquid *power* it confers. In this respect, more than in any other, the "capital" economy differs from the "market" economy. Indeed, it turns the "market" economy upside down.

> The capitalist merchant described by Marx ... begins with money (M), acquires goods (G) and returns regularly to money, in a pattern MGM: 'he parts with his money only with the intention of getting it back again'. The peasant by contrast, usually comes to sell his goods on the market in order to buy immediately whatever he needs: he begins with goods and ends with goods: GMG.[2]

If capitalism be defined as the central accumulation and centralized use of money as an instrument of objective *power,* with the focus of that definition on the *power* that capital or money represents *in the abstract* rather than on the money itself, then the ends of capitalism can be seen as no different, essentially, from those of the centralized *direct-action* social, political and economic power that is the preferred control mechanism of communist and fascist States. The exercise of this *money* power, and access to it, may have been more democratic than the exercise of raw political power, but its *bottom line* ethic also has always supported purposes *fundamentally at odds* with the requirements of community life that we seek to maintain or re-create through Community Economic Development. Indeed, that we must make special efforts to re-create healthful community relations, to re-establish institutions of mutual support and non-economic caring, of social and political and economic decision-making, and of sound and sensitive environmental management — that we have created a whole discipline to do that — probably proves the point.

The Market Alienation of Value

The growth of any economy *out of* a prior economy must involve first the abstraction of value created within the first economy, and then the subsequent removal of that value from the first to the second economy, in the senses both of *willing surrender* and *separation* involved in Karl Marx's use of the term alienation.[3] Braudel claims that the "capital" economy was built upon value extracted from the "market" economy, and just so, it is the everyday presence and activity of ordinary people and their capacity to survive, creating value in the process, that underlies the "market" economy and supports our whole economic "three-storey house," as he calls it.[4] He also observes that a result of any community joining the "money-market" economy is the eventual alienation of the value created in the economy of ordinary material life out of its home community to some larger centre, either by political or economic intent or through the pure and simple functioning of market and money. But, along with the loss of that *created value* we also suffer the loss of other *values* as well. There is no reason to assume that today is different from the period Braudel studied.

The Trouble With Money

When the "market-money" economy first became generalized in Europe, the standard of living tended, not to *rise*, which might be expected if the money apologists view of the money system as a wealth-creator is accepted, but to *fall*.

> A quintal of grain [in France and similarly in all of Western Europe] cost the equivalent of 100 hours of work until about 1543, then remained above that critical line until about 1883.... It is always serious when the 100-hours-for-one-quintal line is crossed; to cross the 200 is a danger signal; 300 is famine.... Thus, for the centuries covered by this book, real prices moved in an unfavourable direction.[5]

The world "market-money" economy destroyed the economic insulation of peasant and native communities. Once the world "market-money" economy had penetrated them, it made such profound and radical changes as to destroy almost everything that we could possibly mean by *community,* and it destroyed not merely the distinctiveness of those communities and the relationships of their members to and within them, but also community *ethics* (beliefs about how we relate to one another and to the world around us) and *morality* (how we act out our beliefs about those relationships).

> What did [money] actually bring? Sharp variations in prices of essential foodstuffs; incomprehensible relation-

ships in which man no longer recognized either himself, his customs, or his ancient values. His work became a commodity, himself a 'thing'.

... Any society based on an ancient structure which opens its doors to money sooner or later loses its acquired equilibrium and liberates forces that can never afterwards be adequately controlled. The new form of interchange disturbs the old order, benefits a few privileged individuals and hurts everyone else. Every society has to turn over a new leaf under the impact."[6]

How remarkable. Money creates poverty! It creates poverty where before there was none because it enriches the few at the cost of the many. The few, of course, can view that with equanimity as *the creation of wealth*. And the end result of simply being able to turn value into a universally recognized and liquid abstraction ultimately transformed all of us and our entire world.

Money in the countryside was only rarely used as capital, it is true: it was used for land purchases the aim of which was social promotion; and even more of it was hoarded.... But money still played its part in destroying old values and relationships. The peasant who was paid a wage, duly noted in his employer's account book, even if he received so much of his pay in kind that he practically never had two coins to rub together at the end of the year, had grown accustomed to reckoning in money terms. In the long run, mentalities were changing; and so were work relations, easing the passage to modern society, though never [so] as to benefit the poorest.[7]

The value that people created through their work with and upon their resources was abstracted into money and that money was hoarded as someone else's legal, restrictive land entitlement, or hoarded as someone else's *capital*. In either case, its value was taken out of circulation and kept unavailable to the community: hence the poverty. This is the same process we undergo in recessions. Money withheld from circulation causes depression because less is circulating. Even if banked in the community, it is unavailable to it. More of this *reified, commodified abstract value* collected and held in certain places means less wealth available everywhere else.

Destruction of Community, Culture and Skills

Braudel tells us that the process of community disintegration began as the world market penetrated into our bucolic communities, and social, economic and labour relations changed.

> In the eighteenth century, the Basque country was tending to become a thoroughgoing 'national market', hence the increasing commercialization of rural property.... As a consequence, land ownership became concentrated in a few hands and the already poor peasants underwent further pauperization, being obliged in larger numbers than ever to pass through the narrow gateway of the labour market, in town or in countryside.[8]

One can readily see that, if the community's labourers, whose support source is internal and from within the community, begin to direct their labour and its products externally into the exogenous *labour market* rather than back — inward — to endogenous activities in support of continued local sustenance (that is, to support their source of support), then the material substance, or value, which is created within the community to support them is transferred out of and beyond the community. And once the *value added*, the product of labour once internal to local "root" economies, could be turned into an abstraction and sent away from its originators, then the *labourers themselves* soon followed. This process would accelerate increasingly as money came into more general use as the principal *arbiter* of what skills, labour, time and resources (the *natural money*[9] possessed by all of us) can be translated into spendable value. Eventually, almost nothing could be traded until demanded through someone's willingness to pay money for it.

In this way, the world "job-money-market" economy, by developing and using a *universal commodity money*, was able to extract first *capital* resources, then *physical* resources and, finally, *human* resources out of and away from our communities, and dedicate them to the ultimate use and advantage of the few at the expense of the many. Those skilled in local land husbandry moved to new skills and new places. Cultural-economic skills, knowledge and processes, adapted to place and transmitted for hundreds of generations, and essential to the maintenance of *ordinary material life* in those places, were forgotten in as little as one generation as new knowledge, skills and processes became necessary. Culture, skills, capacity and place — all that makes *community* — was lost.

In her book *Sultans of Sleaze: Public Relations and The Media*, Joyce Nelson details the modern trans-national corporate version of this historic reality. In her chapter entitled "Multinational Free Lunch: The Zones That Eat The World," she identifies the *special trade zones* established to create and preserve *favourable business climates* for multi-national corporations:

> ... The conditions of work ... are so appalling that it would be more accurate to call them slave labour camps ... [and] there are usually very lax, or no, environmental regulations to hamper corporate industrial processes.[10]

Nelson details how these special zones are fuelled by surplus labour, people who are literally refugees from *The Green Revolution* of the 1960s, in which hi-tech Western corporate agriculture, devoted to export crops, dispossessed Third-World people from their land and sent them flooding, jobless, into the cities.

This has occurred before, of course. It is the legacy of *The Industrial Revolution* in Europe. Throughout history, in fact, people have had to struggle to retain and maintain their substance within local communities and prevent the loss of their culture, their identity and their land to the ultimate alienation of their autonomous self-determination by the advance of "the market" and whatever form of imperialist central control went before it. They often became the rebels, renegades, robbers and bandits (or the local heroes) who raided the treasure caravans or the stage coaches, or sailed the pirate ships, to regain their alienated wealth. They have not always been exclusively *economic* activists.

Retaining or taking the wealth produced by people within their communities in the ordinary run of their everyday lives, or requiring them to occupy themselves in one set of tasks rather than another, or to work for others instead of for themselves, or to leave their communities to live where they can be more useful to others — all the substance of who decides what you and I are to do in and with our lives — have always been the matter of politics, war, trade and commerce.

The world "market" and "capital" economic system, everywhere and always, has trampled our borders, breached our hedges, broken down our fences, extracted our substance, and altered the ambience, the meaning, and the physical structure of the places where we live. It has moved whole communities. In the 1950s in Newfoundland, the outports (old and self-sustaining fishing communities) were closed down because they were uneconomical. They could not cheaply be provided with schools and roads and shopping centres, so the people were moved to larger centres. In our present economy, workers are encouraged, even financed, to migrate to industrial centres, to move to where the jobs are. Rural communities throughout North America are denuded of populations as more and more, especially the young, must "pass through the narrow gateway of the labour market," where "work becomes a commodity," and "the self a thing."[11]

Those who would control us have always attacked and criminalized our indigenous cultures and our self-sufficient economic bases. The modern form of criminalization is to label popular and community activists "communists." Modern industry's denial of our access to clean food from the natural world also has a long history. The Spaniards outlawed the growing of amaranth, South America's high-protein food plant, once a staple and now almost lost, because it permitted the natives to be independent. The English enclosed the common lands, depriving their peasantry of the capacity to live independently (inventing the crime of *poaching*), driving peasants into the cities and towns as labour. In North America, it was those dispossessed and de-cultured European peasants who, as settlers, repeated the oppression of their own masters to make aboriginal people dependent on trade with The Hudson's Bay Company, and who would now make them fully dependent on *jobs* and *the market*. Howard Adams writes:

> Systematic colonization...operates to conquer and methodically create a dependency syndrome within indigenous people, who are at the same time having their land and resources seized by imperialist invaders."[12]

> As far as Indians were concerned, fur trapping did not in the end provide as good a living as their indigenous economy of agriculture or buffalo hunting, since the more they became involved in the fur trade, the less they could farm and hunt. Indian councils became concerned over the large number of their people exclusively dependent upon trapping.[13]

We were all, of course, once *indigenous peoples*. For Canadian aboriginals, community development efforts by our federal and provincial governments are still based on market-serving employment and the development of an entrepreneurial middle class in what used to be co-operative, classless and self-sufficient societies, as a 1986 report made to the Manitoba government suggests:

> Community workers and development agencies pursuing this strategy can be said to be acting as agents of social control since they aim at social integration of potential community leaders into the economic system as a whole.[14]

In tribal communities, ownership or control of your own land, upon which you can grow, hunt or gather your own food, is seen as the essential basis of freedom. The Hudson's Bay Company needed the natives to gather furs and persuaded them to give up much of their old hunting in favour of fur-trapping, and much of their old diet in favour of tea and bannock. Today, *marketeers and capitalists* in Third-World countries want to grow cash crops and have dispossessed the natives of the best land they used to cultivate for themselves, turning them into labour on export-crop plantations, or dumping them, excess to a machine-oriented agriculture, into the cities.

In Third-World countries now, land from which people can feed themselves is often not available: it is dedicated to "market" uses, and Joyce Nelson (in *Sultans of Sleaze*) has detailed the fate of the modern urban migrants. In North America, most of us have been so long disconnected from the land, and are so de-skilled and de-cultured, that we wouldn't know how to feed ourselves if we each did have five acres. The land that our grandparents (in the West) or their grandparents (in the East) turned into farms now agglomerates to multi-national agribusiness corporations, and our dreams of personal autonomy have changed.

Our *urban* version of the dream of autonomy, self-sufficiency and self-determination is usually to own not our own farms but our own small businesses, so that we may have, if not the independent capacity to grow our own food, at least self-directed and independent access to market sources of wealth. This is often a goal of Local Economic Development. But even if we were to choose entrepreneurship within the money-driven "market" economy as the basis of our independence, not only must we then still submit to the vagaries of the international "market" economy, which is largely controlled by the "capital" economy, but we must also recognize that the small entrepreneurs within the money-driven "market" economy are now going the way of natives, peasants and small farmers. They are becoming wage workers as the businesses they built up fall under the control of national and international conglomerate corporations dedicated to what they call *world class* styles of organization, corporate behaviour, and economic reach. Joyce Nelson aptly notes that this is simply a replication of 19th-century Europe on a global scale.

Behind all the platitudes and rationalizations of modern world (trade and market) development, there is still the same need to expand and extract, to abstract and alienate, to alienate and concentrate, that stood behind the old-style enforced world trade and the colonization of empires. Force, coercion, persuasion and seduction are merely different methods of bringing ever more people and ever more resources into the "market" and "capital" economies, and centralizing that conjoined economic system in fewer and particular hands. The world of the "market" and "capital" economies requires and achieves our enlistment, one way and another, brutally or subtly, in the same old process. It is now identified as the expansion of trade in the "market" economy and called *development*, but it still sustains itself by consuming our substance, no matter how great or how small a portion of it is theoretically returned to us to keep us viable.

The Futility of Local Economic Development

In an article entitled *Bio-regions as Econo-regions*, published in *Planet Drum Review*, Peter B. Meyer, an associate professor at the University of Pennsylvania, addresses the issue of regional economic autonomy as opposed to central economic control. Like most local economic developers, he fails to take account of the structural problems of money.

> Efforts to increase regional self-sufficiency and to upgrade an area's economic conditions through 'bootstrapping' (local self-help) invariably bump into the brick wall of a massive concentration of productive capital in an ever-shrinking number of major corporations and banks. These large organizations have no commitment to, or interest in, 'place' ... [not in] the physical/biological locales in which they operate, or in people, the tools with which, and on whom, they work ...
>
> Without commitment to place, the distribution system for capital resources sends funds where the greatest (short term) profits can be realized and then moves the funds as soon as better opportunities arise elsewhere.

> Centralized capital and economic power thus create in-
> stability in the (local) economic environment ...[15]

In essence, Meyer is arguing for *regional restraints* on money. There are such efforts as *ethical investment* funds, which put *moral restraints* on money, and they are successful. But their success lies in the fact that they are, for the most part proving to be *more profitable* than general investment portfolios. Any Local Economic Development effort must also, in the long run, rely for its success on the greatest value that the money invested in it can chase deriving from its use and circulation within the community or econo-region.

Of course it is possible to manage money in more community-supportive ways, but that presents a constant problem in financial (and political) artifice requiring a consistent intent and will to do so, even — perhaps especially (or why is the special effort needed anyway?) — in the face of less-than-satisfactory returns. It would require a degree of *stoicism* (the philosophy that human will is the dominant factor in human affairs) that would be unreasonable to expect in financial and political leaders in a community. It might be available in some community leaders for a long time, or in any for some time, but I believe it would be very difficult to sustain a generalized stoic local will in all communities — or any one of them — in the longer political run.

It is not that those who send money elsewhere — the *managers* of the game — *willingly* ignore or are hostile to community, and so are (or cause) the problem. Even legal constraints or social sanctions would not address the problem. It is not a matter of will at all — not a matter of money being *sent* out of our communities — *it runs away all by itself,* because its managers or owners are constrained — always — to seek its greatest possible increase. The problem is a *structural* one, not one of *management.*

Money Runs Uphill

A rich community is one in which money stays to be re-spent six to eight times before it flows away up the hierarchical pyramid to some central location. A northern community of fifty families may have a welfare income of a million dollars a year, or $20,000 per family, but, typically, that million bounces right out of the community, spelling *poverty.* If it were re-spent only three times among the members of the community, that would mean an average income of $60,000 a year, and that community would be well off.[16] Nevertheless, *since money always goes where it will find its greatest increase, it will always leave sooner or later.* Any economic or political system that relies on money cannot avoid the centralizing influence of its structure, and political wills that might resist that influence are notoriously short-lived, if not altogether lacking.

Lacking a continuing stoical political will, local economic self-determination becomes entirely a matter of trying to attract at least as much money as that which escapes. By definition, then, although Local Economic Development may occur, local *self-determination* is lost to the determinants and determinators of the "market" and "capital" economies. These, also by definition, are largely beyond any local, regional, and now even national, control. Braudel makes it clear that the structure and organization of our entire world-wide culture, society, politics and economy has, since 1600, been dedicated to supporting and facilitating trans-border value exchange. Is mere local political will going to stand in the way of the trans-border out-migration of money? It never has.

Economies know no borders.[17]

The global marketplace generates a terrible dependence that further impoverishes the already destitute and leads rich countries like Canada to sell off energy and forests that should be retained for future generations ... all for the immediate benefit of dollars.[18]

Traditional ways of measuring the economy have treated each country as a separate entity. But with the rise of the global marketplace, things have changed in ways that economic theorists are just beginning to understand, let alone measure. How can [national] central bankers control the supply of money and credit when so much of it has escaped beyond their borders to the free-wheeling, and unregulated, Euro-market?[19]

[People today are] looking for institutions where they can put their money and the money will stay within the community and be cycled and re-cycled from investment to consumer goods and back again. Right now we put our money into institutions and it could be down in Argentina buying guns or something like that because the bottom line says you can get eighteen percent down there or twenty-two percent and only twelve percent in Canada. So much money haemorrhages out of the country ...[20]

Such haemorrhaging is not new. The modern world has been built upon a trade and commerce that has always been world wide in scope. It has always fed upon its constituent economies and economic regions, and was very early driven by a money which was universally movable. It has always functioned, and now functions — always and everywhere — to abstract real value, to alienate it from the people and regions who create it, and transport it out of their communities to some centrality under the control of a very few people.

The present-day trans-national corporate manifestation of this centralization of value and control is merely the phenomenon of nations now experiencing what has been happening to the "root" economies of tribes, villages, communities and regions for half a millennium. I find it simply not credible that the destructive *structural* effects of the system — any system — can be alleviated through efforts undertaken within, and using the methods and structures of, that same system. And the problems of the money system, the "capital-market" economy, *are structural.* They are built-in faults of the system: they are *systemic.* This new thing, liquid value, or *commodified abstract money,* is to us and our communities as the honey bee is to the flower.

Honey Bees and Money Bats

The honey bee alienates nectar from the flower and hives it up in a honey store to nurture the hive's increase. Capital alienated from communities does also come in to communities as currency, credit and cash, as *"new" capital* that can be used to stimulate new economic growth, rather as the bee serves the flower with pollen gathered from other flowers in order for the flower to become fruit. *But honey-bee money has a sting.* The symbiosis between the flower and the honey bee results in a random and, generally, balanced distribution of pollen from flower to flower. The distribution of capital realized from any locality, however, is not random, it is determined, and driven by one determinant only — the necessity of its own increase. There is certainly no guarantee that the capital alienated from any one community will return to that community and not to another. It will always go to the community which will provide it with the greatest value-load to take away again. And none of the decisions that would see it return to its originating community, or that might constrain its behaviour within that community, are that community's to make.

There may be such a thing as healthy competition among contributing communities in any region, and between the satellite communities and some central core community. Local Economic Development finds its field here. But logic dictates that there has to be an unfavourable trade balance for all satellite communities with respect to the larger central core community that they relate to. All the satellites will lose in competition with the central community, which is why it is central. And there will always be some among the satellites who lose out also to other satellites and wither. If the alienation of value endemic to an unfavourable trade balance is to be avoided, the model that must be invoked is that of the network — of autonomous and approximately equal communities — and not the pyramid of superior and inferior communities. And the movement of such goods as do move between self-reliant communities — which would only be of prudent surplus production — would have to be between or among communities directly, not by means of an interposing superior central community trading our exports in and our imports out.

Developing any community economically within the money system *goes against the fundamental imperatives of our economic system.* No national or international chain outlet in any of our communities, for example, will be there for long if the value it takes out of the community is not, overall, greater than the value it puts in. Your national or international merchandising chain-store or franchise operation uses goods to get money, not money to provide goods. *Consumer City* is not an outlet, it is an intake. Some of my associates prefer the analogy of the vampire bat to that of the honey bee. Or, to return to my original metaphor: using money, we willingly impale ourselves on an extractive spit, and all our politics and all our vaunted economic freedoms can deal only with who turns the handle, how fast, and where the fat, juice and gravy run to.

Chapter Four

HOME AGAIN, HOME AGAIN
How We Lost Our Sense of Home, and What We Need to Do to Regain It

Money, Markets and Cities Co-develop

The world "market" economy and its facilitator, "money" developed *together*, conjoined elements of a single historical phenomenon which also includes our nearly universal urbanization.

> A world economy always has an urban centre of gravity. News, merchandise, capital, credit, people, instructions, correspondence all flow into and out of the city. Its powerful merchants lay down the law, sometimes becoming extraordinarily wealthy.[1]

The market and money created a new kind of wealth for *The Bourgeoisie*, the middle-class burghers engaged in trade, whose development of wealth was encouraged by the European nobility as a tax cow they could milk for the cash to buy armies, but whose influence soon rivalled and finally eclipsed that of the monarchs who had fostered, protected and taxed them. The power of money wealth was much more democratic than the power of divine right and inheritance, or that seized by concentrated military power. It was that reality that gave rise to the old German proverb "City air makes you free," which recognized both the growing independence of cities against the older power of landed gentry, and the power that the new money wealth conferred on any who could get hold of some. But the democracy, provenance and profligacy of this power did not change its structure and its effects.

Market and money together mandated the development of modern Western European towns and cities after the Middle Ages, and the evolution of their modern appearance, physical structure, functioning and character as the centres of the new mercantile and, eventually, industrial order.

> Urban growth did not happen simply because our
> grandparents decided that they would like to live
> together. Nor was it the result of rational social planning.
> Rather, some places grew into cities because they were
> more successful economic units than other places. That is
> ... they were better located for the realization of profits.[2]

The development of modern cities cannot be considered apart from that of money and the world market. Modern *commodity money,* the world "market-money" economy, and cities co-developed. Even the development of national States was an ancillary correlative.

Cities as Distinct from Towns

Jane Jacobs claims, however, that mere market trading was not enough for the development of our modern cities as economic units.

> The great Mediaeval fairs of the twelfth century were, of
> course, immense centres of trade where great numbers of
> merchants gathered. But the fairs did not become
> manufacturing centers and they did not become cities
> either. They proved to be ephemeral. Today they are
> deader than Troy; even their names — Thourout, Mes-
> sines, Bar-sur-Aube, Lagny — are hardly remembered.
> Yet such Mediaeval cities as London, Paris and Hamburg,
> which started several centuries earlier than the fairs as
> smaller trading centers and perhaps as centers of
> seasonal trade at that, early became centers of general
> craft manufacturing too ....[3]

The first evolutionary difference from the fairs was probably in the element of permanence and protection supplied by the walled town as fortress, which permitted — or perhaps mandated — the establishment of production as well as trade in the same place: a greater concentration and depth of economic activity, and the control of it. Contrast this reality with our present urban reality, where very little of what we purchase for ourselves is made in the places where we live. Is our world market returning our cities to the hollow and relatively powerless economic status of the Mediaeval trade fair? Is that the true sub-text of our modern urban malls, with their festival marketing of goods made elsewhere? If our cities are only places in which to reside and to shop, and lack primary local production of the necessities of life *for those who live there,* then the answer is, *yes.*

The second, *qualitative* difference that evolved between life in the 10th-century cities (as Jane Jacobs defines cities) and life in the earlier, self-sufficient agricultural towns lies in having added to *basic first-level* local self-sufficiency the local manufacture and local provision of those *additional* amenities necessary to the *good life.* This essential nature of a *city* seemed, to the self-sufficient peasants or natives, a matter of *luxuries* — that *higher standard of living* which we now accept as the normal standard of urban life. Their wonder, and generally negative moral opinion, are both recorded in folk tales like *The Country Mouse and the Town Mouse.* Import replacement by local industry is, of course, nothing more than self-sufficiency at the more luxurious *urban* levels. Local industry providing for local needs *and wants* is, then, along with "market" and "money," also a necessary concomitant of the development of our modern cities. But there are further evolutionary steps.

As self-reliant communities, virtually City-States, the transformed and transforming little cities of Europe were probably at their most free, autonomous, self-sufficient and democratic at about 1000 AD. That was before they began to expand from merely replacing their imports with local production to producing, in their turn, goods for export to non-self-reliant towns. That was the road which led both to urban greatness and to the eventual loss of self-determining autonomy through a greater and more widespread integration of communities into the "money-market" world economy, as the social disease of *industrialism* seized us all by the markets. It was that competition for import resources, markets and comparative trade advantage that led to the apocalyptic and suicidal competition for *greatness* which we have known as the European tribal, national colonial and world wars.

The third step that set the cities that did manage the local self-provision of former luxury imports onto the growth curve to *greatness,* then, was the *additional* capacity to begin to *export* their import-replacing manufactures (of both necessities and luxuries) first to their own hinterlands and then to other centres. They became also *suppliers to,* rather than only *recipients from,* the world market. This is beyond industry, a totally different kind of enterprise akin to what we today would call *marketing,* moving effort from production into the task of finding — and competing for and protecting — markets for production. It probably also represents some trip-wire of *decline,* for the exports of *great* cities must be the debilitating imports of *lesser* cities, importing whereby they compromise their own self-reliance and stunt or retard their development. Such compromises, for reasons of trade, were and are often *enforced* by some sort of direct or indirect coercive power.

The Industrial Revolution grew upon and out of this context, fueled by *mass production* and *mass consumption;* that is, production beyond what the producers themselves can consume. Perhaps the Industrial Revolution is misnamed: it ought to be recognized as the Market Revolution, both because it precipitated the savage competition for exotic markets, and because that is also what it became, once the early industrialists stopped viewing their workers as throw-away factors of production and began to view them also as customers. Both those market revolutions continue to be advanced today, justified as *competitive world-class development,* but we can see the pendulum swinging again toward the development of new foreign markets (marketing empires) and away from the development of at-home, reasonably wealthy worker-markets.

Once developing export markets became important, the cities — and eventually the States — of Europe became mutual competitors on the larger economic stage, and the battle over power and decline was joined. We begin to see what Jane Jacobs calls *transactions of decline.* These are the artificial supports of non-productive activities, areas and regions with which power centres seek to retain dis-affected people, regions and groups in a state of engagement with the larger, unitary polity or trading block rather than drifting off to some elsewhere.

But, with such *transactions of decline,* Jacobs says, centralized empires seeking to shore themselves up sow the seeds of their own destruction as their resources are drained in non-productive uses, like armies, or in transfer payments such as regional re-distribution of tax money among Canadian provinces, special regional development efforts, massive farm-aid programs and aid to fishermen, and even the transfer payments devoted to family and individual welfare.[4] It is a delicate balancing act between growth and decline. It may, consciously or unconsciously, be what is behind the present intent of the Canadian federal government to lay off its non-profitable obligations to provincial and city governments.

Capital Cities and the Urban Lifestyle

What made the local manufacture of import replacements affordable was the new urban *money wealth* available for investment in local production, which facilitated the development of the *great* cities, which organized around themselves the European Nation-States. By the 17th Century some cities had undergone a fourth evolutionary transformation, according to Braudel. Not only had they become the competitive centres of economic strength in a world-wide market network, they rivalled, in economic power and influence, the nominal personifications of the national States they had fostered, their monarchs and their courts. The royal courts of Europe (Versailles in France and Westminster in Britain, for example) were attracted to those new principal cities (Paris and London) that had grown up within their national political dominions. They were attracted for essentially the same reasons that every other element in the developing nations had been attracted: influence and wealth at the centre of real power, by this time counted, registered and expressed in and as quantities of money. And the combination of King and Court with the newly rich large towns, the combination of political legitimacy and power with the new economic power and influence, created something else again:

> In the sixteenth century, demographic growth had still favoured all the towns indiscriminately whatever their size — large or small. In the seventeenth, political success was concentrated on a few towns to the exclusion of others. Despite the depressing economic situation they grew unceasingly, and continually attracted people and privileges. These [capital] towns ... represented enormous expenditure. Their economy was only balanced by outside resources; others had to pay for their luxury.[5]

Can you hear the busy buzz of honey bees and the rustle and squeak of money bats?

> What use were they, therefore ...? The answer is that they produced the modern states.... They mark a turning point in world history. They produced the national markets, without which the modern State would be pure fiction. The British market was ... primarily the result of the ebb and flow of merchandise to and from [the city of] London ...[6]

Braudel does not explore whether the new "capital" cities may have *contributed* to "the depressing economic situation" that seems to have accompanied their development as they drained wealth from their peripheries to their centres, although his thesis supports that notion. Self-sufficiency went out the window as some of Jacob's *transactions of decline* entered, and even trade fortified with manufacture was not enough.

Trade was obviously one of the driving forces behind the monstrous agglomeration [that was London], but ... taken all together, profits did not add up to the civil list allocation granted to William III, 700,000 pounds. London, in fact, lived primarily off the Crown, off the high, middle-grade and minor officials it maintained.... It also lived off the nobility and gentry who settled in the town, representatives to the House of Commons who had been in the habit of staying in London with their wives and children since Queen Anne's reign (1702-1714), and from the presence of holders of government bonds whose numbers grew as years went by....The same thing happened to Paris....These wealthy classes and reluctant spendthrifts supported "a multitude of merchants, craftsmen, servants, unskilled labourers" and "many ecclesiastics and tonsured clerics!"[7]

The new *capital cities* also created a new man, perhaps the necessary forerunner of Adam Smith's *rational economic man: modern urban man.* Europe's monarchs, not about to bow readily off the stages of power in favour of those who possessed and created this new wealth, provided the final essential elements that created the modern city: the marriage of legitimized politics to economic power. Perhaps even more important in the long run, they created the urban lifestyle and culture which we now consider our normal due. The Royal Style, the mystique of Royal Power and Eminence, the notion of *Great Culture, of Urbanity,* became the essential feature of *The City,* adding to its commercial viability, and to its attraction to all levels of society — bourgeois, trade, labour and servant class alike.

The Urban Consumer-Kings

A Canadian National Film Board documentary called *Mobility* suggests that, by the year 2000, most of the world's population will reside in twenty megalopolises of some ten million inhabitants each. Most of those will exist (or subsist) in Third-World suburban shantytowns. Braudel points out that this is nothing new:

A town would probably cease to exist without its supply of new people. It has to attract them. But they often come of their own accord towards its lights, its real or apparent freedom, and its higher wages. They come too because they have already been rejected first by the countryside, then by other towns.[8]

The movement to the city is ancient. The old Greek for that phrase is going *eis ten polin*, which is the recognizable root of the city name *Istanbul*. But Braudel says that that migration accelerated and took on a new character with the modern development of the world "market" and "capital" economies and the development of our *great* capital-mercantile cities and the increasing use of *money*. Braudel describes Naples in the 17th and 18th Centuries:

> The poor ... were so crowded that their life encroached and overflowed onto the streets. The majority of beggars [did] not have houses [but found] nocturnal asylum in a few caves, stables, or ruined houses.... Next to them an undeveloped petty-bourgeoisie of half-starved artisans scraped a bare living. Above this totally deprived mass let us imagine a super-society of courtiers, great landed nobility, high-ranking ecclesiastics, obstructive officials, judges, advocates, and litigants. These privileged people did not always receive rich livings. A little money was enough to move a man into the ranks of the nobles.[9]

One social critic at the time wrote, no doubt hyperbolically, but aptly: "Our former butcher no longer practices his trade except through his assistants since becoming a duke."[10]

People will do just about anything for the magic elixir, reified, *commodified money*, because it permits us to *rise above our ordinary material life*. This is what we all come to the cities, and stay in them, for. The urbanized, consumerist life that most of us live now, even on our farms and in our towns and villages, derives not from our peasant and native forebears' life in country *towns*, but, by means of the magic of *money*, of *value extracted, abstracted, alienated and re-commodified*, from that parasitical and profligate lifestyle of the royal or ducal courts that annexed themselves to the wealthy, independent, European merchant trading towns of the Middle Ages and turned them into *great capital cities*.

We are now learning to rue the day that the Royal Symbols of power and affluence, the Royal Culture of essentially non-productive luxurious exploitation, became the lifestyle model for the newly rich and powerful. That model subsequently became the life ambition for all of us below who aspired to it and now take it as our minimal social and economic — and ecological — right.

The Unbalanced Life

Our consumer society, with its belief in leisure pastimes, its expectation of entertainment and spectacle, and its central concern with the provision and consumption of exotic material goods, is something quite apart from the *ordinary material life* of most people in most places throughout most of human history. Yet, just a generation or two from the rural peasant turnip field or the forest or grassland hunt, we now have come to think of that regal lifestyle as ordinary. *Urbanization,* which is at once effect, facilitation and support of the "market" economy, according to Braudel, is the name by which we all, merchant, worker and moneycrat alike, have grown accustomed to living as hangers-on at the court of a vanished king. It is a regal abstraction that feeds compulsively and coercively off "outside resources." It is precisely this life that is no longer *sustainable* as we mine other peoples' ecosystems by means of our ever farther-flung commercial empires, and try to tell them they can join our unsustainable courts of abstraction.

All of us who are employed at jobs within the urbanized and far-flung "money-market" economy, or who otherwise get our necessary support from it, are part of the circular MGM-GMG game.[11] We are rewarded more or less for our part in the generation of more *capital* and our legitimization of the game without much thought as to whether our own productivity is ultimately *real*, in the sense of being *primarily,* rather than *secondarily,* productive. Much less do we concern ourselves with whether the foundation of our productivity, the productivity and forgiveness of the earth's ecosystems, is infinite. For the *capitalists,* the *money itself* is the object of the game: MGM. For those of us *employed* by the capitalists, the object is the *regal consumerist lifestyle*: GMG. It is a velvet trap, seductive and destructive. George McRobie in his book *Small is Possible* says:

> One of the principal characteristics of industrialization
> … is its over-riding tendency to create a more and more
> dependent population. This dependence, this external
> direction of people's lives, is most evident in the case of
> their employment, over which they have virtually no
> control, either as regards its availability or its quality. It
> also applies to other aspects of daily life.[12]

The problem addressed by Community Economic Development, one of the "other aspects," is the autonomy, self-reliance and sustainability of local peoples — *re-empowerment*. However, the effect that arises from economists not perceiving or dealing with the difference between two distinct economic cycles has been the internalization by the market (and us) of the interests of capital power — interests fundamentally at odds with ours and with a free market — in order to retain our regal privileges. *We have willingly disempowered ourselves.* Local Economic Development does not address this empowerment issue except through the discourse of money, and the discourse of money, we have seen, is other-directed.

> Orthodox, conventional economics, technology and applied science, and administration, are designed to serve an efficient system of production and consumption and not to develop the capacity for people to look after themselves. The conventional structures are those that support a system of economics whose starting point is the production of goods, and for which purpose labour is (merely) a factor of production.
>
> A structure that supported an economic system whose starting point was people — economics as if people mattered — and regarded goods as the natural and inevitable result of making everyone productive, would look very different.[13]

One thing neither would have is either the form GMG or the form MGM but the form PGP — people producing goods for people, and doing so directly, for their own purposes and according to their own needs. A better acronym might be NPN — proceeding from needs to production to needs satisfaction. In any case, the form of the economy — its basic systemic design — would be that of a *real-goods* economy, the "root" that gives rise to and supports all else, an *unorthodoxy, apart* from the world market economy, which those who operate and apologize for the "capital" and "market" economies dare not let us contemplate.

The "root" is not very far from any of us. It was only by the Education Act of 1870, allied with agricultural depression and urban puritanism, that the imaginative cultural life — the art and folk-ways — of the British tribal system was finally broken.[14] The de-culturation process that began with the Romans, and continued through the Holy Roman Empire, and the witch-hunts of the Middle Ages that destroyed the tribes' spiritual and political leaders, was officially concluded only 64 years before I was born! How tenacious! And the tribal-village ethic is, even now, not yet quite out of reach. It persists, if only in our nursery tales, as a *golden age* memory. Many things are remembered as golden. Caring, self reliance and autonomy are high among them. The golden memory often shows up in TV commercials that extol the *natural* way of life. It persists in the handing down of traditional cultural gardening and craft habits and skills. Some new feminists are reaching back for parts of its spirituality to support their struggle for the re-empowerment of women. I believe we can still reach back for that tribal, non-monetary, self-reliant economic style as well, and use it to liberate our communities from the same oppression.

Re-balancing

It takes very little ground to feed one person for one year — an acre or two, and in some places and for some people, even less. It takes much in the way of imagination and cultural knowledge. We have lost much of that knowledge, but we can regain it, and there is more of it to be had from modern research and technology. There is a living to be had on the fringes. Food can be grown in sewage, often solving two problems at the same time. Small technologies can re-cycle the detritus of our consumerism, for a start.

Any community with any sort of land base and available labour can *begin* to become self-reliant. A community could provide its own essential goods and services for people who also remain partly connected to the "market-money" economy and continue to enjoy some of its advantages when they need or want them. There is already a comprehensive body of work and experience on community development, and even specifically on how to develop local self-reliant economies in urban and rural settings. The work of David Morris and his Washington-based Institute for Self Reliance is notable.

> The city is becoming an ecological nation. As such, the city maximizes the long-term value of its finite piece of land by creating elegant, biologically based systems. Local self-reliance is the goal. The term 'local self-reliance' is defined in various ways by different disciplines. To the ecologist, local self-reliance means 'closed-loop systems' where the wastes of one process become the raw materials of another. To the economist,

local self-reliance means capturing for the benefit of the local community the greatest amount of 'value added' to the original raw material through processing and marketing. Local self-reliance, to the biologist Russell Anderson, is 'a type of development which stimulates the ability to satisfy needs locally'. It is 'the capacity for self-sufficiency, but not self-sufficiency itself.' Self-reliance represents a new balance, not a new absolute.[15]

Community Economic Development seeks, along with *economic* development, the re-establishment of the ecological sense of *kinship* with one another and with place which must underlie the concept of *community.* We are presently making our cities, and ourselves within them, *commodities* to feed the corporate *golem.*[16] Our challenge is to begin to make of them natural places that will feed and sustain ourselves and our cultural, social and economic lives. I am aware of two responses that seek to redress this imbalance. One is the view of Pat Mooney, a co-director of the Rural Advancement Fund International of Brandon, Manitoba, whom I interviewed for *City Magazine.* The other is the view of Peter Berg, Director of the Planet Drum Foundation, of San Francisco, California. Both call for a re-activation of our vital and organic links with the places that sustain us. Pat Mooney thinks it is time we re-peopled the country. Peter Berg (like David Morris) thinks it is time we countrified our cities.

No large urban area in North America is sustainable at present…. Cities aren't sustainable because they have become dependent on distant, rapidly shrinking sources for the basic essentials of food, water, energy and materials. At the same time they have severely damaged the health of local systems upon which any sensible notion of sustainability must ultimately depend. Water courses have become dumps for everything from petrochemicals to sewage, nearby farmland is continually lost to housing developments, soil and water tables are poisoned by seepage wastes from garbage buried in landfills, fossil-fuel emissions increasingly mar the purity of air, and the small refuges for wildlife and native vegetation that still remain are constantly reduced or threatened.[17]

Peter Berg and the *Green Cities* movement accept our nearly universal urbanization, and propose that we work within our cities to make them *natural*. Pat Mooney and his colleagues want to change the urban-rural imbalance.

> Ultimately, city people are going to have to move to the country [and] repopulate rural areas. There's got to be industrial strategies, taxation policies, wage and employment strategies, the whole gamut, to actually encourage more small-holdings out in the countryside.... The fact is that you need voters, you need neighbours out there if you want to keep the school buses running, if you want to keep the schools running, if you want to have any shopping at all, then you need folks, and the tax base has got to be altered to reflect that need. And I think that, for a lot of people, it's a very viable way to live, an increasingly viable way to live.[18]

I believe that Pat Mooney and Peter Berg would agree that, whether we live in the city or in the country, we all must learn to think and act in land-connected ways again. There is a living model which we can learn from in the economic and community life of the Old Amish communities in the United States.

> Where Amish are active, countryside and town are full of bustling shops and small businesses, neat homes, solid schools and churches, scores of roadside stands and cheese factories. East Central Ohio even has a small woollen mill, one of the few remaining in the country. Compare this region with the decaying towns and empty farmsteads of the land dominated by large-scale agribusiness. The Amish economy spills out to affect the whole local economy.[19]

Braudel seems to say that, historically, in the confrontation of community and centralization, the abstraction of value we know as *money* has always carried the day for the forces of alienation and central control. The cultural, political and economic dislocations here and in the Third World that serve market ideology are tragic enough. Even more so however, in my estimation, is the commitment of those who would assist people, supposedly in their own best interests, toward an irreversible enlistment in the "job-money-market" world economy. The usual goal of Local Economic Development, working within the dominant economic system, is like introducing the suckling pig to the rendering pot.

All of our customary efforts to develop communities economically and socially come down to the matter of fitting people into the royal life of the trading, manufacturing, capital city.

1. Job training exists to help the former peasant or native learn skills to replace skills no longer thought to be relevant (and which are then lost), and so become acceptable for employment in the new order;
2. Local economic development is undertaken to assist the aspiring and established townspeople or rural immigrants to set up shops and businesses as *petits entrepreneurs* within the world market system;
3. Social development is predicated on educating and acculturating the new-comers to the practices and ethics of the market economy, and the royal tastes of our vacant monarchical court.

Such goals, tied to an unsustainable economics, are also unsustainable. They are, fundamentally, culturally normalizing and therefore, at base, they constitute a *political agenda*, particularly with respect to aboriginal populations, and continue the destruction of cultures.

This kind of development effort is a political agenda, also, if it refuses to consider, and add to its tool kit, alternative development possibilities that are congruent with (for example) the existing social norms of aboriginal reserves, or the alternative economic and cultural tastes of others who are not comfortable with the money-market ethic and morality or who are suffering debilitation from its operations. It is a political agenda, also, if it addresses the needs of those of our rural villages and towns suffering job loss and depopulation only by means of and within the economic system dedicated to the world market *that has brought about* their job loss and depopulation.

We can counter the forces of alienation and central control with local value retention and locally autonomous economic management, and do so with other than *market* ethics and morality. To develop *communities,* I submit, *demands* that different ethic. We need to expand and re-invent our *ordinary material life* in both its ethical and practical dimensions. For capitalist and consumer alike, the money-market-dependency game, a forced and artificial cycle of production and consumption, is now fatally threatening the world's resources, ecosystems and bio-sphere, as well as the social fabric and general well-being of our society. Murray Bookchin writes:

> Capitalism has transformed itself from an economy surrounded by many pre-capitalist social and political formations into a society that itself has become 'economized'. Terms like consumerism and industrialism are merely obscurantist euphemisms for an all-pervasive embourgeoisement that involves not simply an appetite for commodities and sophisticated technologies but the expansion of commodity relationships — of market relationships — into areas of life and social movements that once offered some degree of resistance to, if not a refuge from, utterly amoral, accumulative, and competitive forms of human interaction. Marketplace values have increasingly percolated into familial, educational, personal, and even spiritual relationships and have largely edged out the pre-capitalist traditions that made for mutual aid, idealism, and moral responsibility in contrast to businesslike norms of behaviour.[20]

I think Bookchin would agree that we must go home again. But where is home now? Is home where you grew up, or where you moved to? Is it where your family is, or where your job has gone? Where your heart is, or where your hat hangs? Where you live, or where you work? And why are those separated? Alvin Toffler suggests the answer.

> ... The very word 'economy' was defined to exclude all forms of work or production not intended for the market, and the prosumer became invisible.
>
> This meant, for example, that all the unpaid work done by women in the home ... was contemptuously dismissed as 'non-economic', even though ... the visible economy ... could not have existed without the goods and services produced in the ... invisible economy.[21]

Home means where it all comes together for you.

Chapter Five

LADYBUG, JIG!
Parsing the Root Economy

The Home Economy

Ordinary material life — the life of *home,* where the *hearth* is — is much more complex than Braudel takes time or space to describe. There have always been within it distinct and separate internal economies of trade and of gifting, and further internal divisions of quite distinct and separate value exchange vectors, significance and moral effect.

The word *economy* comes from the ancient Greek word for household, *oikos,* and *nomos,* the word for steward or, in its feminine form, housewife. The *oikonomos* was the household manager. The "root" economies identified by Braudel are still the non-monetary economies with which most families function, or which operates among friends and neighbours.

This homely economy is the economy of family, friends and charity, and not the economy of the bargain. This is our *primitive* economy, in the non-pejorative sense of that word, our *first* economy. Some think of it as a *feminine* economy: the *hearth* is a symbol of both female and home. But, however characterized, this is the economy in which those who need, receive, and those who can, give, without close reckoning. It is the economy in which people simply do the necessary things for themselves and one another, and get on with living.

Long before the ancient Greeks, most tribal economies functioned structurally that way. They still do. Who can, does — who needs, receives. Riane Eisler suggests that there was a long neolithic period in Europe which seems to have had no war and in which people seemed to have lived co-operatively and co-equally in what she calls a *partnership* society, as opposed to later societies which she calls *dominator* societies.[1] Karl Marx did not invent the formula *from each according to capacity, and to each according to need.* It describes the primitive economy of most of human history, like that native to North America, as described by Howard Adams:

There were no poor and needy by comparison with other members, and likewise no wealthy and privileged; as a result, on the prairies there were no classes and no class antagonism among the people. Members of the community were bound to give each other assistance, protection, and support, not only as part of their economics, but as part of their religion as well. Sharing was a natural characteristic of their way of life. Each member recognized his or her responsibility for contributing to the tribe's welfare when required, and individual profit-making was unknown. Everyone was equal in rights and benefits. Some native communities still function communally in this manner, particularly in poor areas. Very few members set themselves apart from the community and attempted to accumulate material wealth for themselves.[2]

The Gift Economy

Marx's compassionate formula failed in the gigantic, bureaucratic, detached, objective central economy that claimed to be Marx's inheritor, and it simply is not appropriate to the "market-money" economy, which necessarily functions with a different ethic. Lewis Hyde writes:

> Tribal peoples usually distinguish between gifts and capital. 'One man's gift', they say, 'must not be another man's capital'.... A gift ... should be consumed, and not invested for growth. If such transferred wealth is added to [a] clan's capital and kept for growth and investment, the subclan is regarded as being in an immoral relation of debt to the donors of the original gift ... and something horrible will happen.
>
> What happens in fact to most tribal groups [who capitalize gifts in the European way is that] the social fabric of the group is invariably destroyed.[3]

It is important to consider this distinction.

A market exchange has an equilibrium or stasis: you pay to balance the scale. But when you give a gift there is

momentum, and the weight (or energy — like in collid-
ing billiard balls) shifts from body to body.[4]

The economy of the gift has a sacral function of validating and
verifying community. The gift is given in the expectation that it will not
be hoarded by any individual. The gift, or the value or energy it represents, must be passed on, not back: it can neither be kept nor reciprocated. Given without the demand for immediate reciprocal return, it is
given without regard for the recipient's present ability to either pay for
or return the gift. Thus it affirms each person's unconditional *inclusion*
in community, his or her *rights* as a member of that community. It affirms the reality of *shared belonging.*

The gift does return, but usually along a circuitous route that
goes around most of the community before it comes back. It
celebrates and solidifies *community.* A market exchange is different.
Immediate and direct reciprocal return is both intended and required, and if return is not immediate but delayed, performance of
that return is *secured* by some instrument or other. The remarkable
thing is that, although we are overwhelmed by our market practices
and morality, we also have the gift economy tenaciously with us. We
still have a remnant of the sacral ethic of the gift in our vague dis-
comfort with the morality of *accounting* for a gift monetarily. It's the
thought that counts.

The gift celebrates the fact of relationship, the reality of community. There is significance in the fact that the same bassinet has been
used by three or four generations of related infants, that my grandchild
sleeps where I was, as an infant, laid. The gift exchange, on both sides,
belies the kind of *alienation* that is endemic to the idea of ownership —
private, *exclusive* use. Questions of the distribution of wealth and
ownership (of means of production or of anything else) become irrelevant. Who owns the bassinet? Who cares, or even remembers?
Surely what is important is that the infant is sleeping in it.

Usership, not ownership, is what is important. In a gift economy,
the bundle of rights which we speak of as "ownership" is constituted
differently and there are different kinds of rights concerning different
things. The gift affirms realities other than those the market does.
Diametrically different from the vector of market relations, it is also
diametrically opposite in its morality. The "ownership" rights bundle,
for example, does not include the right to destroy what is "owned" —
the absolute which defines "ownership" for us — it instead includes the
obligation to *preserve,* even to *enhance* the gift.

In a culture with an active gift economy, the receiver of a gift has the right to enjoy it privately — for a while. But it eventually must be passed on, or people will think he figures he "owns" it, and that he is an unnatural creature. Unnatural creatures are not suffered to live among human beings. And when it is passed on it will usually be enlarged, or accompanied by additional gifts, for essentially the same reason. Try putting that concept alongside the reality of how we use our environment and its resources. We are in an immoral and unnatural relationship with our earth and its ecosystems, one no rational human being could possibly countenance. What ought to be done with us?

"Male" and "Female" Economies

The most primitive of societies are the *hunter-gatherers*, those who live on what they can catch and kill or find and dig up. The name suggests, again, two economies. In a hunter-gatherer society, the *gatherers* (mostly women and children) feed most of the tribe most of the time with a natural harvest of roots, berries, fruits, vegetables and small game. Gathering is a regular, close-to-home activity with a necessarily steady, immanently present sedentary, conservation ethic and morality of repetitive tasks undertaken in co-operation with co-workers. I see in this the prototype of Braudel's *ordinary material life*. It is significantly what we have characterized as *female*. The *hunters* (mostly older boys and men) provide important dietary protein supplement, but not, in most cases, the dietary staple. Hunting is an erratic, ceremonial affair necessitating an ethic and morality of risk-taking that is part of an activity pattern characterized by long absences from home and long periods of waiting or careful tracking punctuated by short periods of violent and exhilarating activity and, while it is undertaken in co-operation with fellow hunters, it is competitive with respect to the game that is dominated, chased and killed. I see in this the prototype of the "market" economy, where we still use hunter language. It is, significantly, what we have characterized as *male*.

The ascription of gender to these activities, however, is not necessary to differentiate the two sets of human endeavour and economic styles: the activities alone characterize them. One, the competitive economy of the hunt, herding, trade and war, is *outer-directed*, and the other, the co-operative economy of the hearth, planting and gathering, is *inner-directed*. Our general "market-money"-based, capital-driven "world-class" economy of competition would seem to grow from, or at least parallel, the primitive outer-directed economy of the hunt, herding, trade and war. But the internal economy of the hearth, planting and gathering, in which the sustaining, sacral flow of *the gift* can function day by day rather than as a rare *charity*, seems still to be with us, although in a devalued state. And the two distinct economies still comprise very different and distinct behaviour patterns and substance, and foster and require diametrically different ethics, morality and values.

Home and Market Morality

We know what the ethics of our market-place economy are. They are clearly based on *domination* mythology derived from the hunt. We may like to imagine what the ethics of a generalized economy based on the internal co-operative community economy of the egalitarian *partnership* society Riane Eisler describes might have been like. That would necessarily be the project of those who speak of *feminizing* the economy, using the short-hand gender-code word to refer to the internal economy of hearth, home and community. But it might be that this inner-directed economy must *remain* inner-directed to remain a *partnership* economy, and that *any* outer-directed economy must be accomplished with the outer-directed *dominator* ethic and morality of the hunt and of trade.

Jane Jacobs makes a similar point in *Cities and the Wealth of Nations*, although she separates the categories differently:

> Military arts derive from the hunting and raiding life, economics from the making and trading life. Many assumptions, intuitions and virtues that work very well in the one serve badly in the other.[5]

She is aligning "economics" here, as it originally was, with the "making" activities associated with manufacture in the home-place — the *oiko-nomia*, or house-keeping, of the old Greek City-State. Management of the extended Greek household was devoted to sustaining the life of the entire household in the long term, manufacture was for use value, not exchange value, and the benefits of increased wealth were enjoyed by all. The assumptions, intuitions and virtues of the market-place, in the ancient Greek world, were matters, not of *oiko-nomia*, but of chrematistics; "… the manipulation of property and wealth so as to maximize short-term monetary exchange value to the owner."[6] Clearly, what we call "the economy" is properly a matter of chrematistics, a word derived from *chrema*, meaning "goods" and *chrematiso*, meaning "to conduct monetary business with." It clearly does not mix with oiko-nomia — market values do not mix with home values.

It is the entire point of this book that we re-learn that difference, and make a more extended *oiko-nomia* — extended farther from the family to the entirety of our local communities — once again the centre and mainstay of our "economic" life. It will help in that re-learning, to understand that the products and values of the internally-directed *partnership* economy are not comfortably displaced into a *competitive* context. They are not properly to be monetized or capitalized. You cannot healthily operate the dynamics of a family with the values of the market-place or military camp. *But the reverse is also true.* You cannot operate with the open morality of the family in the hard world of the market-place, where you must function with the necessary values of the *dominator* economy. If one believes in the necessity of a *Yin/Yang* balance between the so-called masculine and feminine forces of life, then we each must become skilled at both kinds of ethics and morality. What we must become *very* skilled at is recognizing where and when each is appropriate and when not, so we can choose the proper mode to function in — and apply the *family* morality to a *community oiko-nomia* that replaces *chrematiso*.

Re-inventing Ordinary Material Life

Three facts about the "market" and "capital" economies are significant. The first is that they are separate and distinct economies. The second is that they function in tandem to form our present economic system. The third is that they are still linked to, and dependent upon, the "root" economy. And of that, it is significant that none of us, even the affluent, ever leaves the "root" economy of *ordinary material life* absolutely. We all give and receive non-monetary resources daily in this largely forgotten and overlooked economy, within our families and our neighbourhoods and among our network of friends, associates and colleagues. These are the *gifts* that sustain us. We pay them too little attention.

This "root" economy is still the economy that people live in when they fall through the floor of the "market-job-money" economy, and still acts as the essential support base for the "market" economy, contracting and stretching itself as the "market" economy waxes and wanes in what it can provide. The "root" economy is the ultimate socio-economic safety net that is fundamentally necessary to keep home and hearth together, maintaining us, and our families and our communities through hard times, so that we can even *have* a market economy again when times improve. There is a whole range of economic activity still within this economy of home and hearth that is available to us, or can be re-captured. We can contemplate building upon these realities, and the shadow memories from our tribal and village past, to re-structure the inner-directed activities into an expanded local *internal-partnership* economy that re-invents our *ordinary material life* at the scale of *community*.

There are also other economic activities that were originally found in the *inner-directed* economy of the home-place, but which have now been industrialized and abducted into the *external-dominator* economy of industry, trade and commerce. Starting with the home and moving out from there, we can hope to re-capture some of these for the homely community economy we are building. I believe this to be the necessary re-balancing that we must do in order to counter our excessive reliance on the market, and on its ethics and morality of aggression and competition.

A Matter of Choice

The American "New Economist" Hazel Henderson said on CBC-Radio's *Ideas* series, *Citizens at the Summit:*

> An economy is simply a set of rules that is devised by a culture in order to promote its cultural norms and what that culture thinks is valuable (what they are 'optimizing' for) ... Every grand economic theorist ... described and rationalized a system that was already in place ...[7]

We have a clear and simple choice to make. If we wish to function according to a different ethic and morality — and that is clearly what we must do to overcome our excess exploitation of our resources, the over-taxing of our ecosystems and biosphere, and the degradation of our fellow human beings — we must function in a different economy. That has to be what we are saying when we say that we need to develop the *community* as well as the *economy* of that community. It also has to be what we must mean when we talk about a sustainable economy of restraint. We need to write the economic theory of the home-place, and write it larger than it is now.

It is also evident that we cannot simply invent a new economic style and require everyone, overnight, to begin functioning in a different mode. If we are to achieve a new economics, it will have to evolve — or be evolved consciously — from something already in place and familiar. The new, expanded economic theory of the home-place must, of course, be different from that of the "market" economy. We need not only to write — or recover — the economic theory of the home-place, and write it larger than it is now, we must write it sufficiently larger than it is now, and sufficiently well, for it to supersede our present economic style and become the new economic norm. There is a great deal already in it that we can deliberately choose, a great deal that is familiar to us that we can grasp and adapt: its ethics and morality, its style, its products and relations of production — even its currency of exchange. Nothing needs to be invented, nothing unfamiliar needs to be invoked. Hazel Henderson continues:

> What I think is that the new economic theories are going to grow out of what's happening now in every country, and what's happening is a resurgence of local level initiatives and they are, many of them, entrepreneurial. And they include self-employment, small business, the growth of co-ops, the growth of alternative, limited-purpose currencies to make up for the deficit when the national currency is not available to a local community to complete the trades they need to make with each other.[8]

In a money-mediated economy, we see clearly — from the evidence of practice — that the idea of what constitutes wealth is distorted by its focus on the abstraction rather than on the reality. Alan Watts, a pop-religious writer of the 1960s, called the Great Depression of the 1930s not so much tragic as absurd. All the same materials, all the same factories, all the same farms, all the same people, all the same skills, were all still available, and all still in place. There were stockpiles of food and goods and raw materials available. But the economy was paralysed, and people could not get even necessary things, because there was no money. But money is not value, it is only the measure of value. To say that people cannot exchange value with one another because there is no money is like saying you cannot build a house because you have no feet and inches. The Great Depression was an ideological, not an economic, crisis. It was a crisis of the imaginary — money — rather than a crisis of the real — the goods and services that were still available to be matched to people's needs.

Our society may not be able, stoically, to continually choose that which is good for it and us and avoid that which is not. E.F. Schumacher is a little more optimistic — has a little more faith in human stoicism.

All history — as well as all current experience — points to the fact that it is man, not nature, who provides the primary resource: that the key factor of all economic development comes out of the mind of man.[9]

In any case, even though it is clear that what is required is that these new economies be *developed in practice* before they are *described in theory,* I believe that, by first unchaining our habits of exchange from the market practices we have been taught and so long constrained within — by acting out at the practical level — we can begin to actualize a choice to adopt a new, analeptic economic system. It is within our power, now, to begin functioning economically in a manner that would eventually produce — structurally and without the necessary continuing exercise of stoic will — desirable effects that are opposite to those undesirable ones which are endemic to the economic system we have allowed to develop. We have models to guide us.

The Informal Economy

We can call the "root" economy the primitive economy, the tribal economy, the neighbourhood economy, the community economy, the prosumer or the family or the inner-directed or partnership economy. It is all of these; but I choose here to understand them all as *pre-money* economies. The "cultural norm being optimized" here, the "set of rules being devised" to facilitate it, need have nothing to do with *money.* Even when we use money in these homely economies, it tends not to be accounted in quite the same way or to quite the same degree that it is accounted in the money economy. That is what is meant by *informal.*

In an informal economy, formal accounting is uncomfortably held to be, somehow, inappropriate. And that is exactly correct, even if largely unconscious. "That's close enough," or "we'll call that even," we say. The essence of these "root" economies is neither wealth nor money, it is *survival, survival, survival* — for which *sustainability* may now be another word. Neither word can apply to the money-market system of economic organization, nor, I suggest, to local economic or community development efforts undertaken within that system.

The Invisible Economy

There is, fundamental to the "root" economy of ordinary material life, the ordinary — and economic — life of the home. I have said before that we accept it unthinkingly. The reality is much worse. The most resounding indictment of our present economic system is that this foundation of all else is invisible to it. Formally invisible. In all likelihood, *deliberately* invisible. New Zealand parliamentarian Marilyn Waring has documented this invisibility in her book *If Women Counted: A New Feminist Economics.*

> ... as a member of the New Zealand Parliament from 1975 to 1984 ... I underwent a rude awakening as to the importance of the United Nations System of National Accounts (UNSNA). I learned that in the UNSNA, the things that I valued about life in my country — its pollution-free environment; its mountain streams with safe drinking water; the accessibility of national parks, walkways, beaches, lakes, kauri and beech forests; the absence of nuclear power and nuclear energy — all counted for nothing. They were not counted for in private consumption expenditure, general government expenditure, or gross domestic capital formation. Yet these accounting systems were used to determine all public policy. Since the environment effectively counted for nothing, there could be no "value" on policy measures that would ensure its preservation.
>
> Hand in hand with the dismissal of the environment, came evidence of the severe invisibility of women and women's work. For example, as a politician, I found it virtually impossible to prove — given the production framework with which we were faced — that child care facilities were needed. "Non-producers" (housewives, mothers) who are "inactive" and "un-occupied" cannot, apparently, be in need. They are not even in the economic cycle in the first place. They can certainly have no expectation that they will be visible in the distribution of benefits that flow from production.
>
> These injustices result from the System of National Accounts, an international system of economic measurement. Any annual report of the World Bank, the International Monetary Fund (IMF), United Nations (UN) agencies, or national governments, is based on national account statistics. The UN uses national accounts to assess annual contributions, and to appraise the success of

regional development programs. Aid donors use the UNSNA to identify deserving cases, need being determined by per capita gross domestic product. The World Bank uses these figures to identify nations that most urgently need economic assistance. Multinational corporations use the same figures to locate new areas for overseas investments. Companies project the markets for their goods on the basis of the national accounts projections and plan their investment, personnel, and other internal policies.

And that's only part of the story. For individual countries, the uses made of national accounts and their supporting statistics are manifold and have far-reaching effects. They are used for creating frameworks or models for the integration of economic statistics generally. They are used to analyze past and current developments in the national economy and are the basis of projections of the possible effects of changes in policy or other economic changes. They are used to quantify all areas of what is considered the national economy so that resource allocation decisions can be made accordingly. Governments project public service investment and revenue requirements for the nation — and plan new construction, training, and other programs necessary to meet those needs — all by using their national accounts. They are used to forecast short and medium-term future trends. They are also used internationally to compare one nation's economic performance with another's.

Early national income accounts were evolved ... in order to justify paying for wars. Since the institutionalization of national income accounting by the United Nations, however, the motive has expanded. A major reason that only cash generating activities are taken into account is to ensure that countries can determine balance of payments and loan requirements — not as a comparative exercise, but as a controlling exercise. Those to whom money is owed (First World governments, multinational banks, and multilateral agencies) now impose this system on those who owe them money. They are interested only in seeing the cash generating capacity of the debtor countries, not their productive capacity. But whatever the change of motive, two things are constant. Those who are making the decisions are men, and those values which are excluded from this determination are those of our environment, and of women and children.[10]

Marilyn Waring, however, much as she subtitles her book *A New Feminist Economics,* does not advance a new economics — only accounting adjustments to the old. And if I am correct, and that old economics is fundamentally and structurally colonialist as well as male-chauvinist, then absorbing the value of women's work and the environment into it will only make these susceptible to full economic colonization. Put boldly, if the invisible work of the home, usually described as "women's work," were monetized within the structure of our present monetary system, it would be subject to the same abstraction and alienation as all other valuable and value-creating activities. The result, I believe, would not be a "feminizing" of the economy, but the ultimate subsumption of "feminine" economic qualities into the dominator economy — in other words, the ultimate triumph of patriarchy. I believe a safer route is to construct a truly *new* economics, with a different ethic and different institutional and monetary structures — a new "feminist" economics, if you will — upon the base of the reality that now is invisible, making it very visible indeed, but carefully preserving its ethic and values *separate* from, if parallel to, the present economy.

Poverty and Affluence

In the foreword to Volume Two of his work, Fernand Braudel uses the phrase "release from the prison of self-reliance" in referring to moving away from dependence on ordinary material life, and release from this *prison* into the *economic life* of the market is one of the changes that money and the "market" economy wrought on peasant societies.[11] It is the generally accepted view of Western industrialist society that *self-sufficiency* is a lamentable state in which the individual, family, community, village or region has *only* their own resources to live on. But we need not accept that view uncritically. Vandana Shiva says it is an extremely biased view.

> Culturally perceived poverty need not be real material poverty: subsistence economies which satisfy basic needs through self-provisioning are not poor in the sense of being deprived. Yet the ideology of development declares

them so because they do not participate overwhelmingly in the market economy, and do not consume commodities produced for and distributed through the market even though they might be satisfying those needs through self-provisioning mechanisms. This cultural perception of prudent subsistence living as poverty has provided the legitimization for the development process as removing poverty....

... Traditional economies are not advanced in the matter of nonvital needs satisfaction, but as far as the satisfaction of basic and vital needs is concerned, they are often what Marshall Sahlins has called "the original affluent society."[12]

The "market" or "money" economy, with the access it provides us outward to regional, national and world trade (and the access it provides those forces in to us) has released us from the "prison" which Braudel saw (with some justification) as limiting human economic and material life, in comparison with the modern world "market-money" economy, and with the variety and freedoms (local dislocation and destruction notwithstanding) that it affords. But *development* into the world "market-money" economy manifestly does not remove *poverty*, except as the culture of development self-interestedly describes it. What it removes is *self-reliance*, replacing it with *dependence*.

Such development also removes *self-determination*, replacing it with an economic colonialism that becomes internalized by the nations, by the peoples, and by the people which it subsumes. The anti-communitarian practices and values of the money system are encoded in our concepts, our methods, our technology and our politics. We have internalized them into our very style and manner of being. It will be difficult to put that process into reverse, but it is practical — and perhaps necessary — that we do so.

The Dual Economy

In writing about community-based economics, David Pell and Susan Wismer (Guelph, Ontario planning and development consultants) advocate a dual economic approach, allying a local, home-grown economy to the national economy.[13] The practice could be seen in natural operation in 1982 in Papua-New Guinea, in a report to *National Geographic Magazine*:

Papua-New Guinea can be described economically as having two circuits. The upper one is urban-biased and cash dominated. Characterized largely by mining and timber projects, it is more strongly integrated into the world economic system than is the second or lower circuit. This larger circuit is based on the traditional subsistence activities of the rural majority....

The expansion of the public service was in part due to the need of the government to legitimize itself by tackling the problems of poverty, malnutrition, literacy, rising unemployment, and lawlessness. Many officials now realize that a lot of the country's problems are ... the product of development. Thus, the government recently withdrew a request to the United Nations for famine relief, perhaps fearing that such a precedent would increase the country's dependence on outside donors.[14]

In 1982, the natives of Papua-New Guinea were living in a money economy for the benefits that it can bring, but relying on a parallel, non-monetary, real-goods economy, their traditional economy, for the satisfaction of their basic needs. They seemed to be able to balance the two, unwilling to trust the money economy for life's essentials, but using it for the extras — including adapting it to the native *big-man* political ceremonies (akin to Canadian West-coast native *potlatches*) where vast amounts of money can be spent with nothing much *real* being lost.

If we consciously take money out of our *local* economic equation, at least for the essentials, we could focus our attention cleanly and directly on finding and committing — or developing — the local resources that would match our local needs and skills, and we could establish such a parallel local economy in our own communities, wherever they are. We might also be able to adjust our basic needs to fit our available resources, and get a handle on sustainability.

A Local Real-Goods Economy

Commercial barter clubs (actually businesses) are operating now within our dollar economy.[15] These function by accepting the consignment of goods offered for barter for other goods: that is, participants first put goods into the hands of a broker for a *credit*, subsequently spending that credit for other goods offered by the broker. They effectively by-pass temporary *shortages* of money, but they are still functioning only within the "money-market" economy and retain all its disadvantages to local development except that of scarcity.

Barter goods used in such a fashion are, in fact, a *money* according to classical economists[16] (although not a *common money* in Galbraith's definition) and can (unless subject to strict rules and regulations, and strict enforcement of them) exhibit all the essential characteristics of money — including inflation and devaluation, hoarding and limitation of supply, and the artificial increase known as interest or usury. I would argue, however, that there can be very important differences between Galbraith's common *money as we know it* and some forms of exchange mediation which classical economists would still call money. I will argue that difference in the second part of this book, as we set aside the common *money as we know it* in favour of a method of facilitating production, distribution and exchange in a cashless, *real-goods* economy which is based on *barter*, but uses the concept of *credit* along with a membership network to accomplish the by-passing of money, its shortages, and its ethical fall-out.

Establishing a cashless real-goods economy could be managed in any locality in a manner similar to that of the commercial barter clubs, but it would have to be done with a different ethic. The different ethic would have to permit balancing the needs that exist within the community with the resources that it possesses and the capacity of that community to fill those needs from those resources. That is simply a matter of auditing basic local employment capacities, skills and resources, then similarly auditing local needs, and then matching the two.

In such an exercise, there will be considerable overlap or matching of resources and needs. Local resources can be quickly mobilized to meet local needs. Immediately, local production and distribution of basic goods and services according to local need will create a local, real-goods economy. A lot of organizational effort will be required, but real *development* work need be done only where there is no overlap — that is, where you must find or develop resources that are absent, or modify needs. Imports may eventually be replaced, for local economic development reasons, and preference given to local production, but that may be a second step, after mobilizing local production to meet local *unmet* needs. Imports that cannot be replaced by *any* local production — oranges in Yukon, for example — will, of course, continue to be imported. But, if the exercise is to reach its ultimate success, only goods and services that *cannot* be had, or substituted for, locally, will be imported. This is the *new system* economy of the 21st Century, asked for by E.F. Schumacher:

> The economics of giantism and automation is a left-over of nineteenth-century conditions and nineteenth-century thinking and it is totally incapable of solving any of the real problems of today. An entirely new system of thought is needed, a system based on attention to people, and not primarily attention to goods (the goods will look after themselves!) It could be summed up in the phrase, "production by the masses, rather than mass production."[17]

We begin this *new system* economy simply by paying attention to peoples' needs in *real* goods and services, and their capacities within their communities to fill those needs from their own resources. We need absolutely, however, to focus on the *real* needs, capacities and resources, and by-pass the *demand* ethic embedded in the *money* system. Demand in the *money* system is something that can be expressed *only* with money: no money or equivalent, no *demand*, no matter what *need* may exist. Money only serves to obscure the true economic picture of needs and the capacities to fill those needs, and it must be abandoned in this Community Economic Development model.

Once need and capacity are identified, irrespective of money demand, the next step is to organize productivity and consumption by the collective choices and decisions of individuals within the community so as to meet the specific identified needs of both the community and the individuals in it. All that is lacking is the means to facilitate exchange. We may not be ready to simply produce and exchange according to capacity and need. But this lack is the simplest of all to remedy. We just write new rules, as Hazel Henderson suggests, to authenticate what we have already chosen to do. There is more to say on that later.

The Economy of Enough

Such a *new system* local economics could — if an environmentally conservationist ethic is also brought into play — also be what Bob Goudzwaard, an economist with the Free University of Amsterdam, called the *economy of enough.*[18] I suppose it might be possible to mandate both a local economy, and a real-goods economy within our dollar economy by the exercise of regulation and continued stoic political will. But such command economies have failed spectacularly in Eastern

Europe. The better approach would seem to be to create a strictly local economy, free of the distortions that capitalism very soon introduced into what we now call the world free-market economy, a local economy founded on fulfilling need rather than answering to demand, and using a differently structured means of exchange.

By drawing a local boundary around such a community economy by means of the kind of special local currency Hazel Henderson mentions, we might make it relatively easy, as well as useful, for local resources to fill local needs, and realize a different kind of ethic as well. We would make it *easy* by not requiring people to have available sums of our *universal commodity money* to pay for that needs-fulfillment, but by enabling them to do so with the personal resources of time, labour and skills — *the natural money* — which we all already possess.[19] We would make it *useful*, by ensuring that there is a wide range of locally produced needed goods and services available for the *spending* of this *natural money*, a means to spend it, and a market to spend it in. This would free people from the bottle-neck of money, which now gets in the way of our capacity to spend our *natural money* until some employer requires it and so permits its translation into our *universal commodity money*, and only then into the market. It would also remove local primary sustenance from the *anti-community* manipulations of the capital economy. A local market in locally produced goods and services facilitated by a locally mandated means of exchange could be managed and operated according to whatever ethic and morality — economic, environmental or social — that the people within the community have or care to work out. Nor is it necessary for such a local economy to be isolationist, even if it is aggressively self-reliant. It is highly unlikely that any locality would be totally self-sufficient, and trade between localities would be desirable, even if it were not necessary. That could be accomplished by replicating the model of the local economy at the regional level, by mutual-agreed confederation, and so on.

Being *needs-based* rather than *demand-based*, and removing from the economic equation *commodity money*, with its drive for non-productive increase through *interest*, the drive for excessive exploitation of resources might also more easily be removed. *Competition* in production might be discouraged in favour of *complementation*. None of this would necessarily do away with the spectre of over-consumption of resources if needs out-run them. But over-use would, at least, not be a built-in foundation of the economic support system. A *sustainable* economy would move into the realm of possibility.

The Spanish Anarchist Collectives

Such economies, outside the "market-money" economy and based both on the concept of filling *need* with *enough* and not *excess*, and on so-called primitive communitarian *ethics*, have existed successfully in this century and in an industrial context. In my lifetime (I was two years old in 1936), the anarchist collectives of Spain functioned in just that manner.[20] The industrial workers who formed the anarchist collectives (in the midst of revolution) were barely-transplanted village peasants. They still had, and valued, their communitarian, near-tribal culture and values, and their social and economic systems. They carried them, relatively intact, from their villages into the industrial towns as they migrated in neighbourhood groups into the industrial age. That is significant in the context of the proposition I am putting forward in this book.

It is also significant that, where these peasants did form governments, they frequently tended to burn the money they found. I would say they recognized its function and role in the destruction of their former lives. But the most significant fact of all is that their economic structure *worked very well,* both at local levels and between localities. They proved, at least until they were destroyed militarily by both the communists and the fascists, that a modern industrial economy could be managed in something like a tribal or peasant village communitarian, non-monetary style, if given peace in which to develop it.

I submit that something like these Spanish anarchist collectives ought to be the model for Community Economic Development, not for political, but for purely functional environmental and economic reasons. It makes no sense to me to try to build a newly self-sufficient, supportive and non-market-oriented community economy upon an economics that is structured for a purpose and end that is just the opposite of what Community Economic Development wants to achieve. It makes every sense to build it upon the systems, values and procedures that, at one time, did define the self-reliant, autonomous communities which transferable money destroyed.

The Sustainable Economy

To achieve a sustainable economy, *money has to be set aside* — at least money that functions as our money does in the matters of alienating and transporting value across our local borders and as the sole arbiter of *supply* through *demand.* It has to be set aside in favour of a system which focuses attention and meaning on the production, distribution and exchange of the *real* goods and services that are required by a population, and upon defining those requirements according to *need* rather than *demand*. We need to do for *community* what John Friedmann suggests we must do for *families*. That is to selectively *de-link* from what he calls the "exchange" economy, what I am calling the "market-money" economy, and what Braudel calls the "market" and "capital" economies:

> Selective de-linking is portrayed here as a voluntary act. But for many workers it may present itself as a choice that is forced, for instance, when their jobs are suddenly declared redundant.
>
> ... With the prospect of further industrial decline, social polarization, economic stress and hyper-inflation, it is not unreasonable to suppose that households (ed: or read "communities") will become increasingly self-reliant, using from the economy what they need for the self-production of their lives, and little more. The trend is already underway.[21]

Along with money, we will also be able to set aside its internal demand for constant increase and the profit motive, both of which drive resource depletion in the *economy of excess*. In fact, we can't do that *until* we set *money* aside. Setting aside *money* and *demand*, we can also set aside the concept of *payment* with its requirement for advance or immediate and exact reciprocity, and replace it with something like the familial ethic of mutual support.

The functioning of a nurturing relationship among members of a convivial community could also make more possible a nurturing relationship between the individuals in it and the environment that sustains them. In an economy that lived off local resources, it would be evident that the life of both individuals and community is directly sustained by the health and productivity of the local ecosystem. Establishing a sustainable Community Economic Development on this model, we might establish communities which can be economically, ethically and morally, and *environmentally* more sustainable.

Sustainable Community Economic Development

It is now quite possible for us to accomplish such a de-linking on a community basis. Those non-monetary communities of the heart, sentiment, emotion and memory can be re-constituted to form a significant part of a new, modern *dual* approach to economic life. It cannot be done in its old, primitive fashion, of course. We are too de-cultured to return successfully to a circumscribed, prosumer, tribal communitarian life and too acculturated to a life of individuated freedoms — which are usually expressed as freedom *from* domination by smothering *tribal* communities and families — and to the "Royal Urban Lifestyle." Even in our family life, we are extremely individuated. For most of us, any extended family life exists only at weddings and funerals. But I believe that those cashless communities of self-defined and indigenous cultures, whose economies were based on productivity for use and on the tribal *family-support* ethical model, can be specifically useful models for creating a new economic style in our modern, individuated urban context.

To re-establish community and a communitarian economics, we need a form or fashion in which to re-establish the ethic and practices of the tribal economy that yet recognizes our modern individuation and does not close off all of the advantages and pleasures of our urban, courtly life which the market economy brings us. Fortunately, with our present statistical and information techniques, our modern computer technology, and our modern communications technology, such a method of re-organizing our basic economic life locally is eminently possible once again. It can be done as a practical rather than an ideological pursuit, still using our money-habits of exchange facilitation, but in a convivial rather than a competitive way, and without seriously compromising our larger, market-oriented life-style. It can even be done without requiring *community* to be a homogenous geographical entity. Part two describes a practical program with which those changes can begin.

Today.

PART TWO

The LETSystem in Winnipeg

Chapter Six

THE LOCAL EMPLOYMENT
AND TRADING SYSTEM
Recognition and Presentation

The Rescue of Community

Are we concerned with cities and towns as anything more than agglomerations of population, jobs, services, accommodation and commerce? Are we content for them to be, like the Mediaeval fairs that did *not*
become cities, essentially venues for trade? And by trade, do we mean
the alienation, through the devices of *festival marketing* and the uses of
universal commodity money, of value created in our various home-places?
Are we satisfied to live in cities that are essentially key structures in our
trans-national systems for the extraction, abstraction and alienation of
our vital resources beyond our control, and little more than places for organizing us efficiently into large groups conveniently available to our
various uses as labourers and consumers in those systems?

If the answers to those questions are no, then we should be looking
to radically different tools, forms, patterns and facilitation methods
upon which to base our primary economic life. Such a change may well
be necessary to re-establish our cities as the sources and venues of
economic life *for their inhabitants* that they once were. It will be necessary to rescue them from becoming disempowered adjuncts to a life
that is ordered from some different and wholly artificial, if not inimical,
plane, and restore their holistic sense of *community*.

The best that can be hoped for Local or Community Economic
Development within the dollar-driven national or world trade systems
is to reach some kind of balance of trade in which value imports are not
exceeded by value exports. No such statistics are usually kept for
municipal jurisdictions as they are for provincial or federal ones: cities
are not seen by our economics as economic units — partly because they
are not self-reliant in our economic system. If those statistics were kept,
however, maintaining a local balance of trade level would be no easier
and no different from the same attempt on the national level, where we

are now witnessing the general surrender of national self-determination to international trading blocs. Our political choices are now moving in the direction opposed to national, let alone regional or community, self-reliance. Community Economic Development needs a radical method to bring about the revitalization it pretends to.

This second part of this book describes the LETSystem and advances it as a simple and practical way to initiate this revitalization. The LETSystem is not central to a new local, real-goods "root" economy. What is central is the conscious development of primary production capacity and the balancing and structuring of the inputs and relations of the economy to cover, as completely as possible, the full range of human and community necessities — at least the fundamental necessities of food, clothing, shelter and culture. But something like the LETSystem is the necessary key to *unlocking our addiction to commodity money,* and the destruction that follows upon that addiction, and to *unlocking the restrictions that universal money-use* has placed upon the *natural money* we all possess in our learned and innate skills, and in our time and labour. The system helps to make whatever physical resources we may possess freely available to serve *us* once again.

The LETSystem provides the conceptual breakthrough that shows us that we *can* disconnect from our uncritical assumption that the money system is the only possible way to organize an economy. It focuses our attention away from money and onto the real substance of any economy, the goods and services it produces and exchanges. It permits us to imagine *another way* to make a living, to facilitate exchange, or to conduct Community Economic Development, and it provides us with a simple and practical way to begin to do that.

Initial Exposure

The Local Employment and Trading System was devised by Michael Linton of Courtenay, British Columbia, in the early 1980s. My first exposure to the LETSystem was through a documentary on the Sunday evening CBC-Television business program *Venture,*[1] which was broadcast (for the second time) in the fall of 1986. I was already a graduate student in the School of City Planning, Faculty of Architecture, at the University of Manitoba. I was also reading Jane Jacobs' book, *Cities and The Wealth of Nations.*[2]

In that book, Jane Jacobs — an urbanist and our foremost critic of the old-style city-planning profession — claims that cities and their regions, and not nations, are our appropriate economic units and the actual generators of our wealth. Since information about an economy's health comes from the demand and value fluctuations of that economy's currency, Jacobs claims that we cannot get accurate feedback information about our true economic health when we use national currencies that are based on the false 18th-century assumption of Adam Smith (in his book, *The Wealth of Nations*) that nations are our basic economic units.

What Adam Smith thought he was describing as the economy of Britain, Jacobs claims, was actually the economy of the City of London and its (very extensive) region. *Urban currencies*, she says, are required in order to get accurate readings about the activity going on in our economy, which all takes place within the true economic generators of our economy — city regions. Without those readings, which we cannot get with a national currency, we are not able to make any rational sense of our economy, or do any sensible economic planning at all, on any scale, because we really cannot tell what is working in our economies and what is not, nor where adjustments and remedies should properly be applied.

If we had regional currencies, so-called *regional disparities*, for example, would be recognized as the differences in wealth, or strength, between separate economies, and solutions to those disparities might be sought in more practical forms. Without the fine-toothed tool of urban currencies, however, we do a lot of economic blundering. It was immediately apparent to me that a LETS economy, creating what is effectively a local, bounded currency, might fulfill that minimum requirement which Jacobs insists is necessary for the accurate measuring of our economic performance and, not surprisingly, also the minimal requirement for managing the rational economic development of any city and its region, either for its own self or as part of the conglomerate of urban economies that we call the national economy.

I was part of a class in City Planning, under the direction of Dr. Kent Gerecke, that was researching alternative economic models for the City of Winnipeg on behalf of a short-lived effort by a collective of grassroots organizations: The Winnipeg Initiative. This was an economic development initiative that was organizationally assisted by the office of Cyril Keeper, a member of the New Democratic Party, then Member of Parliament for Winnipeg North Centre. In September 1986, as part of our research for The Winnipeg Initiative, the class invited Michael Linton, the designer of the LETSystem, and manager of the system operating in Courtenay, to make a presentation to us in Winnipeg.

Linton briefly explained to the class the LETSystem's genesis, theoretical basis and development, as well as how it worked and how he went about presenting it to public meetings. Such presentations relied in large part upon learning and playing a Monopoly-style game which enables a group to experience how a LETSystem functions.

In *LETSPLAY*, attendees go through a process of mock economic exchanges, as in the game of Monopoly, using a list of items which vary in price, and in the percentage of their price demanded in our customary currency (Canadian dollars) and in the LETSystem's internal nominal currency, *green dollars*. Monopoly money is used to stand in for ordinary money, and the *green dollar* transactions are recorded on a graph as plus or minus positions relative to a zero vertical axis.

Linton told us that he considers *LETSPLAY* to be the principal tool for introducing and teaching the LETSystem. Once the game is learned, he says, people know how to function within a LETSystem and anyone can set up and operate one.[3]

The class decided to ask Linton to present, on November 3, 1986, an academic seminar on campus for the university community and an evening game demonstration and discussion open to the public at a central location, sponsored by The Winnipeg Initiative. About twenty people attended the afternoon university session, mostly from the School of City Planning. About thirty people with avowed economic development interests attended the evening session.

LETS Theoretical Background

At the afternoon university session, Linton detailed the theoretical background and practical experience of the LETSystem, notably that:

- our customary "official" currency has no substantial value, but is only a "re-presentation" or measure of value;
- using a centrally distributed measure of value of limited and scarce supply to mediate all our socio-economic relations limits those relations;
- our potential for prosperity is limited according to the local or individual supply of the exchange medium that we use as a value measure;
- permitting economic relations to lapse simply for want of the measure of value rather than the substance of value is fundamentally absurd and not necessary;

- many of our society's ills, including personal and regional poverty and both economic depression and economic depravity, are caused by the limitations of our money system and its structure;
- a system which records value and value exchanges between people directly can replace scarce money in the exchange of goods and services possessed and needed by people in any community;
- such a system has the effect of creating a nominal local or personal currency which is created by each individual as he or she needs it to facilitate economic transactions, and in whatever quantities are needed;
- such a nominal local currency can be supported by individual commitment to the community to return equal value to that community, into and through the system, at a future date;
- such a self-created, self-reliant and self-serving economic system can be both convenient, secure, and safely self-managed to the local advantage of any community, and could protect it from the vagaries of the general money system;
- such a direct system, by-passing centrally issued, distributed, limited money, overcomes structural problems of our customary monetary system with a currency of markedly different structure and morality that also has salubrious moral effect.[4]

Money Theory and Community Economic Development

The designer of the LETSystem presents the system as a way in which individuals can create their own currency, legally claiming for themselves the empowerment generally considered to be restricted to governments and what are called *credit grantors*, usually meaning the centres of economic power that govern our economy. In an economic transaction in the LETsystem, Linton claims, each individual creates the amount of currency necessary to facilitate that transaction. Each individual backs his or her *personal* currency by means of the commitment to return into the system equal value in the future. The aggregate of *individual, personal currencies* backed by individual commitment becomes, in effect, a *community currency* backed by the community's collective capacity to create value out of its own resources of material and the work and capacities of its members.

It is important to note that it is the collective guarantee of committed individuals and the resources, goods and services available in their community — together with the capacity to *realize* the available resources as goods and services — that underwrites the LETSystem and its currency, not the individual guarantee of a collective entity like a bank or government based on its power to legislate and command, or on pre-existing wealth in gold or some other substance of value, which our national monies are based upon.

Linton calls the LETSystem's *personal* currency *green dollars*. He claims, with some justification, to have designed the first significant advance in money theory in 2,000 years. While personal money systems have been known before, it is not likely they have enjoyed the LETSystem's simplicity and sophistication. They have certainly not enjoyed the ease of operation made possible by modern computer technology.

I found, eventually, that presenting the LETSystem as an alternate or personal *money* system was not an easy task. Prospective seminar attendees reacted with suspicion to the notion of creating their own money. It sounded vaguely illegal to them. They feared a breach of the federal government's imagined monopoly on money creation. It is not, of course, a government monopoly, since private credit grantors are the ones who create money in our system. Even merchandise coupons are a limited and bounded currency. People tended to look for a scam, especially when the matter of membership fees was broached.

Later, I myself generally encountered such fears and suspicions in promoting the LETSystem in Winnipeg. They derive, I think, from presenting LETS as a *money* system, from the mere fact of talking about another way to create *money*. While Linton presents it this way in order to provide a familiar format in which people can begin to function in a new way, I ultimately decided to choose a less troublesome descriptive format — that of the very familiar *barter* exchange.

Linton makes the further claim that the LETSystem itself, because of its structure, improves the economy of any community by increasing trade and keeping wealth at home, and so builds up a community economically. Because it does that, he feels that it should be welcomed by merchants in any community, and that a community's merchants can be a source of the federal-dollar financial support that is still necessary, unfortunately, for operating the system. In fact, to date the LETSystem has never been generally welcomed by merchants, anywhere. Merchants tend not to be overtly interested in non-monetary trade, and it is not until a LETSystem included a large number of merchants that internal trading could approach the level and variety possible with *money*. An unwillingness to think of economics in anything other than in terms of our customary money has also proved troublesome in other quarters.

Linton also claims that the two basic functions of a LETSystem are sufficient to achieve the effects of both community and economic improvement. The LETSystem requires people to deal with *one another* in their economic relations, and it requires them to *deal* with one another in their *economic* relations. It generates social contact and the community solidarity that comes from relating to one another for economic reasons, and it generates economic contact and the improved local trade that comes from relating with one another for social reasons. The LETSystem enables and requires the members of a community, in short, to *communicate* at a fundamental, practical level. Linton believes that the necessary inter-personal communication, together with the economic advantages of dealing with one another instead of with value-alienating forces, are sufficient for both social and economic development.

The elegance of Linton's creation lies in the fact that such changes in community relations can be achieved without requiring of its participants any special knowledge of social or economic theory or matters of ethics and morality, or even any volition or concern for such matters. All people need to do is use the system, conducting their economic affairs in a familiar style but merely in a different locus, and change will result. What Linton calls a *convivial* rather than a *competitive* community can be achieved *structurally*.

In my experience, however, while Linton is not wrong, the LETSystem has not proven *sufficient in itself* to achieve significant levels of community economic development. In fact, in Linton's own LETSystem, use has fallen off. Concerning this, Linton has said to me that if people find the system of use, they will use it, and if they do not, they will not, and either is O.K. In other words, he still believes that the *system itself* is its own best advocate and that active, *hands-on* promotion and active and intentional internal development of a LETSystem is not, or should not, be necessary. I believe additional effort is required, and that it can only help if LETSystem members approach their use of the system *conscious* of its potential for change, and *desiring* that change.

LETS Hands-off Style

Linton's approach is very much a *hands-off* one, and the LETSystem is organized to function with an absolute minimum of human administrative effort and involvement. Trades are arranged between members who find each other by means of a want-ads style publication and who then come to their own terms on valuation. The person in the position of buyer then uses the telephone to record the trading information on a telephone recording machine at a central location. That information is regularly transcribed in writing and entered into a computer data base program. Subsequently, regular records, invoices, receipts and statements of members' accounts are issued and delivered.[5]

The LETSystem's techniques work very well. But many people still need and desire — and miss, in all the technological communication — simple, direct human contact and the physical, tactile confirmation of even *commercial* relations that a money transfer provides. This is quite ironic in a system that seeks to promote social contact among its members in their economic activities. The technology makes it *simple,* but it also seems to militate against the building of *community.*

Linton also believes that the system, once understood through the playing of the simple game he has designed called *LETSPLAY,* can be initiated and operated by anyone, and that anyone, understanding it, will also wish to initiate, operate and use it. I found neither to be necessarily the case. He also believes that its general application as an alternative economy among a generalized middle-class population is its future. I found that ideologically disquieting, for those who need rescue most from our money system are the poor. They are also the hardest to speak to about the system, because they are, if anything, more focused on getting money than anyone else in our society.

Reservations were expressed privately to me, after the seminars, by several people, that the LETSystem seemed, indeed, ideal for the self-employed, least useful to the employed middle class who might best understand and be able to operate it, and most difficult to explain to the habitual and very poor who would find it most useful. All these reservations, I discovered, were justified.

The self-employed can sell their products or services for a combination of the normal currency of the country and the LETSystem's nominal currency, covering their costs with conventional money and taking some of their profit in the nominal currency, and they find the LETSystem very useful indeed. The middle-class employed find that the time they need to produce goods and services for their neighbours in the LETSystem is taken up with earning money at their jobs. The unemployed and the very poor, who need alternate sources of support and who have the time to spend doing tasks within the system, have — like merchants — all their attention focused intensely on acquiring money — or, in this case, jobs or their welfare rights — and do not listen well to ideological or theoretical exhortation based on establishing a different economic system.

Alternative Economist Guy Dauncey, who has written on the LETSystem in his book After The Crash, suggested to me during a week of seminars he presented at the School of City Planning that he believes active and continuing *leadership* is required both to begin a LETSystem *and* to bring it to successful operation. That leadership has to be local. Operating at long distance, Linton cannot supply that leadership to the other localities which he organizes. Experience also proved that LETS leadership needs to be generalized and collective. One or a few people taking decisions and making plans soon becomes a bottle-neck. LETS works best with large numbers of its members taking responsibility for its continuance and spread.

Detailed and prolonged instruction in the LETS accounting and data management computer program is also more necessary than Linton supposes.[6] It is simple to operate, but not easy to learn in one sitting.

These difficulties are merely logistical problems, but they do interfere with the simple self-start of a LETSystem following from a purely theoretical understanding of it and a simple game-playing familiarity with it.

The LETS Presentation

The participants in the seminar were polite and attentive as Linton presented his arguments and played a copy of the *Venture* TV documentary about the LETSystem in Courtenay. Such scepticism as there was among the attendees was expressed principally through a lengthy and unresolved discussion around the possibility that an individual might make purchases with the self-created LETS nominal currency and then subsequently renege on the commitment which backs the internal currency by failing to return value equal to that which had been received.

There was an almost Orwellian experience of *doublethink* on that subject — the capacity to believe two things, both of which could not possibly both be true at the same time. The group could agree that any and every purchase was *paid for* up front in the nominal currency, and that that currency thereafter continued circulating in the system with undiminished value, even if its originator subsequently defaulted. Yet they also insisted that a defaulter would have had something for nothing, even if he was subsequently barred from the LETSystem for default, and should be materially punished in some form. That he or she would not be so punished, or otherwise materially deprived, was taken by many to indicate that the system would not work, notwithstanding that others continued to use the system quite undeterred and unaffected by the default.

I believe that those who are concerned about defaulting are making an incorrect connection with our present money system. The familiar defaults and failures of our present money system are failure to pay for goods on time, breached agreements, theft, and bankruptcy. These things happen to governments and other credit grantors (or money creators) all the time. Something similar also happens to individuals when, for example, trust, savings and loan companies default on their obligations to depositors, who then lose their deposits. That's what deposit insurance is all about. Yet, no one says the money system cannot work because of this defaulting. In a LETSystem, there can be no default on payments, because *green dollar* transfers are always completed in full to close every transaction. There is no other way to record them. Those familiar money paradigm models do not — cannot — apply.

In fact, a defaulter in a LETSystem does "get something for nothing," not by virtue of the fact that he or she receives something that was not "paid for," but by virtue of the fact that he or she failed to support his or her own self-created currency. This is akin to what happens when a nation ceases to exist, and its currency is no longer of any value, because it has nothing to support it — like Confederate dollars after the U.S. Civil War. Massive defaulting by most members, of course, would lead to a LETSystem collapse, but the mere fact that defaulting could occur, or even the fact of some actual defaulting, does not mean that the system "cannot work," as some claim. Absorbing any losses from defaulting (a kind of self-insurance) is automatic in the LETSystem as long as it keeps functioning and honouring the defaulter's (indistinguishable) "currency" which has already entered into the system. The guarantee of the defaulter's currency is, in effect, taken up by the LETS community as a whole.

In fact, a default is essentially inconsequential in a LETSystem — there is, effectively, no consequence to an individual default, just as there is no consequence to an individual negative balance. How much defaulting would lead to loss of confidence and collapse of the system is a moot point. More important perhaps is that a default is a failure to continue the essential circulation of trade. It is for this, and to prevent system collapse, and not for moral reasons, that defaulting is discouraged. It is not, however, punishable except by the sanction of loss of membership.

If a particular LETSystem wished to do so, of course, it could make its membership a matter of contractual obligation, in which case defaulters could be held liable for the value of their defaults in a court of law. If a LETSystem were generalized in a large community, that might be an advisable course to take as a general discouragement to mass defaulting. However, LETSystems are now established — as the acronym suggests — on a basis of voluntary association and voluntarily assumed responsibility, and no LETSystem has undertaken a more hard-edged course. The instance of defaulting in over a hundred locations around the world has been utterly negligible.

The example of people cleaving to two mutually exclusive opinions on the question of defaulting — that the defaulter's currency is still circulating but that he got something for nothing — does serve to illustrate, however, the difficulty people have in accomplishing a *paradigm shift* on the subject of money theory. They are right, but they find it difficult to figure out why they are right.

We have so internalized the imperatives of our now customary money system that we cannot easily conceptualize a system which functions with a different set of assumptions. People find it difficult to conceive that something that functions so like a currency — and sometimes is even described as a currency — can be so easily self-made, and so they discredit it. They require such rationalizations as that the defaulted value is absorbed as a loss by the community as a whole, like self-insurance paid for after the fact, or they have to work it through in ever more complex terms of familiar money theory, as I have just done, to make it comprehensible to the money system. But torturing the rationalizations of the money system to describe LETS — while it can be done — eventually just gets absurd. In fact, a wholly different kind of thinking is needed to properly understand the LETSystem and its non-currency.

The LETSystem is the beginning structure of a *new paradigm* for economic life — or, perhaps the return to an *old paradigm* in a new context and form. Part of the difficulty people have in accomplishing the necessary *paradigm shift* to internalize an understanding of the LETSystem derives, I think, from the presentation of the LETSystem's notation system as a *money,* which is the *old paradigm*. Doing that leads us to hang on to the concepts of *buying and selling,* as we consider the LETSystem, rather than crediting the alternate terminology — which Linton himself promotes — which is *acknowledging and providing.* I eventually found it preferable to abandon the money terminology altogether and concentrate on the essential mutuality of embedded community relationships that is implicit in the structure of the LETSystem. That is, I decided to shift all the way to the *new paradigm,* if I could, and not get stuck half-way.

The new paradigm involves the old practice of *gifting*, and the old concepts of the mutuality of the right to consume and the corresponding responsibility to produce within and for a community. It should be noted that it took me about two years of theorizing and writing to purge (even imperfectly) monetary concepts from the vocabulary with which I now describe the LETSystem and its functions. Our indoctrination into the money system and its imperatives is terribly deep.

Eventually, and somewhat reluctantly — and for reasons external to the LETSystem — I did have to return to the notion that LETS users *do* use a kind of money. It was necessary to do so principally because classical economics sets its definition of money so wide that *everything* is money now, and economists can't talk about economics or an economy in any other terms. In that respect, we are all classical economists. But I did eventually find a way to satisfy *old paradigm* economic thinkers and still be true to the *new paradigm* of community gifting, by falling back on the notion that everything is money, and considering the money that is in use in a LETSystem to be, not the *green dollar* markers equal to a dollar in which members measure the value of their goods and services, but *the goods and services themselves*.

In the LETSystem, the money that is used is what could be called the *natural money* of our own skills, time, labour and resources. It is these that we spend in the money system, of course, but only by translating them first into money — which is the fundamental problem with money, because money — the medium of translation — is scarce and becomes a bottle-neck that controls, and, controlling, impedes our free spending of our "natural money" resources. That "natural money," however, is always, generally speaking, readily available to all of us at the personal and community levels, where it is usually visualized as *barter* or *working for kind* not *wages*, and it is the power to spend that directly which is freed up and magnified in the LETSystem, through precise records keeping and a larger vision.

This *natural money*, in the LETS context, is limited only by the *availability* of those skills, time, labour and resources, and by their usefulness — that is, by the *extent to which they are needed*. If I am ill and incapacitated and so am unable to provide something to someone else, I am as short of the wherewithal to trade as I would be, lacking money to spend, in the money system. Likewise, if I had a skill or a resource that no one wanted, I would be quite unable to trade with it. Similarly, even if I had the resources with which to trade, but what I wanted was unavailable, no trading could occur. The supply of our "natural money"— our resources of material and human capacity — is not actually unlimited, nor is the need for what is available really infinite. To say the same thing another way, the ultimate value of *green dollars* in any application depends on how readily they can be "earned" and "spent," and that depends on capacity and need within any community, and on the willingness and capacity to trade. *It is the trading activity itself which constitutes an economy*, and not either the amount of a monetary or other symbol that its values are recorded in or the simple presence of mutually matchable capacities and needs. The LETSystem is no automatic guarantor of local economic development — the development work still has to be done. But — specifically — *neither need nor the capacity to fill that need is limited by the supply of some arbitrary and artificial exchange-facilitating medium in a LETSystem*, and that is the essential LETS difference.

The second part of the afternoon seminar was taken up with a discussion of special applications of the LETSystem in a City Planning context. The principal application discussed was getting around money shortages for specific short-term development enterprises. A co-operative housing project or the construction of a church or community building or other physical development project can be facilitated because the LETSystem, just like money, can be used to translate effort of one sort into effort of another sort.

Construction workers, for example, can be *acknowledged* (that is, in the old paradigm, *paid*) in the internal nominal currency for the work that they do, out of a supply donated or pledged by others who earn it through volunteering other sorts of activities of which they are capable. So a hairdresser can charge customers in the internal nominal currency and provide that to the LETS building fund, from which it is transferred to the construction workers. Hairdressing is thereby translated into carpentry, *without* the intervention of cash money.

Such translation of volunteer effort is applicable to any group project, and can be a valuable function of the LETSystem in Community Development. That, in such cases, LETS is an adjunct to rather than a substitute for the money economy, does not diminish its value. The *combination* of our *natural money* with the more ordinary *coin of the realm* is a feature of most LETS exchanges. Combination exchanges merely mean that the individuals in the exchange are simultaneously functioning in two different economies — in the national or world economy facilitated by money (especially when what is being exchanged originated therein), and in the local economy of self-created work and goods.

Most of the other discussion of applications germane to City Planning centred around the development of community empowerment

through increased control of personal and community economic activity (and, therefore, development) and the enhancement, through
necessarily increased interaction within the community, of the sense of
community itself. It was this discussion that gave me the context for undertaking LETS in Winnipeg. The evening workshop was attended by
eight students from City Planning and sixteen people reached through
the Winnipeg Initiatives mailing and an announcement at a meeting of
150 economic, community and social development workers. Note the
small response from development "professionals" — about 10%. That's
a response level we will come across again. The evening session
covered much the same ground as the afternoon academic seminar, but
also included *LETSPLAY* — which made for a lively and entertaining
evening, but did not generate a significant commitment to join the system.

Initial Reactions to LETS

The reactions of the seminar group and the evening workshop
were typical. I later noticed a fairly consistent division of reaction
among groups to which I presented the LETSystem. It must be noted
that my presentations were to groups whose leadership had expressed
interest in advance, presumably on the basis that the group would be
sympathetic to the notion. Nevertheless, the response echoed that of
the Winnipeg Initiatives professional group. A small percentage (about
10%) of any sizeable group immediately and enthusiastically recognized both the nature and the benefits of the system. Most people
received the notion open-mindedly and were prepared to be convinced
after serious examination of the answers to their questions. Another
small percentage (about 10%) reacted with an almost panic-stricken
denial of the concept.
    This latter 10% minority refused to credit any reasonable answers to
the objections they raised. The objections were usually the ones about
defaulters and about legal recourse to remedy for unacceptable work or
goods, but also about possible government opposition and income tax
problems, and about bank and big business opposition. One might add
legitimate organized labour and union objections, and ideological opposition from the *self-made* business successes of the money paradigm,
which I have encountered in other forums. All of these objections are
readily answerable. But the answers are not always believed.
    Legal recourse for contract performance is the same as in the
money system, with an earlier and accessible arbitration possible

within the administration of the system. There are no taxation problems: Revenue Canada accepts the nominal currency as fairly representing the value of goods and services traded. Taxation on transactions using it follow the same rules as for money, and so, on the other hand, do tax deductions and tax credits. (Accountants, however, do have difficulty with it — a problem of educating the accountants.) Bank and big business opposition is more probable, since money-dealing is their bread and butter. But the LETSystem largely avoids banks and big businesses. Small and local businesses should be able to see the benefits to them, once they identify their real interests as being other than those of banks and big business. Of course, that is the usual *class interest* argument familiar to leftist apologetics, and it never has worked very well in general. It is also quite reasonable for organized labour, particularly in the service industries, to be suspicious of the LETSystem. *Green dollars* might readily be substituted for real dollar earnings in small scale operations. The solution is to use them as *bonuses* and not *salaries*.

Old ideology does remain a problem. In Linton's own community, he reports, most local merchants do not support the LETSystem: he says they consider it to be a *communist plot*. It has also been described as right-wing economics like Social Credit, apparently because the creation of its internal currency *follows*, and does not *precede*, the economic activity that it facilitates. The amount of currency, then, depends on the trading going on. This is similar to the money-supply theories of Social Credit, in which money, as a gratuitous credit, is issued equally to every person, the amount depending on the actual economic activity of the period immediately preceding the issue. Social Credit, however, is a centrally controlled and administered *money system*, with an issued currency backed by the single corporate entity of the state. The LETS currency — if you insist that there is one — is *created by each exchange itself* and is not an *issue*, and is backed by the collectivity of individuals assuming a community responsibility. The mistaken identification with Social Credit is another misapprehension, I think, that comes from insisting on using the old *money paradigm* to describe LETS.

Undertaking LETS in Winnipeg

After hearing Linton and observing the seminar and workshop, I undertook to associate myself with *LANDSMAN* — the LETS parent organization — and with the LETSystem:

1. I was ideologically convinced of its value as a more moral, practical, democratic and socially responsible means of facilitating economic activity and organizing our socio-economic relations than is our present centralized money-capital system;
2. I saw in it the potential for generating a community planning and development thrust owned by the members of the community itself and independent alike of any government approval process and of any private commercial encroachment, which, when fully operational, could provide independent, self-created, self-managed and self-directed employment for any community;
3. Its unique private-democratic community development approach and community power ethic was an appropriate subject for study toward a degree in the Community Economic Development field of City Planning.

In the end, the idea did sell itself, as Linton suggests, but only to the minority and a small portion of the majority. I undertook to organize and operate a LETSystem in Winnipeg and study it in practice and in theory as a thesis and practicum in Community Economic Development, in partial fulfillment of the requirements for a degree of Master of City Planning — now successfully completed.

Linton had, when we first contacted him, recently formed *Landsman Community Development Services, Inc.,* a private (shares) corporation registered in British Columbia and operating in a non-profit (non-share) mode. *LANDSMAN* has been held distinct from the LETSystem itself as a vehicle to be used to promote the development and external proliferation of LETSystems, gain assistance and funding for that purpose, and to administer community development trust funds that might be generated (in official currency) by LETSystems. Such dollar funds he anticipated generating through higher membership fees to commercial members such as retail stores, professionals, etc., and made available to members for community and business development by means of a development fund. I advised Linton that I would represent *LANDSMAN* in Manitoba, developing and overseeing LETSystems in this province, to which he agreed.

Formal association with *LANDSMAN* began with the registration with them of *LETSWIN,* a Winnipeg LETSystem, based on a nucleus of six participants in the academic seminar and the evening workshop, plus myself. Late joiners from those participants plus family, friends and acquaintances brought the total membership to fourteen by the end of the first quarter of 1987, six months after the first decision to contact Linton.

LETSWIN published its first bulletin of wants and offers in December of 1986, to the initial seven members, produced on my own CPM-based computer, before the *LANDSMAN* accounts and data management program had been received. The LETSystem was underway, in Winnipeg by January, 1987.

It was a disaster.

Chapter Seven

GETTING STARTED
Establishing the Winnipeg LETSystem

Getting LETSWIN Started

LETSWIN (LETSystem, Winnipeg) was in place and operating in January, 1987, but on a very tentative basis. The name was registered as a business name, accounts established and bulletins issued. The system failed in at least two respects — operation and use. And there's not much more than that to fail at. In the first place, I had not been adequately prepared for operating the computer program which manages the system, and more importantly, even though I hurried out and bought a telephone answering machine in anticipation of calls with trading information, no one used the system for trading.

During his presentations, Linton had described the *LANDSMAN* LETSystem data management program, which he wrote, as simple to operate. So it is. But only after it is sufficiently explained and demonstrated in a hands-on workshop and one has had some experience, under guidance, of its rather lengthy procedures. This I was not able to get during Linton's quick visits, and I was unable to travel to Vancouver for proper workshopping.

Linton was able to give me only the briefest demonstration of basic routines while he was in Winnipeg. These included setting up a dummy membership list, entering new members, entering advertising (want and offer) requests for a circular or bulletin, entering acknowledgements of transactions ("payments" made in the internal nominal currency), performing the daily routines which interconnect and alter the membership list, members' accounts, their acknowledgements, and their ads in the bulletin (and acknowledgement or payment to the local LETSystem for those ads) and which record the continual changes in the information data base, and then performing the month-end routines that produce the bulletin, a membership list, and members' account statements.

A computer-managed data base is not necessary for operating a LETSystem — all the necessary entries and transfers are simple, and recording transactions can be done by hand — but it functions most readily with computer technology. The LETSystem computer program is written in Microsoft Corporation's dBase II for use on an IBM-compatible MS/DOS computer. It has since been re-coded for use with dBase III, and several free-standing versions, not requiring the user to have copies of dBase, have been developed and are available from *LANDSMAN*.

After I received a copy of the LETSystem program from *LANDSMAN*, and using IBM-compatible MS/DOS computers available to me as a student at the University of Manitoba, it still took me several days — with professional assistance — to sort out the procedures. Establishing the initial accounts was simple enough, and the first balances were of accounts that had started at zero and had undergone no changes. Recording subsequent changes in them (after the first statements there were transactions to enter concerning membership fees, etc., although not yet any inter-member trading) and then closing and re-opening them with changed balances was a more mystifying procedure. The February month-end balances were wrong.

It is probably not practical to start a project before you have thought it through and prepared it adequately, no matter what the pressures — a lesson applicable to both Linton and myself and, I suspect, to Community Economic Development generally. Perceiving the program as one that *does not work* (in fact, it does) has disaffected people in other localities who were initially enthusiastic about the LETSystem. My experience with organizing *LETSWIN* also underscores the necessity for a continuous, experienced development presence rather than a *fly-in* and *muddle-through* approach.

For self-starting, LETS requires a good deal of familiarity with both book-keeping or banking procedures and the use of computers. Otherwise, it takes a period of continuous, detailed and specific *hands-on* training by someone familiar with the system and its program. Eventually, Linton produced a detailed manual for the computer program, and the problem was reduced, but that was a year later. At the beginning I abandoned the LETS program and devised a simple system using my own non-IBM-compatible computer for keeping the exchange records: essentially, keeping the records by hand, although in a spread-sheet program. That this is even possible speaks for the LETSystem's simplicity.

Sorting Out What To Do

In 1987, *LETSWIN* existed as a core group, expanded slightly by isolated and individual proselytizing and recruiting, with the LETSystem being presented as Linton presented it — an alternative money system. From this core group, as required by the LETSystem practices and procedures, a board of advisors fundamentally interested in the LETSystem sorted itself out. From these people, in rather infrequent meetings, ideas and approaches for developing and introducing the LETSystem in Winnipeg were forthcoming.

During the first quarter of 1987, two key notions developed from these interchanges, and from the needs and possibilities perceived by those who had been attracted to the LETS idea, and from their challenges and questions.

Henk DeBruyn, Director of the Indian Family Centre at 470 Selkirk Avenue in Winnipeg (a facility owned by the Christian Reform Church and serving a native community of some fifty families), asked how a non-profit corporation like the I.F.C. could be integrated into a LETS community. He wanted to know, basically, how his organization would fit into a general, alternate LETS economic system involving a full community like that of the North End, which includes a full mix of retail, wholesale and manufacturing establishments. His question took the form of asking how IFC could go about acquiring *green dollars* to pass to its clients, employees and volunteers as wages within that alternate economy.

Brian Emond, a social worker with Child and Family Services, Province of Manitoba, asked how the LETSystem could benefit the clients of his agency. During the same period I came into contact with Eric Rempel, of the Mennonite Central Committee's Committee on Native Affairs, re-directed to me by Linton after an enquiry to him in British Columbia. Mr. Rempel wanted to know how LETS could be used around a locally owned grocery store on an Indian Reserve in Northern Ontario, to break a near-complete welfare dependency.

A fundamental dichotomy was evident from these questions. LETS is a self-managed economic and monetary system. Its very ethic is centred on the notions of people doing things by themselves and for themselves, including co-operative management and operation of the LETSystem. The whole LETS concept is one of being freed from reliance on outside agencies, and of its participants being enabled to manage their own economic lives. The DeBruyn and Emond questions seemed to be infected with the fundamental assumption, rooted in the *charity* aspect of our present economic model, that the facilities to combat poverty are to be provided by some central agency. This is a paternalistic notion which can, I think, only perpetuate dependency. It is certainly incongruent with the purposes and style of a LETSystem.

This dichotomy became strongly evident to me when presenting the LETSystem to an inter-agency meeting arranged by Emond. It did not arise from anything said or done by the social service agency representatives at the meeting, but I was suddenly aware that I was speaking to a group of people whose careers are bound up with servicing *the poor,* and who are dependent upon *the poor* being *always with us.*

I am sure that all the people at that meeting, and Rempel and De-Bruyn and their associates, are sincere in wanting *the poor* to become self-sufficient. I am equally sure that bureaucracy itself is powerful enough to eventually put insurmountable blocks in the way of any effort to *deliver* the LETSystem through social service agencies. Paternalism in the social service bureaucracy is no doubt *structural,* and pervades everything that is done despite the best wishes and intent of those doing it.

DeBruyn's IFC could, of course, acquire and pass on *green dollars* in a number of ways, but the short answer to DeBruyn's basic question is that IFC should have *no central economic function* in a LETS economy. Rempel's question about how to use LETS to *break* welfare dependency, and Guy Dauncey's comments on leadership, provided the framework for addressing this issue.

A central agency or agencies could undertake the *leadership* role in a LETSystem and consciously lead their clients toward their own economic self-determination. But it should ultimately phase itself out and pass leadership to its clients or members. The agency might then still function within the alternate economic system, but it would not necessarily have any *special* economic function or role within it. And that is the long answer to DeBruyn's basic question.

DeBruyn's approach, while I had imagined it (with its strong fundamentalist church base) to be paternalistic, also centrally and strongly espoused the notions of his agency's clients eventually paying, *if only* (SIC!) in *green dollars,* for all the services they now get for nothing. Implicitly, at least, he was anticipating my long answer to his question. Rempel saw his task as *breaking the welfare dependency* of the native community he was working with. Both saw the task as eventually achieving the economic independence of their clients from any agency. Both were attached to private, rather than government, social service agencies.

These private workers seemed to best express, in a practical way, the necessary route to take. Nevertheless, bureaucracy is not exclusive to government agencies. Bearing in mind that the LETS ethic is fundamentally inimical to what drives social service agencies and their private or public bureaucracies, I proceeded to conceptualize my approach to introducing LETS in Winnipeg:

1. It should be a community development tool first, rather than contingently, as Linton had expressed it, and it should use a whole-community involvement approach rather than the simple trading approach;
2. It should not be merely a trading club for the educated middle class or an agency tool, but a way for the poor and disadvantaged to enfranchise themselves economically;
3. It should be based on addressing the problems posed by DeBruyn, Emond and Rempel, and the similar but less sharply focused efforts of other (and community) economic and development outreach programs concerned with the hard-core poor.

Structural Decisions

The product of wrestling with DeBruyn's question was a series of organizational charts outlining the structure of possible LETSystems, from the simplest LETS *club* to a fully developed complete LETS community economy. The charts are used in Appendix I, *Building Community With Barter Credit*.

The charts display the roles of producers and consumers, wholesalers and retailers, the non-profit sector, and the LETSystem itself. The role of the non-profit organization — or N.P.O. in the charts — is structurally analogous to the position of a government, to answer DeBruyn's underlying questions about the *leadership* role his organization could take. Any organization in that position could receive *green dollars* in tithes (as a government does taxes) through the same mechanism by which the LETSystem itself receives *green dollar* income as service charges. The LETSystem itself, then, would assume the associated role of a central bank, like the Bank of Canada.

Ultimately, the N.P.O. might receive payment in *green dollars* for the services it renders. I believe that would initially present a difficult conceptual threshold for the N.P.O's clients to cross. But, once crossed, the N.P.O. should probably then remove itself from a governing position, assume an *ordinary-citizen* position in the alternate economy, and pass the *governance* of the system to a body derived from the membership itself — a government, if you will.

The same model, answering Rempel's question, would serve the needs of an Nature Band Council, who literally are in the position of being a government — and, of course, would not have to remove itself from that role. The *payment for services* would, in that case, take the form of *tithes* as *taxes*. This is only an indirect answer to Rempel's question, however, which was how ownership of a store would help remove the band from welfare dependency.

The direct answer here is that simple ownership of the store would not achieve that removal. Band ownership of the store, especially as a co-operative, would improve the reserve's economic conditions and self-reliance somewhat, because profit from operating it would remain with the band. But it would not alter the fact that the *products sold* at the store would still have to be brought in from outside the reserve, and the band members' money would still bounce quickly out of the reserve and not circulate. You see how difficult it is to engage in community economic development within our money system? The solutions sought do not address the necessary goals, in this case productive self-reliance!

The provision or production of products by the band members *for themselves* is the only thing that would fundamentally alter their economic status. This *import replacement* process is identified by Jane Jacobs as the first step toward self-development taken by the independent towns in the Middle Ages, the step that set them on the road to becoming cities. They grew to be truly themselves only by replacing the goods that they had been importing with goods of local manufacture. Reserves could do the same, starting with basic sustenance needs.

Native Reserves have the added advantage of having very little monetized economic structure to dismantle, as well as imaginative roots still in the tribal-style economy the LETSystem emulates. This approach to economic self-reliance — a truly native approach — contrasts with the usual approach by Local Economic Development, which takes the form of investment in some industry to manufacture goods for *export from* the reserve, and which, I submit, merely further guarantees its dependency on the market-money economy, to little good effect. The same is true of any distinct community, isolated or not.

Investing for *export* of locally produced goods is the *second* step identified by Jane Jacobs in the development of cities. A native reserve or other small community, especially if it had developed a unique set of products distinctly its own, might well develop an export industry. It is important, however, that this be the *second* step and not the *first*, because taking the *second* step before taking the *first* only provides wages in lieu of welfare, it does not provide *development*. Wages are better than welfare, but without the capacity of a community for self-provisioning, providing wages in lieu of welfare leaves the community still firmly within the market economy, and much of the money that comes in as wages would still eventually bounce out of the reserve, just as welfare income does. Such measures provide money, but do not build an economy. It is just as Jacobs says: "Golden eggs, being gold, do not hatch goslings."[1]

The reason golden eggs of export production do not hatch the goslings of development, of course, is that they don't necessarily remain in the community, and their continuing production is still vulnerable to all the *external* vagaries of our dominant economy. Organizing the capital investment to begin such projects is also a problem, usually resulting in a debt load that hampers the development. Nobody hands out golden eggs for nothing, or if he does, it requires a continuing exercise of stoic will — and charity is not development, either.

If a community did organize its self-reliance on the LETSystem, and then began exporting into the market economy products developed in a LETS-capitalized (that is, human energy-capitalized) local venture established to provide goods or services *for the community first,* care would have to be taken to use the cash realized from export sales *only in dealings with the outside world* and not internally. The local economy could spring a leak.

The production of basic necessary products by members of a reserve (or any other small dependant community) for use by, and exchange among, themselves — and not requiring large capital investment, the continual good will of external agencies or the beneficence of the market — is the only way to make a fundamental change toward self-reliance in a dependent community's economic status. For the substance of its success, of course, it depends upon the community having both resources and skills. But in the beginning, neither of those has to be extensive if the community is prepared to start small and build surely. The LETSystem can facilitate this kind of active, local economic development.

The DeBruyn and Rempel questions set the course for my approach to LETS as a development tool, and ultimately resulted in the research and findings of the first part of this book. It became, in my mind, a matter of developing a community, complete with its own, independent economic structure — which is now what I mean by Community Economic Development — and doing that within and parallel to, but separate from, the dominant economy. Dealing with Rempel's question gave me the goal, dealing with DeBruyn's question the form, and the LETSystem the method.

Ultimately, I came to think it advisable for any LETSystem to separate a governing body out from the LETS structure and charge it with the task of overseeing and delivering the LETS service — much as the Bank of Canada is separated from the federal government. *LANDSMAN* had separated itself generally from LETSystems as a promotional and development tool for LETSystems. Making that kind of separation in connection with each LETSystem would make the *leadership* that Guy Dauncy claims is required for successful implementation of the LETSystem something *separable* from the day-to-day functioning and operating of the system itself.

Such considerations, I think, move the LETS concept considerably beyond its initial incarnation as, essentially, a *trading club,* and into the realm of a formal *tool* for Community Economic Development, available for use by any agency or group — even governments — but most effectively taken up by development-minded citizens themselves.

Allying With a Local Economic Development Initiative

LETSWIN was accepted as a working group in the general Winnipeg Initiatives Community Economic Development project. As such it was embedded in a presumably sympathetic network which had provided some of its initial core membership. But W.I. supporters did not automatically take out memberships in *LETSWIN,* despite so-called *full* support. In hindsight, it seems to me that the error was in thinking of *LETSWIN* as one project of The Winnipeg Initiative, whereas it ought to have informed the whole, as a fundamentally different manner and method of Community Economic Development. But this was not, at that time, a practical proposition.

It was impractical because the concept of undertaking full-scale economic development in one of our major cities by using the LETSystem would have been impossible to sell to a group centred on economic development within the present dominant economic structure. As a mere *adjunct* to a project committed to orthodox financial thinking, albeit trying unorthodox *new-wave* methods and approaches, the LETSystem could not be seriously considered, and it was not — not even properly by me, given my un-developed appreciation of the LETSystem at the time.

This experience was echoed among my personal network of acquaintances, some of whom had joined *LETSWIN* even though they fell short of being convinced that it would really work for them, or that they really needed it. Their conceptualizing of (personal or community) economic development was also centred on earning money or getting jobs, or organizing the opportunities for both within the dominant economy.

I recognized from these experiences that it was going to take a considerable length of time for the new LETS idea to percolate through the public consciousness in Winnipeg, even to the point where it might be merely *considered* by new groups and new individuals. It has taken about three years for that to begin to happen after constant operation and regular publicity.

Looking For a Constituency

The most frequent response to my early approaches to people about joining the LETSystem was that the LETSystem is a good idea (for some other, undefined *them*) but prospects tend to feel they would have a difficult time earning *green dollars* since their time and their skills were absorbed in full-time employment. Even detailed discussions about what they could do for *green dollars* (essentially, all the *uncommercialized* ordinary life skills most of us possess, do for ourselves and family, and could do for others) did not result in a desire or commitment to begin changing the patterns of their lives so as to begin doing those things and earning *green dollars* in those ways.

We are all too much private individuals, and not enough community members. In fact, our kind of democracy, as well as our kind of economic organization, is predicated upon individualism — our rights are those of individuals, not communities — an issue that arose in the constitutional debate in the question of native self-government rights *versus* those of individual (usually female) natives, and in the similar question of the rights of English-speaking Québecers *versus* the collective rights of the *Québec Nation* to protect its francophone identity. The experience found its echo, too, in the fact that no trading in *LETSWIN* had occurred by March, 1987 month-end.

I sought to gain the understanding and support of the Church and The Economy Committee of the Winnipeg Presbytery of the United Church of Canada. The Committee Chairman, Carl Ridd, a previous acquaintance, was enthusiastic in his reaction and did publicize the existence of LETS through his committee's projects and his contacts with other United Church ministers and congregations.

Through this contact I became aware of a community outreach program conducted by Young United Church in the West Broadway/Maryland neighbourhood. Private contact informed me of a similar program in the same area operated by the Broadway Optimists

(Community) Club. I learned of a Mennonite Church in the Wolseley district of Winnipeg which had an economic outreach program and an interest in housing development. Learning that there were all these development initiatives underway, I began to believe that a systematic approach to existing groups *already active* in some form of community or economic development was the way to proceed.

Approaching already committed organizations seemed to be the way around the short-fall from automatic commitment and use by nominal supporters of the system, including proponents of self-help among the disadvantaged. I had not yet learned adequately the strength of the drive for success within the dominant economy.

What About Businesses?

It began to seem necessary to approach merchants early in the process of establishing *LETSWIN*. In Courtenay, Michael Linton had approached merchants with a list of committed members who could provide new customers for them if they would accept *green dollars* for a portion of normal purchases. I reasoned, however, that involving merchants *first* would provide a positive answer to the first question usually asked by any prospective member: *what can I get in the system?*

With the hope of being able to attract membership by means of goods available in the system, at least for part of their price, and the thought of using merchants counters as a point of introduction for the LETSystem, I approached the Riverborne Community Development Corporation in the Osborne Village Area. Osborne Village is a high-profile, middle-class, smart and trendy shopping district and living neighbourhood that *generated itself*, rather than being fostered by some special program. The merchants there are firmly connected to local development initiatives. I hoped to activate the Development Corporation in a leadership role with respect to the Osborne Village merchants.

In the event, I spent a frustrating hour describing LETS to the Executive Director of the Riverborne Development Corporation, whose primary aim seemed to be convincing me (or himself) that the system *could not work*. It should also be noted that one of the Osborne Village merchants of my acquaintance, a bookstore owner, reacted favourably to the LETSystem idea when I approached him briefly. However, having failed to excite the Development Corporation, I did not pursue the project.

Feeling very strongly that the *general* participation of businesses in a community would be a key to success of LETS as a community development thrust, I also pursued the *100+ GROUP* organized in the Selkirk Avenue area. I found, to my dismay, that it had fallen apart, and that it had done so specifically because of the attempt to inject resident influence into the development of the area. A key pillar of the LETS economy is involvement and control by its members.

It is probably true that merchants overall tend to view *business* development as the totality of *community* development and want no interference from non-business sectors. On the face of it, that is a peculiar notion, since it is the non-business sectors who are the foundation of their businesses — if they see themselves as drawing their business from their own locality, which, of course, may not always be the case. As with the *second-step export* model of development, they tend to view increase and growth as something that comes from *outside*, not from *within*, their communities. It is an unfortunately common conceptual bias in our economic system. LETS, of course, takes a completely opposite approach.

That cast doubt upon the usefulness of approaching businesses at that time. Although I still felt — and feel — that the participation of the business community was — and is — essential to the success of LETS, I was uneasy about getting off on the wrong foot and being misunderstood by the business community, as had happened in Courtenay. At a meeting of the *LETSWIN* Advisory Board on April 22, the majority expressed the opinion that businesses would be interested only to the extent that they would recognize immediate financial gain from participating, such as targeted advertising, increased custom, tax advantage, and the capacity to realize hard goods and services from expenditure of *green dollars.* I eventually developed an approach to business, incorporating those ideas, but not at that time.

Some at that critical meeting felt that businesses would have to be much more sure of *value pay-back,* possibly by means of a cash guarantee supporting their holdings of *green dollars,* before they would consider getting involved. Much later, Linton in British Columbia and the LETSystem in Ottawa addressed this same question by organizing a *LETSFUND* to do just that, guaranteeing payback in dollars of business members' unused *green dollar* holdings. That, in effect, is in imitation of our early banks, which once held in gold and silver the equivalent of the paper currencies they had issued and which were circulating, guaranteeing to redeem that paper currency with real gold or silver at any time and at anyone's request — a retrograde step. At that time, however, we found no solution to the problem of uniting producers, retailers and consumers in a convivial, alternative development effort, other than by slowly building confidence and trust.

On April 22, the Board considered the choices between taking an initial business-like approach to business (i.e., presenting *LETSWIN as* a business) and taking a populist co-operative approach. While I leaned to the former, the majority of the group favoured the latter. The choices presented themselves as merely different points of entry into what would, in any case, become the same, complete, parallel economy with the usual four sectors: Private or Business, N.P.O. or Public, Consumer, and Employment.

The task I had set myself began to look very long and large, indeed.

Chapter Eight

TRIAL AND ERROR
Casting About for a Community

Yes, We Have No Communities

To undertake a community development effort one must first have a community. When we were de-cultured by the market economy, we lost our sense of community, even our understanding of what community is. There is no guarantee that our cities, towns, villages or neighbourhoods are *communities* any more. They tend to be agglomerations of districts (residential, commercial, business, industrial), developments, suburbs, and neighbourhoods in which very few of the neighbours are neighbourly. A new, culturally neutral word has been coined for what these are: conurbations. We tend now to *communicate* with other kinds of groupings — affinity groups, occupational groups, groups — even neighbourhoods — organized according to economic status, or around some industry. Our geographical communities tend to be artificial, shallow, and incomplete; mere vestiges of what used to be *community*.

I now firmly believe that our present social networks, neighbourhoods and affinity groups are, *definitively*, not communities. They lack an endemic and full-ranged *economic* life. I am now certain that an economic life of internal production, distribution and exchange, with all three elements present, is *fundamental* to community — that they are in fact what *defines* it. It was probably always the most significant factor in defining a community, although not recognized as such, when communities were geographically isolated.

I would now *define* community *necessarily* as a self-supporting, self-provisioning economic, social and political entity, with all three of *those* elements also requisite, and with the *economic* element being primary. On that definition, we have very few communities in our modern North American society. I have said in Part One of this book that we have *elements* of community economies still with us, but nowhere do they cohere in a self-aware and *conscious* manner as the core of any community outside the family, and often not even there, except perhaps in remote aboriginal reserves and a few villages.

Something like these conditions for community are described by David Pell and Susan Wismer (Wismer, Pell and Associates, Ltd., Consultants, of Guelph, Ontario) in their article about northern native communities.[1] They also identify the LETSystem in connection with expanding what they call the native *informal* economy. However, it would be impractical to suppose that we must re-organize our living space into small geographic units, the way '60s drop-outs and past Utopian-intentional communitarians tried, in order to organize local economies and re-establish *community* as I am suggesting. If we cannot have both, we would do much better to define *community* as a self-reliant, self-producing and consuming cultural rather than geographical unit, and stay where we are in our familiar spaces, most of which are urban.

Jane Jacobs, defining what she calls an *errand unit* on the CBC-Radio morning program *Morningside* with Peter Gzowski (September 5, 1991), said:

> I think that people make a mistake when they suppose that in some mechanical fashion you can draw borders and do a cookie cutter arrangement of communities that will suit everybody in them. One of the things that a city affords is lots of different kinds of opportunities and they may be in your errand unit, they may be somewhere else in the city, they may even be somewhere else in the city region and [they may even differ] for different family members. Forget about trying to circumscribe what a community must be in terms of all functions for all persons.[2]

Some shared, self-reliant economic life, not necessarily a shared physical geography, is, I think, the *essential* post-modern definition of *community*. That definition can be achieved by any grouping of persons within our present conurbations, not necessarily living in the same neighbourhood — although being close could only enhance the sense of *community*. Jacobs' sense of the *permeability* of our typical urban groupings would only afford a more complex weave among inter-related communities, it would not militate against the notion of a *producing community* producing, distributing, exchanging and consuming its own products — establishing, that is, its own extensive interior economy — although I am sure such permeability would gradually diminish, and a more dense, if still extensively inter-locked, range of communities would evolve.

The LETSystem is uniquely capable of drawing people together into such a social and economic network. Defining small, productive and self-reliant communities within our larger urban entities has the added advantage of permitting us to retain the amenities of modern urban life, and access to the international *market-money* economy, while we replicate the advantages of small community life. I also think that a shared social and cultural life will be enhanced by, and could even derive from, a shared economic life. The *political* dimension of *community* as defined from our borrowing from Friedmann may not be immediately satisfied within a non-contiguous economic community, but I am sure that, with *economic* self-reliance, *political expression* of that self-reliance will not be long in following in some form.

As Michael Linton proposes it, the LETSystem must create its own community, and its first attraction to me is the potential to do just that, irrespective of physical geography. The system has the potential to establish its own *community* because it attracts members who are, first of all, like-minded, and who then can (or ought to) *communicate* and *deal with* one another with some regularity. LETS provides the *economic* dimension to what otherwise might be simply a social grouping, and, with its *communitarian* ethos, it does so congruently.

A second possibility is for the LETSystem to inform an *existing* affinity group and turn it into a *community*, adding to its other ties those home-grown relations of production and distribution. The third possibility, really a version of the second, still remains. That is to add that home-grown economic dimension to the geographical entities we now call communities, like villages and reserves or their urban equivalents, neighbourhoods, and turn them into true, self-reliant *economic and political communities* instead of the adjuncts (and often seriously sidelined adjuncts) of our national and international market-money economy that they now are.

Creating or Finding a Community

After the April 22 Advisory Board meeting, I tossed and turned until 3 a.m. throwing about ideas for names, titles, approaches, formats. The best idea seemed to be to establish a visible store-front operation, a Community Employment Exchange (*COMPLEX*) to be undertaken by existing agencies like the Indian Family Centre, which would match the skills of the unemployed with the unmet needs within a specific neighbourhood, with *LETSWIN* performing the facilitation function of bypassing absent money with *Work Credits* (*green dollars*) accounted by its computer program. Such a program could operate in specific areas like Selkirk Avenue in North Winnipeg, or West Broadway, a transitional area closer to the centre of the city, and could also link participating neighbourhoods together through *LETSWIN*.

This format led me to consider doing essentially the same thing on a city-wide basis through the participation of a prominent radio station, to whom it could be a promotional venture and through whom what still seemed to me to be the important linkage to the existing business community could be achieved via their participating sponsors. In my haste for large-scale success, I imagined CJOB sponsoring *COMMUNITY JOB CREDITS*, in massive co-operation with city-wide church, business and labour groups.

I took the idea to CJOB and was politely heard. I was asked what the attitude of organized labour might be. My contacts with labour groups thought it sounded OK so long as *JOB CREDITS* did not replace dollar wages. I asked for a meeting of the Winnipeg Labour Council to explore co-sponsorship of the idea, along with CJOB and the Chamber of Commerce, but no meeting materialized. Ultimately, after watching the CBC video about LETS in Courtenay, British Columbia, and having staff play a version of *LETSPLAY*, CJOB turned down the proposal. They claimed that the staff people and their families who attempted the game found it too complicated. They had insisted on doing it alone and without my participation. That was a tactical error, especially since the staff member asked to rule on the matter was a notably conservative open-line host. My participation might have got them over some obstacles, and I would certainly have been able to advance counter arguments to objections.

About this time I was invited to make a LETS presentation to an inter-denominational Christian Socialist group. I did so on June 4, 1988. The meeting sparked a considerable discussion, including observations by an elderly woman about similar attempts in which she had been involved during the 1930s Depression. They issued a personal paper scrip for value rendered, but the system faltered because, although it could offer services, it could offer little in the way of goods — which was my reasoning for wanting to involve merchants early. The *LETSPLAY* game could not be finished within the time allotted in their meeting schedule, so I invited them to continue it by telephone over the two weeks until their next meeting, at which time we would evaluate and comment on the results.

Unhappily, one of the members of the group died in those two weeks, and they never did proceed with finishing the game. Nevertheless, at their next meeting, the last before their summer break, we proceeded to evaluate. While I saw a number of yes-nodding heads during the evaluation, the sceptical and negative reaction, at both the first and second meetings, of a well-known Winnipeg social activist set the tone of the meeting's general reaction.

Unexpected Opposition

This man could not believe the system could work. He found even the game *LETSPLAY* suspect, doubting the results. The usual result of *LETSPLAY* is that participants find that more, and more expensive, items can be obtained through LETS than through the cash money system, and that people can continue to make purchases in *green dollars* even after they go bankrupt in real dollars. He suspected that these results were not real, but simply the result of a bias built into the game.

This negativity disturbed me profoundly, because the man is a leader in the general constituency from which I had expected support — the community of social concern and activism. But I keep running into similar objections from that community. Despite the sense one can make of the LETS idea, and despite the witness of practical experience, there is in some a flat unwillingness to believe that it can work. I can imagine only that this is a result of a deep internalization of money consciousness, intensely focused (by the usual absence of money) into an obsession with its power to "solve" problems like poverty and unemployment.

Money, of course, can solve neither of these problems. In fact, getting money to the poor — much as it alleviates their problems in the short run — really only affirms the kind of dependencies described in the first part of this book. Money provided to the poor inevitably finds its way into the hands of the rich. The true path out of poverty is social, political and, above all, independent economic, *empowerment* — to which the LETSystem is a ready access road.

I now believe that my earlier, uncritical beliefs that Leftists objected to capitalism were unfounded romanticism. In expounding the LETS idea, I find that Leftists of my acquaintance are, for the most part, *ardent* capitalists, accepting quite uncritically the basic workings of the present money system and desiring not the elimination of capitalism by a more egalitarian paradigm, but better management and re-direction of the status quo. They love their money chains! What they want is not to be rid of them, but to have charge of the keys.

Time was spent by some of the Christian Socialists at the second meeting sharing experience that suggests that the money system does, in fact, work very effectively and, *in doing so,* adversely affects general morality (acting in the world) through those workings — but this cannot be changed. One participant talked about someone at a conference of university Chaplains wondering what the Church was doing in the university anyway, since universities are no longer *serious* institutions in the world. Something similar was said of the Church itself, which led to the question of defining what *serious* institutions are. The answer seemed to be that *serious* institutions are those of institutionalized *power* in which people *believe* and which, therefore, *govern.* In our world, these are the institutions of business, industry and commerce, and the language of their discourse is *money.*

These institutions in which people believe are now powerfully entrenched in and by trans-national capitalism. They are, in fact, the institutions which govern us, officially and unofficially. They govern our *economic* lives, and through that, our *social and political* lives, since our governments are likely to be their creatures and, if they are not, are otherwise constrained by the economic realities that the trans-national corporate world does govern, such as where the factories go and who gets the jobs. Governing us, these powerful institutions of the *market* also mediate our *morality* and our *ethics.* No wonder both are those of the market-place!

I wonder if our economic structures, rather than our religious or educational ones, *always* mediated morality in our world. *Power* may well have always mediated morality. There have been ages in which power has aligned with religion to do so, and ages in which religion has aligned with power to do so, finding its morality and ethics influenced thereby. But, I think, no matter how political the religion or religious the politics, *morality* in those times was always, at least, informed by some *idealism,* even if it was what we would consider a perverted idealism or one that rationalized power and its uses and abuses. Economics was informed, or restrained, or at least apologized for, by some set of ethical ideals. In our world, however, even among socialists, the Protestant Work Ethic, supported philosophically by rational empiricists and internalized by all of us in Western society, has resulted, in a rather knotted chain of philosophical apologia, in turning the previous ethic around and in fact, has now made *economics* the unapologetic mediator of *idealism.*

The Protestant Work Ethic equates financial success with godliness. The Empiricists denied spirit in favour of what was observably, evidently present. Existentialism — the foundation of which is that there is no *being* or *spirit* without *object* or *matter* — justifies materialism by conflating matter and spirit. I think what is really new in our modern market world, however, is encapsulated in two realities. One is that the drive for profit mediates morality now *to the exclusion of any other mediating force*, requiring *no* rationalization from idealism. That is what is really meant by *the bottom line*. It is a kind of economic empiricism: what is real is what, after all other considerations, does the money say? The second is that ethic is *generally internalized* right down to the individual level. I also believe that it is probable that the second reality listed above preceded the first — that economic practice resulted in the internalization of that *bottom line* ethic — empirical economic reality became our spiritual social creed and all of the above merely reiterates that we are socially and morally structured by the necessities of our economic life, no matter what they may be.

All the above notwithstanding, I do not, understand how either a modern and liberated Christian or a socialist can recognize that economics — or money — mediates our morality, *and then refuse to consider an alternative system* that even *might* mediate materialist morality to a more co-operative and less competitive end, even to the extent of doubting the instrument used rather than the readings it records. That sounds very much like Galileo and the Pope. As far as I know and logic suggests, the prices set out in the game *LETSPLAY* reflect reality and are not rigged.

On the positive side, the evenings with the Christian Socialists sharpened my perception of LETS as an instrument for *achieving* some ends rather than as an end in itself. Facilitating self-directed economic functioning covers most of those ends: creation of employment, fulfilling unmet needs, expansion of personal money supplies. But even those purposes ought to have ends: what employment, what needs, and the expansion of one's personal money supply for what purposes? LETS is not enough by itself. It must be informed by purpose and, I think, by very *particular* purposes. While establishing a general system may seem logical, perhaps it is not sufficiently *purposeful* to be attractive.

Finding the Right People

A member of the Christian Socialist group who became a *LETSWIN* member shared my amazement that the group as a whole was not enthusiastic and went on to suggest that I might be talking to the wrong people. The group, she noted, consists principally of university, government and church employees, none of whom really want for money and all of whom have very busy lives. They lack, that is, both practical motive to embrace LETS and the free time to create for themselves the employment it demands. I noted that the original Courtenay LETS was developed in a time of great economic crisis for that community. Discussing this notion with others, one suggested taking the idea to the Society for Manitobans with Disabilities. This society represents people who have sharp and permanent economic disadvantage, which, despite a variety of skills, typically keeps them in permanent economic crisis. Further, it is possible that they could benefit as a group from advertising and demonstrating the *abilities* of their members to the general public.

In my impatience, the approach for *LETSWIN* that seemed to me to be the most promising at this point was to identify existing groups that might be willing to adopt the LETSystem to add to their group's cohesion, especially those who might find it a useful way to expand the economic lives of their members. Taking LETS to the Society for Manitobans with Disabilities (SMD) seemed like a good prospect. I also determined to approach the Manitoba Anti-Poverty Association (MAPO), the Unemployed Community Help Centre (UCHC) and the Indian Family Centre (IFC) already engaged through Henk DeBruyn, developing a presentation tailored for each organization and offering LETS as a service that each organization could deliver to its members, thereby solving the *leadership* problem.

I also thought to avoid the expense of monthly mailings of account statements and bulletins by having these organizations include them with their existing mail-outs and newsletters. I recast LETS promotional material away from Linton's description of it as an alternative money system in favour of what it actually is — a sophisticated extended barter system which breaks the necessity of one-on-one bartering and extends the possibilities of barter. I reasoned that people would be less suspicious of a familiar model — barter — than of the unfamiliar, and somehow threatening, concept of creating their own money.

Initial response from all four organizations was good. SMD noted that they already were proposing to encourage their member groups (they are a federation) to begin sharing services and a newsletter that would include a want-ads section of needs and offers of the disabled to one another. The remarkable parallel was most encouraging. MAPO, however, said they had just given up their newsletter for lack of funds, and a meeting with the then Executive Director convinced me that any approach not tightly focused on getting dollar funds for the organization would be fruitless: indeed, MAPO itself is principally focused on getting dollar welfare payments and other welfare rights for its clients, and not oriented to their self-empowerment. UHC has no newsletter nor consistent clientele. A demonstration to IFC members was agreed upon, but not pursued.

A presentation went forward to the SMD Board consisting of a slide presentation describing the LETSystem and a presentation of applications for SMD. The usual questions and objections were raised and, although most Board members were favourable to the concept, they declined to take it on as a project of SMD. They agreed to refer us to one of the Society's member groups, the Association for Independent Living, and similar presentations were undertaken there to Board members and subsequently to society members. These presentations resulted in some individuals joining, but not in the Society or the Association adopting LETS generally.

Opposition, Misunderstanding and Apathy

One reaction I had not experienced before came from SMD. One person wondered if the term *green dollars* indicated that LETS was linked to the *Green Party*. I assured him it did not originate with that political movement, although its concept and philosophy was no doubt in tune with it. Partly to avoid such political confusion in future, and partly to move away from the Linton *alternative money* concept, I eventually determined to change the LETS currency nomenclature, settling on *Barter Credit* as an accurate description of what the LETS artificial currency actually is: barter extended by credit.

Early in July, at a demonstration table at the Winnipeg Folk Festival, I was approached by a funding officer with the Winnipeg Core Area Initiative — an initiative funded by the three levels of government, but operating at arms length from them, intended to re-vitalize the deteriorating downtown part of Winnipeg with both physical and social renewal — who suggested possible funding for LETS from CAI. I spent the next month working out a detailed funding proposal, based on a highly optimistic financial plan predicated on business participation. During this period I also left behind the notion of finding an existing group to adopt and deliver LETS for its members, and moved toward the notion of creating an agency to deliver LETS. Community Circle Services, Inc. was incorporated as a non-profit corporation for that purpose, and the CAI funding was sought under that name.

The key to the CAI funding proposal, apart from some staffing costs, the development of promotional material and the securing of our own computer, was using the Inner City Voice, a CAI-funded newspaper, as the principal medium for publishing Community Circle's LETS Want-ad Bulletins. To diversify funding, I also sought funds from the Kinsmen Club and the Winnipeg Foundation, to cover such particular things as mailing costs and the cost of demonstrations.

Ultimately, the Kinsmen Club proved uninterested, the Winnipeg Foundation was unable even to consider the application because Community Circle had no tax number (charitable status), but the most disappointing of all was the experience with CAI. Despite early positive reaction by CAI project officers and approval by the appropriate CAI board, the project was turned down by the *community* board of core-area residents because they could not see LETS as a *serious* project. After the experience with the Christian Socialists, I assume *serious* has to do with getting poor people either money or jobs. This also has implications, I think, for the *charity* mode of thinking built into the legislation which organizations like the Winnipeg Foundation must work under, and indicates the extent to which very ordinary people are focused on *money*.

The CAI experience was another example of the presentation of the concept being taken out of the presenter's hands. CAI fund-seekers are not permitted to present their own requests to the approving boards. In the case of a novel concept, this is a distinct handicap.

Confounded by Development-Assistance Styles

It is worthwhile here to take note of what I can only call *development style*. Government-supported development programs in Canada are divided into two types: 1) Charitable non-profit projects which tend to continue to rely on government support and; 2) Start-up support for business ventures under various and sporadic development programs. What LETS — and other futurist alternative thinking about Community Economic Development — is all about, falls between these two stools.

The notion of self-reliance is anathema to charitable support, and that includes the support delivered to all non-profits whether from government or private sources, as characterized by the Kinsmen and the Winnipeg Foundation. Tax-deductible donations may be received, basically, by organizations that give money away. Enterprises seeking to build self-reliance need to move rather quickly to self-sustaining measures and status. Much government support afforded in recent years has been provided on the understanding that the supported projects will eventually become self-supporting, which seems to mean not real self-reliance, but that they should eventually find other, usually private, sources of charitable donations — charitable donation being a code-word for tax-deductibility. Such ventures intending to become self-supporting through business activity are difficult for our legislation to recognize. You have to move over to another realm and start talking about investment, expense and deductible losses. Nevertheless, that business-like intent should not automatically preclude tax-deductible support from any source, government or private, especially in setting up. Such projects should still be able to benefit from *charitable status* funding, at least to the extent that they have a good measure of public good in their intent, even if it is, essentially, a business intent.

Alternatively, such projects could be perceived as businesses operating in a public-service rather than a profit-oriented manner, rather like a Crown Corporation. The mere fact that a venture is a non-profit one should not preclude the kind of start-up assistance afforded to businesses without invoking a whole new set of laws. But we have no simple legal models available to private citizens for such a creature, and no such concept among the handlers of public and charitable money in Canada. You are either a business or a charity, and the twain are not allowed to meet. Funders who really want to be helpful should avoid forcing projects exclusively into one or the other pattern.

Linton and his associates in British Columbia have opted for the private sector format and made *LANDSMAN* non-profit in their by-laws. I am more comfortable with the non-profit format, probably because I am more familiar with it, but I recognize that it too needs adjustment to accommodate the business or self-reliant purpose. As a non-profit corporation engaged in community economic development Community Circle is, in fact, an enterprise to do business — essentially, the combined business of banking and publication — in the public interest. But that is not perceived as a *charitable* activity, and cannot be funded for tax credit under our present tax laws.

All of the above took up the summer and fall of 1987.

Chapter Nine

COMMUNITY CIRCLE
Developing the LETS Community

Fall Back and Re-group

Community Circle Services, Inc was incorporated on November 25, 1987. During the winter and spring of 1987, the functioning of the Winnipeg LETSystem lapsed. Although Community Circle had been incorporated, we still did not have a functioning LETS computer program more than a year after the initial LETS presentation in Winnipeg by Linton. At least, I was unable to understand and operate it. We also had no exchanges to record in my own crude system for managing *LETSWIN*. The time was spent in refining the slide presentation, which the SMD showing indicated was too long and theoretical, and in developing promotional pamphlets using art-work from the slides. A great deal of time was taken up with rewriting the LETS promotional literature to purge the concept of the LETS currency as a form of money, and with producing our own promotional pamphlets.

It was a revelation how deeply embedded in our psyche our money consciousness is and how much it is an unconscious and uncriticized part of our language, and therefore our thinking. It is incredibly difficult, for example, to talk about economic transfers without using the terms *pay, sell* and *buy.* In the end, I have returned to an understanding of LETS as using a *currency,* but not the currency that is created by its transactions — or, as Linton talks of it, created by its users — no matter what Revenue Canada and orthodox economics say.

I now recognize that it is the *natural money* of our own time, labour skills and resources that is spent — our goods and services — and that that *natural money* can be spent freely, because simple records-keeping in positive and negative bank-like balances *without either the usual negative-balance penalties or positive-balance rewards* replaces our *universal commodity money,* its *money demand,* its *scarcity* limitations, and its particular rules and consequences. Thus we are able to put our attention where it belongs, on the actual level of need, and the capacity to fill that need, that are present in our community. We are able to act directly — unhindered by initial concerns about money — to match the two where they match, or expand capacities (or reduce needs) where they do not. In short, we are able to engage freely in real Community Economic Development rather than engaging in mere money-manipulation.

During the summer of 1987, I visited British Columbia to attend a couple of conferences and to holiday. One of the conferences was a LETS gathering at Duncan, on Vancouver Island, at which I met and shared notes with other LETS members and operators. They had invited LETS contacts across Canada, but I was the only off-island respondent. The gathering proved to be more social than conference-like, but a lot of education and experience-sharing was achieved informally during the social time. This is a noteworthy model for solidifying the relations of any community.

For a few days after the LETS conference, I visited Linton at home in Courtenay and gained greater familiarity with the LETS program. Apparently the principal problem with the material I had lay in a mismatch between the early dBase II data-base application in which it is written and later versions of Microsoft's disk-operating system (DOS 3 and later). When used with earlier DOS, the LETS program works well enough. That correction, plus my improved familiarity with the month-end closing procedures, the new promotional pamphlets, and secure access to an IBM compatible computer from a new member, put the Community Circle Barter Credit Network into operation in the fall of 1987.

The other conference I attended in British Columbia was an organizational convention-gathering of the Green Party of Canada, and it resulted in a conceptual expansion of my thinking about LETS and its place and purpose. I recognized it as appropriate to the de-centralized and self-reliant ethic being advanced by the Greens, along with, and as an essential part of, *Green* social and political theory. When I discussed this later with Linton, he admitted to being very discouraged by the reaction of American Greens to LETS (as I had been by the socialist's reaction). In summary, he had found yet another version of the *not serious* syndrome when trying to interest the American Greens in adopting the LETSystem as their preferred economic model. American Greens are, apparently, as thoroughly wedded to capitalism as Canadian socialists, and as unable to contemplate either a cashless society or a society without a centrally created and controlled money supply. These discussions further committed me to the investigations which resulted in Part One of this book.

Contact!

It was, however, at a Green Gathering in Winnipeg where I began to make fruitful contacts to develop our LETS community through Community Circle, and where I expanded the Community Circle Board. I began to produce the LETSystem ad bulletins in a format that was more easily readable than the LETS computer program printout, using computer facilities at the University of Manitoba and a Pagemaker desk-top publishing program. The LETS computer printout is judged by most to be confusing and difficult to access, particularly for people who are not accustomed to getting their information from close reading.

LINKS — a magazine intended to link and accentuate the common cause between environmental, peace, and social justice activists — gained impetus from that conference, and Community Circle's LETS Bulletins became a section of *LINKS*. Publication in the magazine seemed to touch the correct nerve. Requests for information and membership began in a slow but steady stream. Participation in *LINKS* also *alienated* what had begun as an active small neighbourhood group of members, whose fundamentalist Christian ethic was offended by an article in *LINKS* on Latin American Liberation Theology. The LETS community was beginning to define itself.

Community Circle also began to get attention from the media — press and radio at least. A full page on our effort, written by Bonnie Bridge on the basis of an interview with myself and Janine Gibson, was published in the *Winnipeg Free Press Sunday Supplement* on May 14, 1989, entitled "No Money Required." Mainstream television did not respond, but two public-access cable TV hosts did full half-hour programs with me in 1988, and each generated additional response from the public. The Community Circle membership grew to forty-six in 1988, 128 in 1989 and to 138 in 1990, 150 in 1991. As of this writing in the fall of 1992 it is 200 and rising.

Slippage!

In 1988, I was still taken with the notion of signing up whole groups of people, which accounts for a large part of the large 1988 increase in membership. We organized a demonstration evening at the central Winnipeg Public Library under the joint sponsorship of the Independent Living Resource Centre. We got several memberships from this effort, but no general commitment to membership and use from the Resource Centre. In the summer of 1988, with a *CAREERSTART* employment grant and the prior agreement with the Crossroads Family Centre Board, Community Circle hired a student to proselytize among the Crossroads membership in the Logan district with a view to having the Centre *adopt* LETS. Again, while individual members of the Family Centre did join, the organization did not.

The Crossroads Board, while sympathetic to and approving our summer experiment among their membership, eventually rejected the notion of any self-reliant relationship between itself and its clients, specifically because the Family Centre is a *charitable* project of its parent church organization. I find that the operators of such organizations, most of whom are fully engaged with their own projects, are unable, as a board, for example, to take the time to understand LETS and its implications. Typically they devote less than half an hour at a Board meeting, which is insufficient time to present the LETS concept effectively. This results in incomplete understanding, for the most part, which results in people trying to understand LETS with reference to the *money* paradigm, which in turn does not result in a clear apprehension of the system or its capabilities, but in confusion and then negative response.

Many of the Crossroads members also attended an adult literacy program called *JOURNEYS*. With this group there was a better result, possibly because its Board is made up principally of its own constituents and does not have members from "outside" or from some parent organization. Its members are committed to becoming self-reliant through increased literacy, and show a better intuitive grasp of the LETSystem. *JOURNEYS* did open an account and offered some of its facilities to Community Circle Members, but it too rejected any leadership role or full participation — for example, the notion of acknowledging its volunteers with transfers of Barter Credit.

I opened accounts for all the *LINKS* workers in order to test the concept of acknowledging their volunteerism in Barter Credit. The concept worked well enough but most of the volunteers did not use their accumulated credits to trade for other goods or services available in the system. It was a project peripheral to their general "alternative society" activism, and very few of them took the time to understand it. A number of them (it was a large and loose group before it settled down to a small number of regular volunteers) never actually became functionally aware of their membership and were soon moved to dormant status.

At this point I finally began to accept that the group membership idea was not working. Individual members of a group were not necessarily committed to or understanding the LETS idea, and group leadership — the Boards — were not being convinced either. It was becoming evident that the members who were joining and using the system were *word-of-mouth* joiners, those who became interested through the membership of friends and neighbours, and joined out of some feeling of personal conviction. Membership growth has continued by word of mouth, encouraged by social gatherings which serve as meetings, and by trickles of enquiries through 1989 and 1990: growth in 1990 was from 128 to 138.

The level of trade did not warrant issuing monthly account statements, so we moved to quarterly regularity; the new members, although fewer, were better traders. Partly due to efforts to sign up large groups of people (which falsely inflated the membership figures), and partly due to a continuing shortage of *hard goods* in the system, trading has been at a relatively low level compared to membership size and compared to claims for the initial months of the LETS system in Courtenay, although there too use has fallen off. I do not believe, however, that the experience of the Winnipeg LETSystem has been spectacularly out of line with the reality experienced by most LETSystems from which I have direct reports (Courtenay and Duncan, British Columbia, Ottawa and Kitchener-Waterloo, Ontario). The literature from other systems — notably in New Zealand — is enthusiastic and reports rapid and sound growth (also best by example and word of mouth), but I have not spoken or corresponded directly with participants there.

Valuation

One of the constant questions from members and prospects has been what people should ask for their goods and services. The question indicates a lack of awareness of self-value, of the value of our own *natural, personal money,* that is quite general. Answering the question is a problem, not because the answer is difficult, but because of distortions introduced into our self-evaluation by the money system.

The first distortion is that we now habitually make our self-valuation in money terms. Unless a dollar value can be attached to what we have or can do we have difficulty *evaluating* our own labour, and, therefore, our own worth. Quickly, now, how many carrots is an afternoon of your time worth? The second distortion is that we are led to make even that money-based evaluation according to the values of some *outside agency,* like an employer. But there is an even more fundamental distortion. We have fully internalized the concept of money-valuation of our skills, time and labour and now believe that they are worth *noth-*

ing unless and until there is someone willing to *pay money* for them. They — and we — are effectively *devalued* by the money system.

The *devaluation* of people by the money system is so complete and pervasive that, if we cannot demand *money* for our *value*, we feel *worthless*. LETS functions to increase individuals' *self-valuation*, especially for those individuals who have been extensively *de-valued* by the money system. LETS is uniquely able to alter this internalized belief in our own disempowerment. It does so by freeing up our capacity to realize value from spending the *natural money* of the time, labour and skills that we all possess without first having to push it through the restrictive bottle-neck of *money supply* and *money-driven demand*. It takes time, but people do learn in the LETSystem that they have value, independent of their demand in the job market. Changing that belief in our own disempowerment is the route LETS offers out of the conceptual poverty that underlies material poverty in our society.

Theoretically, LETS restores a free-market economy. Not imposing any central rules on participants, it leaves them free to set and sort out their own values for their goods and services according to classical economic rules, undistorted by capital and market controls. Also, any LETSystem can operate on its own value system, replicating in economic life the values held by the members of the trading group in their social, ethical and cultural life. Art, and such social acts as neighbourly visiting, can, for example, be more highly valued than they tend to be in the money system.

Within the LETSystem, the Free Market Laws can operate to establish valuation according to, and reflecting, the shared value system of the LETS community. That would, of course, take considerable time, but a coherent and communicating community would, sooner or later, evolve its own valuation patterns from the practices of authenticating its members' own valuation of their goods and services. Eventually, as new value-equations became clear and understood, valuation in money terms might give way to more direct and meaningful valuation comparisons. Thus, LETS might inform the *culture* and *morality* of a community. I have noticed that, while most LETS traders still, generally, make what are essentially *market* valuations of their goods and services as they are encouraged to do, some are developing the attitude that, while providing these goods or services remains important, the amount they actually receive in exchange is less so. The security of their capacity to trade is not dependent on "possessing" barter credit, so *amounts* reduce in importance. What remains singularly important is the *fact* of trading.

Discussions about valuation were frequent in the growing period of *LETSWIN* and Community Circle, and often got very complex. In general, it was evident that the principal target population — the poor and disadvantaged — tend to under-value themselves, although some, in reaction perhaps, tended to over-value their services. They simply had no experience of valuing themselves. But arriving at a valuation for what we have or do, independently of our accustomed market valuation, is never easy, hence the LETS desire not to legislate value.

In addition to the problems noted above with under-valuation or over-valuation, it is the *nature* of value to be ephemeral. Value depends entirely upon who wants what, when, and how badly. Value changes constantly. What is valued today may not be valued tomorrow, because it is needed or wanted today and may not be tomorrow. What is valued by some is not valued by others, and so on.

Part of the complex of valuation problems may also be a (commendable) reluctance to put a value on "social" things that we do, such as occasionally shovelling snow off the old man's walk next door, which is both a vestige of our communal tribal past and, perhaps, a reaction to the demands of the *market-money* economy that attacks those communal values. But I think LETS traders need to go through that exercise in order to learn their own value, before coming out the other side with enough security simply to give, knowing they will also receive.

In practice I have found that people do not usually feel their valuation questions are adequately answered by *you decide,* or *you and your trading partner negotiate that,* or other *Free Market* answers. This is only to say, of course, that no community, even a homogeneous one, is immune from the value system ingrained in us by the market and its dollar messenger, and people who ask about valuation are having difficulty switching away from that externally validated value system. As well, most LETS systems — especially one generalized, for example, to a whole city, as Community Circle is — will experience the normative cultural, ethical and moral influence of the general market-money economy. A native reserve community, on the other hand, might not. They might be able to move directly to a more communal valuation system, since in most cases they have never stopped practising it among themselves.

If it is felt that replicating the general market values within the LETS community is not desirable, and that one advantage of the LETSystem is the capacity to value things and people differently, then some local rules about valuation within the LETSystem are probably desirable, although theoretically there should be none.

Several possible solutions to the valuation problem present themselves:

1. Letting the Free Market decide — the preferred LETS solution;
2. Valuation at the economic level of the producer, replicating inequity;
3. Valuation at the economic level of the receiver, also replicating inequity;
4. Valuation parity, a fixed rate for labour which, added to resource and material costs, will also result in a predictable and reliable price for goods;
5. Valuation equity, pricing labour within a limited range (for example, a top rate that is no more than three times a bottom rate), also resulting in a relatively predictable price for goods.

Compromising between the preferred LETS *hands-off* style and the valuation difficulties experienced by the disadvantaged is probably necessary, at least in the initial stages of a LETSystem. The decision to do so has not yet been made by Community Circle.

Class Problems and Community Barriers

There may also be problems with generalizing a LETSystem over a whole city. The inclusion of a target population such as the comparatively more welfare-dependent clientele at the Crossroads Family Centre together with the more educated and activist population in the Wolseley-River Heights districts — who, among LETS users, are nevertheless often not money-wealthy — created something of a moral dilemma for me. While on the surface it seems to be a good match to pair people who have time to spare, basic skills and a need for greater amounts of spendable currency with people who have little spare time and who often need help with basic things like house and yard work and child care but do not have much cash, I was bothered by the spectre of replicating classical class exploitation, and continuing the role of *the poor* as the domestic servants of the *middle class,* and that *not even* (!) for money.

I don't know if that was ever a legitimate concern — it may be an artifact of my own liberal guilt — but it did result in my not pursuing those linkages. And it raises the question of whether or not LETS works best within a homogeneous group, and whether small neighbourhood systems — one in Logan and a separate one in Wolseley, for example — might be a preferable organizational target. So far, Community Circle has not wrestled collectively with this question.

Trust and Social Contact

One minor difficulty in preparing LETS promotional or explanatory information is that our target population includes people who do not — and some who cannot — get their information from reading. A great deal of social interaction is therefore necessary to spread the LETS concept and the how and why of using it. Personal explanations of how to use it are usually required. This is one of the reasons, having established and defined the system, I am now working to involve more individuals in the management and development of Community Circle. Frequent (much increased) social contact among Community Circle members is an absolute necessity.

LETS can engender contact through trading, one of the primary methods of Community Economic Development, but trading also devolves from social contact. While it seems evident that people will join and use the system according to what is available within it, merely leaving trading contacts to the want ads in the Bulletin — which is to say, predicating contact on the basis of material needs — is not sufficient to develop actual wide use of the system. Moreover, we have found that face to face social contacts lead people to discover things they have or can do that other people want. The social contact broadens people's awareness of their capacity for trade. Community Circle is now embarking on quarterly *LETS TRADE FAIRS*, at which Community Circle members may display and trade their goods and services. New Zealand LETSystems report this as a successful method. By also inviting the public to take part (using customary monetary exchanges), they extend the value of the system to members and introduce the LETS idea to outsiders.

Social contact is also necessary to engender the *trust* which is basic to the LETSystem, although *trust* has not obviously been a problem so far. No one in the Winnipeg LETSystem has yet complained of not receiving value and no concern has ever yet been expressed by providers of value about the possibility of their not realizing value in return — of those who received it not passing it on so that it *can* return. Still, I believe that in a generalized system such as Community Circle, such problems will arise. While all LETS trades are secured by the same laws that apply to trade in general, I look to such organizations as community mediation services to act in such cases to provide a more personal and congenial community problem-solving intermediary (or to the LETSystem itself providing such services) *before* invoking the legal system, with its confrontational context. Such services seem more appropriate to the convivial ethic of the LETSystem as well as being less expensive, difficult and time-consuming.

Habits Compromise Use

The principal factor inhibiting the use of the LETSystem seems to be people's ingrained habits of trade. Our trading habit of shopping at one-stop supermarkets interferes with our taking the time to deal with neighbours for individual items or even patronizing neighbourhood stores. And our habit of not accounting for the gifts of time and service that we do give to and receive from friends and neighbours — the gifts which LETS seeks to expand and generalize — results in some embarrassment when members are asked to acknowledge even such gifts with Barter Credit. It seems wrong to *pay for* such things.

An intentional community in the interior of British Columbia rejected the LETS notion because they already shared their food and other resources freely among themselves. This is a reaction against our internalized *money thinking,* essentially an artifact of the money system itself. People are correct in resisting *monetizing* such exchanges. I believe this to be one of the problems generated by presenting LETS as an alternate money system which I have tried to avoid by de-emphasizing the LETS currency as a money.

In fact, in the LETSystem, it is *positive* to acknowledge gifts with notation in the internal *currency.* When gifts are acknowledged in the Barter Credit received in exchange for a gift, they are acknowledged in a way that can itself be realized in valuable form. The gift does not *die* after one exchange, but is symbolized in a manner in which it can be made again to someone else — thus helping to fulfill one side of the necessary dynamic of the Gift Economy. Gift ethics already recognize that gifts are not without obligation to the receiver, although that obligation may not be to the giver. Simply formalizing that obligation in no way diminishes the ethical value of the gift and, as a negative notation in the account of the receiver of the gift, Barter Credit acknowledgement serves as a reminder that the second half of the cycle — the *passing on* of concrete gifts — must be carried forward for the Gifting Circle to be completed. This is an argument that, to date, has usually fallen on unreceptive ears. People value gifting, in our society, as an ethical expression that counters the dollar-values of the market place.

This is essentially a problem of habits of belief. Our belief system is thoroughly informed — I would say contaminated — by the reductionist rational competitive economic model of Adam Smith. It is easy to believe in humanity's avarice. It is less easy to believe in humanity's conviviality. But we do, overall, succeed in living together. To what extent our present belief system is an effect, rather than a cause, of Smith's philosophical formulation, would make an informative study. But until the case is disproved, I choose to believe that our institutions, like the money system or the LETSystem, inform — or, at least, re-inform by the feedback of a dialectical process — the morality of our society, and that that morality can be changed by a change in our system and style of trade relations.

The success of LETS as a generalized way of conducting our economic life ultimately depends upon a belief in it at least as generalized as our ubiquitous belief in money. The objective of LETS organizers at this stage must be to establish and operate the living proof that such systems can be believed in.

LETS Future as a Tool for Community Economic Development

As 1990 closed, the probable future course of the Winnipeg LETSystem, like that of most others, seemed to be the continuing association of self-identified, like-minded individuals sharing services, much as Linton first proposed. But I had come to believe that its future as a *community development tool* would rest upon whether or not it can encourage the *production* of goods and services by members for members, imitating the *import replacement* function described by Jane Jacobs as essential for the development of early cities, and following the suggestions of Susan Pell and David Wismer that a community-based economic development ought to begin with local production of local goods for local use.

Community Circle is prepared to set up a development fund in cash dollars through the intermediary of the LETS currency. To do that, Community Circle itself will exchange Barter Credit for dollars with dollar-contributing members, and encourage members undertaking LETS-oriented enterprises to use those funds for the necessary supply of materials for production.

I have had an enquiry from a United Church minister in Russell, Manitoba, whose Lenten Homilies reflect the same kind of economic-community thinking exemplified by LETS. It would be informative to see if one could undertake a general community development effort in a distinct community such as Russell, rather than limit oneself to carving out a borderless functioning community within an urban setting.

The most promising recent advance in our LETSystem has been the membership of Neechi Foods Community Store, a grocery store situated in a neighbourhood with a large aboriginal population, which is owned co-operatively by the native community and dedicated to aboriginal community development. One can now get groceries for Barter Credit, and Neechi will be the centre for expanding the Community Circle LETSystem in their neighbourhood through cash-register contacts. Neechi may also receive vegetables produced by a neighbourhood food club's gardening project, also facilitated by Barter Credit, providing an outlet for Neechi's Barter Credit. Barter Credit may also be used by Neechi to carry on trading exchanges with a Wolseley-district bakery to whom they already provide blueberries and wild rice, and whose bakery products they wish to carry.

I look forward to having other neighbourhood Community Economic Development projects adopt and use the LETSystem, either through Community Circle or on their own. Unlike The Winnipeg Initiatives, the key to success will be integrating the LETSystem organically into any community development effort *as a means of recognizing, facilitating and rewarding the essential development effort* — an ancillary to that effort rather than becoming the effort itself.

One should also approach aboriginal reserve communities — the LETSystem is only a modern adaptation of a tribal economy, after all — but I hesitate to approach any native community with the notion that this white man has the answer to their economic problems.

In all cases — neighbourhood, town, reserve — money thinking will be hard to get past, but I look forward to being able to undertake such projects, even if I cannot initiate them, as Community Circle Continues to prove LETS as a tool to engender and advance Community Economic Development.

Distortions and Adaptations

At the time of writing (first quarter, 1991) LETS communities had grown to about 100 in number around the world. They don't communicate at all well with one another, but efforts are going forward to improve that and, in North America, LETS has a computer bulletin board, where information and up-dated software are freely available, on the WEB computer network.

There are also a number of adaptations of the LETSystem which fail to make the requisite full shift from reliance on the money paradigm to reliance on community productivity and so distort the concept. One, in Florida and California, organizes community service work for the elderly in the LETS style, but backed by a government commitment to redeem the internal currency used with "real" dollars. Another — sponsored by the Schumacher Project in Great Britain — is attempting to organize community development using a LETS type of internal currency backed by "real" money raised through bond issues. These are distortions in that they found the security of their system on the availability of money rather than on the endemic capacities of the system and its members — its *community* — and so do not get free of either the demands or the vagaries of the money-market system.

Other systems are operated strictly within the market-money system as brokerage businesses. They organize barter among manufacturers and retailers as a business proposition, secured by member firms' dollar credit and advance commitment of hard goods, and paid for by their services in "real" dollar service fees. Barter business is a multi-million-dollar operation in North America. It was a strange experience to read the literature of such barter companies in Toronto, Montreal and Vancouver, and to see there the LETS concepts and even the language, used for a commercial rather than communitarian purpose. These applications distort the LETS concept because they gleefully enter, rather than leave, the market-money economy.

All of these adaptations fail to get beyond fundamental reliance upon our centrally issued official currencies, and so compromise the essential value of the LETSystem. That is described by Linton as the decentralization of money supply to the field of individual action, responsibility and empowerment. I describe it as the by-passing of money in favour of dealing in the *natural money* of our *real* goods and services. In both cases the foundation of the economy is the willingness and capacity of its members to be productive — the capacity of a community to realize the natural money of its own endemic productive resources and the ordinary skills, labour, time and creative resources that we all possess, individually and as communities. In either case the essential value of the LETSystem is that it frees our communities and the industries, businesses and individuals within them, from dollar-demand restraints. To re-engage the dollar economy as a foundational guarantee for the LETS economy, or to use what is structurally a LETSystem to function within the market-money system, is a backward step.

Although it is a difficult concept to implement, given our deep and intense internalization of the money ethic and money system, *getting beyond money,* getting *beyond the need* for such a guarantee and accepting the *credit of the community itself*, and its capacity to produce, exchange and consume its own goods and services is, I still submit, the essential element of the LETSystem. The true LETSystem bases its exchange facilitation on the true economy that can exist, or be brought into existence, within a community. It works within that community's own real capacities, and real economic activity, however large or small, and works to expand that capacity and activity. Having said that, and while it does not require external justification, LETSystems, unless they are small enough to permit, for example, hand-delivery of communication bulletins and account statements, do generate real-dollar expense. Even if there are no mailing expenses, stationery and computer paper are not usually available for 100% Barter Credit.

Linton himself is now advocating, as in the Ottawa LETSystem, establishing dollar funds to guarantee *green dollars* to entice merchants to take part in LETSystems. Community Circle, has, I blush to admit, determined to accomplish that instead by getting into the commercial barter business on the model of the barter exchange companies. The results we expect from that are a cash-dollar flow sufficient to support the administration of the system, the provision of additional outlets to members for the "spending" of Barter Credit for mainstream merchandise, and with that, a more general expansion of membership. If there are excess funds — profit — from that venture, it will be directed to our production development fund, where it can be applied to build new enterprises oriented to local production, in my view the third necessary element of a local *community* economy.

I salve my conscious about going into the business of barter — like the barter clubs, providing a business service to businesses by facilitating non-cash inter-business trading and taking a commission for the service in dollars — by reminding myself that, while this means functioning within the market-money system, it does at least have the virtue of demonstrating very openly, and to business people, that there is another way to do even "regular" business. That might have important repercussions if we are, indeed, sliding into a long and low economic depression. And what is most lacking from the business-oriented barter operations is the constituency we already represent, and which we are now calling the *family* network — that is, the non-private, non-business sectors of a full economy. By operating two parallel and inter-exchanging trading networks, we hope to have our cake and eat it too.

If you will recall, at the end of Chapter Seven ("What About Businesses?") I suggested that the argument about whether to approach businesses or private members first was merely an argument about what entry point you choose to begin constructing your local economy and what recruitment strategies you might adopt, but that without the inclusion of local businesses your local economy would remain incomplete. A full economy consists of both private and public sectors, each divided between the individual and the collective — private collectivities of commercial venture and the private producing and consuming individual, together with public collective ventures (the non-profit and service organizations and government) and the public socio-cultural individual, or *citizen*. The real problem with the exclusively business-oriented barter businesses is not their commercialism or flirtation with the dollar, but that — not being community development efforts — they leave out the other sectors of the economy.

So, rather than shrink from having Community Circle operate a barter business to support itself and its projects, even if it does seem like courting the devil, we are taking that route. Having a number of businesses use Barter Credit and operate in the LETSystem is not, I think, a matter of us joining them, but of them joining us — never completely, of course, but straddling two economies. And what integrating our Business and Family Networks will mean — when I can receive Barter Credit for cutting my neighbour's lawn and then use it at the grocery, hardware and clothing stores — and when it is possible to do that generally with the value received by people doing the invisible work of the home and community — is that the value created in what are now called the invisible or informal economies can enter the business economy and be made available as an addition to local wealth, without excessive danger that it will be monetized, alienated and capitalized away from the community that created it.

The legal structures we are establishing to accomplish this are the non-profit corporation, Community Circle, alongside a private, for-profit corporation, The Barter Credit Network. Community Circle will be self-governed by an elected Board, contracting for management services with The Barter Credit Network, which will administer the business network and support Community Circle financially through statutory provisions in the by-laws of both entities. Excess profits earned by The Barter Credit Network will be held in trust as business, product and community development funds, administered by independent Boards of Community Circle, with Barter Credit Network members serving as trustees.

That, at least, is our second five-year plan.

Chapter Ten

LETS AS AN ALTERNATIVE MONEY SYSTEM
Ethical and Theoretical Considerations

The LETS "Money"

That the structure of our money is problematic is the claim of Michael Linton, the designer of the LETSystem of economic exchange. Theory and information on the LETSystem in this text has been derived from personal conversation with Linton, and from his writing on the LETSystem. The particular formulation and expression here of the problem with *commodity money as we know it*, and the uses of the LETSystem as a tool for facilitating the exchange of goods and services in what I call a *real-goods*, rather than a *money* economy, are my own.

The LETSystem exchange medium is, by most classical definitions and in the opinion of economists (and Revenue Canada) a *money*. Economists' definition of money insists that such value-records, or credits and debits, is *money*. The LETS currency is, however, a *post facto* money which is brought into being only by the economic activity which it facilitates and which is founded upon the collective skills, resources, time and labour availability of the community — what I have called above our own *natural money*. It is a *record*, merely, of the spending of that *natural money*. It is that *natural money* which is the *money* that should get our economic attention, not the artificial currency it creates as a by-product of its exchange. The LETS currency, as a medium of exchange created by whatever level of economic activity exists, uniquely permits us to monitor our economy qualitatively, whereas our present system of *commodity money* tends to record mere volume of exchange rather than types of exchange, and since the economic activity possible depends on the supply of money and its availability, our present money system not only displaces attention away from "real" goods and services onto the artificial commodity, it fails to record true *potential* of any economy it facilitates. I submit, LETS currency is radically different from any other *created* money, and true to what I have called our *natural money* in being "real," and is, therefore, uniquely useful in enabling us to manage a local economy.

A LETS economy depends totally on people's needs and the capacity to meet those needs, and so can be dedicated to those ends rather than to the ever changing and unreal values of an external, somewhat arbitrary and totally artificial measure. Controlling economic activity through money supply, *commodity money* engenders recession and poverty, and by seeking its own increase artificially through interest, it engenders inflation and excess resource extraction. It also tends to drain wealth away from the communities that create it. A LETS economy, simply by using a differently structured and engendered symbol of value as an exchange facilitator or medium, would be preserved from these effects of money, depending totally on need and the capacity to fill that need, and retaining created wealth within the community.

I maintain that the LETS currency is not *money as we know it,* or what I have called here *commodity money,* since it bears no interest. Linton agrees that it is a money *differently structured,* and describes it as a money *created by its users.* Again, I differ, since the LETS money has no existence prior to the exchange which brings it into being as a money, and so cannot be arbitrarily created by anyone. I think its essential structural difference is not that it is created by individuals as they "need" it, but that it comes into being only *after* the fact of an economic exchange. In any case, the LETS currency, being structured very differently from our *commodity money,* has a very different character which is an additional benefit. It is what Linton calls *convivial,* meaning both co-operative and life-affirming: affirming *the life of community* as well as the *empowerment* of the individuals within that community.

Since money is merely notional in any case, I prefer, and choose, to think of the LETS currency not as a *money,* but *merely* as a record — after the fact — and adopt the position that *there is no money of any kind in a LETSystem,* no matter what the classical economists — or Michael Linton — claim.

Money Problems

Our present *money* economy is based on values derived from the ethic and morality of the hunt, from Riane Eisler's *dominator* society. It is based on the values of competition, exclusion, hierarchy and coercive power inherent in the ownership system. It is based on Adam Smith's *rational economics,* in which each person acting in his or her own selfish best ownership interest produces a collective effect that is supposedly best for all. It is possible to mount an argument that money is based on patriarchal Platonic Idealism, objectively reifying what is actually an abstract. And the concept of gaining a collective good from individual greed may even be a version of *The Great Chain of Being*, in which the impure matter of Earth is directly linked, in ascending orders of greater purity, to the ideal, immaterial Angels and to God, with Man right in the middle. I see in it the Mediaeval alchemical belief that base matter can, by transmutation, become gold. Atomic theory notwithstanding, base most often remains base.

Whatever the theory, the reality is that we are experiencing the *functioning* of the *rational economic* system outlined by Smith as having very destructive side effects both for society and for the environment. Linton claims that its very structure causes problems — the structure of the system, and the structure of the currency itself:

1. Money is created by fiat, the command of some hierarchical central authority.
2. A "material" money, itself a "good," is traded as though it were a commodity.
3. Increase in value abstraction (money wealth) is the greatest good. The results of this structure are familiar to us, although we are not accustomed to thinking about them as structural defects of money.
4. Control of our economy is vested in authority external to us.
5. The supply of this limited "commodified money-good" must be competed for.
6. Money abstraction drives resource extraction, depleting and displacing real resources beyond the level of need.

Much less do we consider our social affects as defects in the structure of money:

7. We lose control of our economic life, the capacity to fill our material needs, and political autonomy.
8. The price of money is always too great for some, who cannot compete for it, creating poverty.
9. Increase in the abstraction itself beyond what it represents is opted for, creating inflation.

The demand to constantly increase the abstraction that re-presents the value found in the combination of labour with resources acts to drive resource depletion beyond the need for it, and the displacement imperative, together with the imperative to constantly increase the abstract value which money represents, adds a tenth and major point: the function of modern money:

10. Our money comes to us in response to the goods or services that we offer only for the added value that it can pick up and carry away: all other results are secondary or accidental.

We have now, in our generally commodified trade-oriented world, internalized at the individual level the abstraction of money as we know it as a commodity valuable in itself, with the endemic problems of inflation and personal poverty that flow from that. But the principal trouble with money, with respect to Community Economic Development, is probably the far distant extent to which it can circulate when it is universal. This capacity to circulate universally has been painstakingly arrived at over centuries of economic development. It may not be a necessary endemic structure of the currency, but it is a common structure of the system as it has now evolved. Attempts have been made to block it. Transfers between national currencies have been made illegal, but that usually just results in a higher price for the illegal (universal) currency in the sequestered (local) currency, without eliminating the practice.

Universal Circulation means that the circulation of any money can become so extended as to become dispersal and alienation of value. The result is the impoverishment of a locality, as the real value it has invested in the representation of value vanishes with the representation. If I work for you and you pay me a dollar — which now represents — *re-presents* — the value of my work — and I then buy a hamburger with it, I have eaten my work, in that my work became a dollar which became a hamburger which I consumed. Is that the end of my work? No. Burger Buff exchanged a hamburger for my work *re-presented* in the dollar you gave me. When they send it to head office, out of town, my work leaves town. My work then has no more existence in our town: I ate the burger that once represented it, and the dollar it became in that exchange left. If, however, I work for you and you pay me nothing, but accept an obligation to work for, or give something to, someone else in town (including, maybe, me) then my work is being passed around as created community wealth.

What if I had bought a pen with that dollar instead of a hamburger — a pen made out of town. Would my dollar — my work — be still re-presented in the form of the pen, and still present in our town even if the dollar has been sent away? Yes, to the extent I might circulate the pen. But the difference between the retail price of the pen and its manufacturing cost has gone. Buzz, buzz, squeak, squeak — the money bats are busily at work.

As detailed in part one of this book, our problem lies in the way we symbolize value — in the fact that we never shifted our currency model entirely away from using things of *real* value, like cattle or wheat, but went only part way, by way of precious metal specie, then money *good for* precious metal, each step more readily facilitating trade, even trans-border trade. Things of *real* value were used to *re-present* the value of other things also of *real* value: *grain=cattle=gold=money*. Money was *accidentally* imbued with the *semblance* of real value because it was equated with things of real value. When paper money was finally divorced from such real commodities, we had developed the fatal habit of thinking of it as a commodity in itself, and thinking makes it so. When my money leaves town, a valuable commodity leaves, probably never to return.

That equation with things of real value came about because money was developed first in the early economies which were trying to *trade* things of real value with other economies — commodity for commodity. In the absence of a permanent, trustworthy and reliable relationship between the economies, some firm commodity was needed as a transfer medium. It was never needed internally, *at home,* where the material of basic sustenance was never traded as a matter of commerce, but shared as a matter of mutual survival. LETSystems manage inter-system trade this way — on the sharing model. If system A sends something to someone in system B, it is acknowledged by a notation in a system B, not a system A, account. Value has moved *one way only.* Value will move back into system A , eventually, *only as some real good or service* is provided to system A. If that is from system B, it might be acknowledged by a transfer back from system A's account in system B — or by a transfer into a system B account in system A. There could be — but there will never be a need for — reconciliations between these accounts. Since the inter-LETS relationship is a secure one, the notation is a record of an obligation that can and will be honoured if ever required, but it is only the original commodity sent by A that is a diminution of the wealth of system A, not the symbol that records the fact of that gift.

Schumpeter's Equation

The 17th Century discovered that *money* could be created independently of *real* value in goods and services. Since money was then becoming accepted as *real* value, it *seemed* that wealth could grow upon itself. It was done through the phenomena of compound interest and the *issued* bank note or bill of exchange. What actually happens, of course, is that, down the line at the bottom end, where real resources are being turned into money, the screws get tightened a few more notches to keep the produced supply of *real* value growing to keep up with the growth of *nominal* value expressed by the new money created by the "interest." In a world of infinite resources that might be OK and, since the world of the 17th Century seemed to have infinite resources and since this process was to the advantage of the powerful, *seemed* became *did*.

In the 18th Century, the problem of how to actually equate real goods and services, bills of exchange, notes of credit, written cheques, precious metal *specie* and abstract paper money, so that they all could be freely translated into one another, began to be addressed. Bankers and money-men used to run about town with bags of gold and silver coins — objects considered to be of *real* value — on one day each year, the day of reckoning and reconciliation when all accounts for outstanding *paper* had to be settled. They began to recognize that reconciling debts with coin of real value that way was un-necessary, costly, dangerous, and ludicrous. Fernand Braudel cites J.A. Schumpeter[1] on the apparent border between money, credit and *real* goods.

> But if it is possible to claim that everything is money, it is just as possible to claim that everything is, on the contrary, credit.... As Schumpeter said, "Money in turn is but a credit instrument, a claim to the only final means of payment, the consumer's good. By now (1954) this theory, which of course is capable of taking many forms and stands in need of many elaborations, can be said to prevail." All in all, the brief can be legitimately argued either way.[2]

In the 18th Century, *abstract money* became confirmed as a commodity in its own right. Credit instruments are *all* money. If that is so, then equally, money is *only* credit, a *ticket* entitling the bearer to *real* goods or services. We can now add unrealized raw resources and our own time, labour and skills to that equation. In our fully commodified world, everything is money, and, equally, nothing is: it's all *credit*, which is to say, *belief* (in Latin, *credo*).

Money Not Needed at Home

Money was never necessary *at home*, where *credibility* is not usually a problem and where real-goods transactions were possible and, unlike with dollar transactions, easily and plainly evident. It will advance Community Economic Development to return to this model and prevent local value — or *credit* — from being expressed in a form which is hard to see and which can escape from the community as easily as money does. One way to do that is to turn Schumpeter's equation on its head and think of community value in terms of the real goods and services which actually make up the economy, rather than in terms of the abstraction that we use to *measure* that real value within that economy — *money*.

As *real* goods, value cannot easily cross outside the borders of a local economy. But — even here — on any scale beyond the family, exchange relations will become harder to track, and credibility will become a problem. Something like money does become a necessity. Exchange, and understanding the dynamics and results of exchange, ought to remain readily visible for the adequate management of a small local economy, even if an abstract exchange medium is employed. It is probable in our society that we *need* an abstraction, a representation of our *real* value, in order to replicate the form of money and money-exchange with which we are familiar and comfortable. The effect, however, of that abstraction must be the same as if our values were kept only *real*. In a locally mandated economy, it can readily be made so — but not with a reified and migrating money.

A system of economic exchange that is fully abstract would get beyond Schumpeter's equation (which essentially leaves our economic system in the 18th Century) and would move on to Schumpeter's insight that money, in any form, is merely a ticket for, or measure of, the value of *real* goods. Working from that assumption, we can arrive at a form to mediate exchange which is convenient to use in our world, yet open and visible. If we then resist the notion that such an abstraction is *money*, at least *money as we know it*, and if we can continue to recognize it as *merely* an abstraction and representation or indicator of original value, we can focus our attention and trading where it belongs, on the *really* valuable goods and services which actually embody our economy. And we can get rid of the un-necessary fiction of *money*.

Michael Linton's LETSystem establishes an abstract form of exchange that is based firmly in solid, *real* goods and services — in the *real* economic potential of any community — but which has a modern, familiar, money-like form with which to mediate and facilitate exchange without either the inconveniences or lamentable ethical fallout that *money* has and creates. Structurally, the LETS currency could, by local option, be re-constructed in something like the form of our present money, and its advantages be lost. There is a tendency among neophyte LETS operators, in order to make the LETSystem more compatible with peoples' expectations of an exchange system, toward making rules that conform more to the money model than the LETS model. For LETS to function to its best potential, however, such *monetized* thinking must be resisted. But the LETSystem is more than a currency, it is a total system of exchange and, although it widely makes its own rules, they must be made only within the general LETS structure; and the essential *differences* of the LETSystem from the present money system, and the reasons for those differences, must be well understood and preserved.

Discarding Money Thinking

Once outmoded *money-as-value* thinking is discarded, the different ethic that flows from using a cashless system such as the LETSystem is worthy of examination.

Whereas the money system is based on payment, on *money-as-value*, the LETSystem is based on credit — belief or trust — which is in turn based on the availability of *real* goods or services. Money apologists will argue as they are taught, i.e., that our money system runs on trust. That is true to some extent, but not structurally. Structurally, all exchanges in the money system must be balanced by *payments*. It only looks like trust or credit because of the variety of styles, forms and timing of *payment* that are permitted. In the dollar system, value is always *secured* up front by some *negotiable instrument,* namely *money,* according to Schumpeter. It may look as though credit or trust is operating when credit is *granted,* but credit is never granted unless the grantor can find you and take away something of *real* value from you (as his *payment*) if you do not keep up *your* payments. He has a *credit instrument* — a form of *money,* not so convenient as cash money, but *money* nevertheless. He has been paid, even though he and his trading partner have not necessarily ended their exchange relationship.

The LETSystem does run on a community of trust because goods and services *provided* are not *paid for* by any actual *money* transfer, although their transfer is securely recorded. A *record* is kept, expressed as a numerical quantity that is simultaneously added to the provider's account and deducted from the receiver's, of the mutually agreed value of what the provider has provided and the receiver received. The provider and the receiver both receive this record in their computerized accounts. Economists and Revenue Canada — and Michael Linton — call this record *nominal money,* because the positive record in the so-called seller's account can be viewed as a ticket of his or her entitlement to other goods and services from other people, as is money. But the LETS record is not what is *commonly known* as a money to most of us. It is different in several ways.

In the money system, the buyer uses money representing value he has *already created* (with the adjustment we call credit not really making an exception, as explained above). The receiver of a good or service in a LETSystem incurs with that receipt the commitment to return value which is *not yet created*. In the money system, the value used in payment is delivered to the *supplier* of the goods or services. In the LETSystem, it is delivered, not to the supplier of what was received, but to *someone else in the system*. In the money system, you are free to take your money, and that means the value it represents and which you received, anywhere in the world. In the LETSystem, *you* are *not free to take the value of what was received out of the community*. Nothing can be added and nothing can be taken away from the aggregate of the LETS accounts. The positive record, the so-called *nominal money*, can go only into another account *within the system*. Neither can the negative record be alienated. The total value of all accounts in a LETSystem is *always* zero — for every positive entry there is an equal and opposite negative one.

Because in the LETSystem the commitment to return value is made to the community and not to the individual, the buyer and seller — more properly called receiver and provider — are quits in any LETS exchange. The record of the exchange creates what looks like *payment*, seen from the perspective of the *money* system, and, although it permits the provider and receiver to be quits just as if it were payment, I submit that it is not: it is true credit — it is *trust*. The provider of goods or services *trusts* in the freely given commitment *and capacity* of all other members, *and of the community itself*, that they will and *can* perform services of value, or provide goods of value, so that he or she can receive value in return, later, from someone in the system. There is no credit instrument that can guarantee the continuing resources of a community, and the only sanction against a defaulter is ostracism from the community, so there is equally no credit instrument — except community will — that can enforce realization of an individual's commitment.

The greatest difference from the money system, however, probably lies in how the currency is created. *Money* is created by the act of credit grantors, LETS currency by the act of individuals creating a credit for their own convenience.

Money is created in advance, and imbued with value in its own right, which must be supported by some real value somewhere. That is the theory at least, and it used to be the case, but the requirement has been more often broached than held to. Attempts to keep paper currency tied to real commodities — usually gold and silver — have been almost everywhere and always subverted by the money-makers. Inflation is the result. In the absence of real equivalents deposited somewhere to support the value of money created, some authority must guarantee that value, undertake to supply — or command the supply — of equivalent value. That is the role of governments, but they choose to guarantee the imaginary value of paper money with more paper — bonds — of equally imaginary value. The value of our money is supported by authority and the strength of our economy alone.

Since, in a LETSystem, if there is no transaction, there is no record, there is equally no currency without trade. That is, the transaction itself creates the currency which facilitates it. The LETS currency has no prior or independent existence and so needs no base (such as gold or silver — or another *money*) to validate it, other than the strength of resources held individually by the guarantor of value and collectively by the community, and their availability for general use. The lets economy is not without limit, but since it is trade itself which creates the LETS currency, lack of currency can never be a barrier to trade — only the lack of trade goods or need for them. The value of a LETS economy lies not in the amount of credit notations that lie in people's accounts — they always equal zero — but in the value of the real goods and services traded, or available for trade *and needed.* The reality is much more evident.

The LETS internal currency is functionally different because the receiver of a good or service *trusts* in the productive capacity and the continuing productivity of the *community* and the individuals in it to realize the commitment to provide future goods and services, not in the imaginary value of a currency. The community makes up whatever rules may be necessary about the nature of that commitment, which is to say, just what those positive or negative records *mean* in practice but, at base, they mean only that someone has given and someone has received. What is to be done about that is a local option. So a decision could be made, for the elderly and infirm, for example, not to require the reciprocal provision of goods or services but to permit them to rack up unlimited negative accounts. Equally, a decision could be made to limit positive amounts held, as a means to encourage trading.

That might be desirable as a counter to usual money thinking, because, while it may be necessary in a LETSystem to permit some *negative* accounts to build up, and possible to do so without serious ill effect, it is *not* optional to permit *positive* accounts to be allowed to build up. A high positive account is structurally as bad as a high (or low) negative account — *both cases stop trade*. But while there may be justification for permitting a negative build-up, there is no justification for positive build-ups. A positive account provides no advantage to the account holder, since positive balances are not necessary for trading, and no interest accrues. What an un-moving positive balance indicates is someone who is supplying a need, but either not needing in return, or otherwise not fully participating in the exchange life of the community. He or she is not, for example, providing employment. Not participating *in both directions* in the economic cycle jeopardizes the cycle.

All of the above is critical, so I shall go over it again in another way. Even if the provider of a good or service in a LETSystem has received what Revenue Canada calls a *nominal currency*, and can use that credit record as *entitlement* for other goods and services from other people, he or she has received *nothing of real value*. Every provider of value does get, up front and immediately, an information record indicating the extent of his *right to future considerations* of value, and this is analogous to having received *payment* — so there is no *debt* involved even though there is *credit*. The receiver of a good or services gets a negative record — recording what the dollar system would call a debt.

But the positive record is of relatively little importance to the individual who has it for several reasons. By definition, every person in the system *already has the right to receive goods or services,* irrespective of the level of credit notations in his or her account, *by virtue of membership* in the community. It is not necessary to have positive sums of what economists insist on calling the LETS *nominal currency* in order to pay out (make acknowledgements in) the LETS *nominal currency*. So, even though the economists and Revenue Canada define the LETSystem *nominal currency* as a money, such a currency, received, is not, of itself, very important *except as a record to guide community action to keep the system functioning*.

Neither is the negative record significant except in terms of a reminder of having received, or of who has received, services. There is no cost to any individual if those services are not "put back" into the system. There will be a cost to the community as a whole if a receiver does not return value. But that community as a whole could decide to accept that cost — in the case, say of the elderly and the infirm — and even make rules about the extent of such "draw-downs." But there is no *structural* consequence to a negative account except the extent to which it diminishes trade — the same consequence as a positive account.

It is very different from the money system for an individual positive account balance to have no positive effect and for an individual negative balance to have no negative effect for the individual account holders involved. While it would be possible for a community to make a rule to introduce interest charges and payment into their system, doing that would destroy one of the advantages of the system — and result in their losing the right to call what they do a LETSystem. They would be on the road to commodifying their LETS currency and imbuing it with all the evils of the present *money* currency. It is because interest is not introduced — coupled with the capacity to trade relatively freely even from a negative account — that the LETSystem is so useful.

Some systems, for example, place limits on the right to draw down from a *negative* account, which is why I say "*relatively* freely" above. In the Winnipeg system we require only that some movement back up toward a zero balance be recorded within a three-month period, which is not hard to manage. The people we hound most are the ones whose accounts do not move toward zero from a *positive* balance. The reason for doing this is that it indicates *less than full participation in the system*, and the system relies for success on the full, *reciprocal* participation of all its members. In other words, it is preferable for a negative account to persistently go farther negative than it is for a (high) positive account to remain high and not move. The negative trader is trading, the high, static positive account holder is not. How and why accounts are changing — or not — is something the system administrators should know.

Accommodation can be made for those who *cannot* contribute as much or more than they need to take — they can be "carried," at local option. Allowances can be made for those who *do* habitually contribute more than they need to take — which may be one reason for a continuing positive balance. But if the administrators of the system do not know how and why such situations occur, they cannot properly do their job of developing their local LETS economy.

A persistently low negative balance might indicate someone who cannot reciprocate, or someone who simply has not found a way to reciprocate, but who could begin functioning more fully with some advice or help. A high positive balance might indicate that someone has needs that cannot be met from within the community. If so, that disparity should be addressed. It might mean that someone does not need what the system provides but is bringing value into the system or community from outside of it. If so, what is being brought in and why should be examined, if the community is to be self-reliant. Perhaps it would be more advantageous to begin to provide locally what is being brought in.

A persistently high and un-moving positive or negative balance in-dicates lack of reciprocity. In the money system, a negative balance would indicate trouble and become the bank's business, but a high bank balance would be no problem and no one else's business. In a LETSystem the administrators must discover the reasons for both per-sistent low *and* high balances. The relative balances, and how and why they change through time, are indicative of the health of the system and how its community economy is developing. The dynamic behind those changing balances is something the system administrators really need to know.

Registering the health of the economy and the way the economy is developing is one of the information functions that money serves in our present economic system. Here too, an excess of positive accounts means that not enough trading is going on — one of the causes of depression is the hoarding of money in savings, keeping it out of cir-culation. The LETS currency can perform all the useful tasks that money does while avoiding its negative side-effects. How it performs these tasks is, most importantly of all, kept within the decision-making powers of our communities.

Although I try not to do so, it is sometimes useful to think of the LETSystem's value markers as a nominal currency performing the functions of money in other respects as well. It is at least a way to match people's present ingrained economic habits of exchange, which are based on the *money-payment* system — although the essential differen-ces must not be overlooked. Classical economic thinkers — that is, all of us — need to reason out the LETSystem within the rational economic vocabulary Adam Smith and his successors have developed. But that vocabulary — and that reasoning — is severely limited by classical economics' artificially limited assumptions, and we need to get beyond those limitations if we are to restore community life, and to do so under our own control — particularly with the way classical economics dis-cards what it calls *externalities*.

Externalities are, in short, all the things that don't fit classical economic theory and which we know as most of the things that make for a good community life — culture, "non-economic" values, and the condition of the environment included. They also include, apparently, the invisible work of the home and family that sustains everything else, which classical economics and its present accounting systems do not accommodate. But to address LETS with the concepts of classical economics is to make an *incomplete paradigm shift*. It is important to eventually discuss LETS within its own paradigm and with its own vocabulary, no matter by what route you begin to understand it. A different ethic and a different reality prevails in a LETSystem, in which matters of debt and payment are not germane, but matters of community and environmental values are.

Also, in a self-producing LETS community, you are dealing economically with people you meet every week, not faceless and forgettable strangers across the world. And you would also be gaining the majority of your living from your own ecosystem, which you cannot, therefore, allow to deteriorate. In fact, I am coming to see the LETSystem as only *an interim step* in a move to a communitarian society in which money is no longer used in any form at all, but is replaced by a deep appreciation of the *realities* of economic life — the equitable realization and distribution of resources from our own ecosystems, by and for people of our own communities. But that interim, like the *money* aberration itself, may be half a millennium long.

No Individual Gains in a LETSystem

There is further ethical fallout from viewing LETS as a means of doing away with money. Only the *receiver* of a good or service has received value in a LETSystem. The *provider* does *not* receive value *as a result of any one exchange:* the provider's receipt of value depends upon *further* exchange or exchanges, usually with other partners — in which case, he or she is only *then* the receiver of something of real value. The receipt of an amount of LETS currency does not represent a material gain, it measures a material loss. At the same time, since anyone *receiving* any good or service in a LETSystem has, necessarily and by definition of his or her membership, an equal and opposite commitment to *provide* substance of materially equal value later, the receiver as well has not experienced a material gain. What seems like a gain is balanced by an equal and opposite obligation. In a LETSystem, *no one ever experiences an absolute increase in material substance,* no matter how much value he or she has received — and certainly not from the receipt of the *nominal currency.*

Now, I know this sounds like purest casuistry, a specious argument. But, I submit, it seems so only from the point of view of the *money* system. Once the shift in paradigm is complete, the argument is sound and logical. From a communitarian point of view, never experiencing individual gain is perfectly logical, once the concept of individual ownership is replaced by the concept of usership, *for the uses of sustaining individual and community life as opposed to the accumulation of wealth.* It is not that all the resources, goods and services of a community are *owned* by the community as a community wealth-hoard. That is simply another attempt to describe a communitarian reality from within an incongruent paradigm. What is necessary and important is that resources, goods and services be readily and equitably available to all, without unnatural let or hindrance, for sustaining and sustainable use. The concept of ownership simply disappears because it is no longer necessary or useful.

The relevant questions in a LETSystem are *all* about whether a good or service is available, whether it is needed, and whether it can be provided and can be used. The question is never about whether it can be had if it is needed. Everyone has an effectively equal capacity to *demand*, to use a money-paradigm concept. The question is never about whether what is needed can be *afforded*, only whether, and how, it is available. The economic questions in a LETSystem are themselves *real*, and not abstract.

The LETSystem has implications that are very profound. It represents a return to the ethic of pre-money communities: that each should produce according to his or her capacity, and receive — and use — only according to his or her need, and should *not accumulate*. The LETSystem also subscribes to the ethic of the *gift* economy: as sure as you possess something now and have the right to use it, in a LETSystem it will, someday, circulate onward.

But if no one gains or loses materially in a LETSystem, if there is no absolute change of *ownership* of a community's commodities, what about taxation? At the moment, LETSystems function, for taxation purposes, within the money paradigm accepted by Revenue Canada, in which the LETS notation, whatever it is called, is accepted as a nominal currency which is considered to represent value, one for one with the dollar, and things are "owned" by their users. Taxation assumptions follow from that. However, there are more profound taxation implications here that might be explored in the future.

If no one receives a *money* in return for goods or work, and if no one experiences any absolute increase in value because of any LETS transaction, in a LETS economy, *no one has an income to be taxed*. If there is nothing but a *transfer* of the use of goods or services, all taxes would have to be on the transfers themselves, and on the *use* value involved rather than any *capital* value. That would be a taxing of pure economic activity — the tax on spending that a sales tax is supposed to be. Sales taxes are usually considered to be regressive because they do not tax that portion of wealth that the wealthy do not need to spend, hence income taxes seem more equitable. But there is a dis-incentive to "save" in a LETSystem. We can presume that everyone will spend for what they need and only what they need, so a sales tax is not regressive. But who would pay it, if no one experienced an absolute increase in substance? The answer is, neither participant, or both, or the community at large — none of which makes any sense.

A taxing of overall economic activity would mean a so-called taxation level dictated by the number, value and amount of total actual exchanges. That is why some people describe LETS as a form of *social credit*. Social Credit, however, is a centrally controlled and administered *money system*, and LETS is neither. The comparison is an artifact of money-paradigm thinking. The fact is that a fully-LETS community would have no need for taxes. The taxation authority, government or otherwise, would be as free as anyone else is to create the LETS currency to facilitate its spending of its resources. As with anyone else, the only limitation to that would be the availability and nature of its resources, and the capacity to deliver services to its constituents that are valued by those constituents — which they, in turn, would acknowledge freely as they use them. Taxation itself may be as outmoded an idea as money, another artifact of an awkward and aberrant *dominance* paradigm.

The Ethical Structure of the LETS Economy

Here is a quick and tentative list of characteristics that we might expect of a full LETS community economy. We can all modify it or make up our own. But it should not be surprising that the opposite of an economy based on the competitive, so-called *masculine* values of *money* will be an economy based on co-operative, so-called *feminine* values, nor that the opposite of an economy based on greed should be one based on generosity.

circularity	*not*	*reciprocation*
locality	*not*	*generality*
reality	*not*	*abstraction*
sustenance	*not*	*power*
co-operation	*not*	*competition*
caring	*not*	*getting*
inclusion	*not*	*exclusion*
community	*not*	*isolation*
sharing	*not*	*alienation*

pragmatism	*not*	*idealism*
choice	*not*	*coercion*
enrichment	*not*	*impoverishment*
contribution	*not*	*extraction*
conservation	*not*	*exploitation*
function	*not*	*status*
rights	*not*	*privileges*
giving	*not*	*taking*
usership	*not*	*ownership*
gift	*not*	*commerce*
home values	*not*	*market values*
family values	*not*	*vendor values*

It remains to be proven whether an information-based, real-goods economy based on homely economics and barter would produce a nurturing, non-linear, non-hierarchical society with the ethic, morality and modality that could be called a *tribal, familial, internal-partnership* economy *of the community* or *of home*. It is arguable also whether such an economy can or should be characterized as *feminine*, although we tend to use that term to describe the values that appear on the left above. But it seems necessary to me that we create a society in which such values predominate against, or at least balance, the more aggressive, outwardly directed qualities on the right above, which we tend to characterize as *masculine*. At the moment the right-hand list of values overbalance the more convivial ones. It seems to me likely to be worth the effort to achieve that re-balancing if a non-consumptive, sustainable and personally richer life could result.

LETS Solves the Money Problem

Since we consider money to be real, we treat it as a commodity. Money is competed for as a commodity, and its supply is limited. The supply is limited in an atmosphere of constantly excessive demand (nobody ever has enough money), so it is a scarce commodity. We know that the price of a scarce commodity always rises until some cannot afford it and demand falls off. We must also know, therefore, that money as a commodity has poverty built into it. As abstract value made essential to life in a competitive system, money also becomes the misplaced focus of a bottom-line ethic in which the money always has to be cared for first and cared about most. This ethic demands that money, above everything else, must always seek its own maximum increase, as if increasing the value or amount of the abstract representation of value could increase the real value that is represented. And that increase in artificial value results in a constant pressure to increase real value — to extract and realize resources.

These *structural* problems of the *money* system start with the fact that its abstraction of value is *imperfect.* The LETSystem is another form for *abstracting* our value, a more complete form, convenient for us to use but not universal, that does not have those ill effects. As a local currency it would be just as difficult, or perhaps even more difficult, to transport across borders as the goods it represents. The LETS currency is a form that is readily and easily available to us. Viewed as a currency, it simply follows the abstraction of value completely to its logical end, by finally surrendering to the notion that money has no *real* value at all, a concept that can be derived from standing Schumpeter's Equation on its head. The structural problems of the *money* system, while they could be re-created in a LETSystem, simply do not arise as an inevitable and concomitant *function* of the system.

A community of LETS communities could be postulated, however, and if taken *ad infinitum,* might seem to restore the problem of the cross-border out-migration of created value. So we must be careful to understand that the *real goods come first,* that *they* are what is being traded, and what *looks* like a currency comes *only after* the goods or services are exchanged. LETS currency is information only, a record of a transaction that has already occurred; it cannot have a prior existence; it is entirely dependent and contingent, and not to be *viewed* as money. Our fully abstracted medium of facilitation is created by, and relates to, only the initial *transaction,* which itself occurs only if there is both a need and a capacity to fill that need. If you insist on thinking in money terms, then the economic activity creates the exchange medium. The activity is viewed correctly, however, as economic activity *for its own necessary sake,* and *only for its own necessary sake.* Ultimately, the apparent loss of currency in the case of out-migration of a LETS currency is countered by the fact that new LETS currency can always be created within the community to facilitate new transactions, so the migration of currency does not represent a migration of wealth. The LETS currency is not itself valuable.

In a LETSystem, it is always the goods that are moving, not an exchange medium. So there is no artificial impediment to exchange, no scarcity to create poverty and inflate currency values relative to goods. The medium itself is also never scarce, so it can't get priced out of anyone's reach. There is also no artificial de-valuation of the currency that can arise from currency speculation or excessive currency creation, so artificial inflation of the medium itself is not possible. The wealth created by the production and exchange of goods and services in a community whose economy was facilitated only by means of information, rather than by a pseudo-commodity like money, could consistently remain (which is to say that the community's productivity would remain) unalienated, within its own borders.

In such a community, wealth would take on an entirely new meaning (or revert to its original meaning of *a sufficiency of real goods*) being not expressed in abstract money, but in *real* things. It properly would not even be expressed in the internal currency, but remain a matter of goods, circumstances, capacities, relationships and values. The true balance of needs and capacity in the community, and how they are matched — community well-being, in short — would become the way in which the concept *wealth* is expressed.

The fully abstracted currency would become, not a measure of wealth, but merely a community economic management tool. The system of recorded plus and minus balances, as people give to and receive from one another, would steadily reveal any disparities between need and capacity, and permit them to be addressed by measures either to decrease the *need* or to increase the *capacity* of the community. The community could not lose touch with itself in an abstraction beyond the care and knowledge of the majority.

There would probably be changes in patterns of economic and work activity as well. *Surplus* value would result, not in sterile capital accumulation, but either in *import replacement* exchanges, and so a richer and more diversified material life, or in increased *non-labour* time, and so a richer and more varied cultural, community and personal life. Given the known result of using *money*, such an approach is the absolutely necessary minimal instrument of regional self-reliance and community economic self-development.

LETS Alternative Money Structure

The exchange notation used by organizations founded by Michael Linton, using his LETS computer software program, has been accepted by Revenue Canada as a *nominal currency* which appropriately describes the values of the exchanges it records, and is the virtual equivalent of the dollar for the purposes of calculating taxable income, tax owed, tax deductions and tax credits. Since most people find it difficult to consider an economic paradigm not based on buying and selling, but on gifting and receiving, it is academically useful to examine the results of considering the LETS notation as a *nominal currency* in the money paradigm.

If our present *money* economy is based on values derived from the ethic and morality of the hunt, competition, hierarchy and coercive power, and these produce structural effects which are problematic, we should consider the structural elements of the LETSystem's exchange medium, and how they might differ:

1. Currency is created automatically by local economic activity.
2. A "non-material" currency is not tradeable as a commodity.
3. Equitable production and distribution of real goods is facilitated. The ill affects of the structural defects of money are replaced by positive affects of a different structure.
4. Control of our economy is vested internally in the community.
5. The exchange medium is always available to all as needed.
6. Resources are not depleted for profit but only for use.

The socio-political affects of the different structure are likewise desirable.

7. We retain locally both economic and political control of our lives.
8. Poverty can only result from lack of resources or capacity to realize them, not from lack of money.
9. Value changes in the currency reflect only the availability of goods.

With no demand to constantly increase the abstraction that represents the value found in resources, and with no displacement imperative or drive to constantly increase the abstract value which money represents, the tenth and major difference is the convivial functioning of our fully abstracted post-modern money:

10. The value produced (or added) in our communities remains in our communities as a currency which continuously circulates at home, preserving and passing on among its members their own created wealth.

The system using a currency with this structure is in place and functioning in upwards of a hundred localities world-wide, facilitating bottom-up cashless trading, and it is available for use by any community group.[3]

Chapter Eleven

THE LETS ECONOMY
An Evolutionary Program

Making a Distinction

As I read Braudel, he makes it plain that merely *tinkering with the features* of our world economy will have only minor or temporary effect. If we are to change our world fundamentally, and it seems we must, then we cannot just turn it top for bottom in some distributive revolution within the existing system. *It is that system that functions fundamentally to alienate our created real value and destroy community.* We have to re-make the home-places of our world in a different, older image:

> Finally, if we are prepared to make an unequivocal distinction between the market economy and capitalism, might this offer us a way of avoiding that 'all or nothing' which politicians are constantly putting to us, as if it were impossible to retain the market economy without giving the monopolies a free hand, or impossible to get rid of monopolies without nationalizing everything in sight?
>
> If people set about looking for them, seriously and honestly, economic solutions could be found which would extend the area of the market and ... put at its disposal the economic advantages so far kept to itself by one dominant group in society.[1]

Sauce for the goose being equally sauce for the gander, we can "... make an unequivocal distinction between" the "capital" and "market" economies and the "root" economy as well, to "... put at its disposal the economic advantages so far kept ..." by the other two economies.

A decade after its creation, the LETSystem of Michael Linton has now taken root in about a hundred localities in Canada, the U.S.A., Great Britain, Australia, New Zealand and Sweden. Using the

LETSystem, we can begin right now, anywhere and everywhere, and without "official" sanction, approval or even involvement, to define an economy based on homely community production and non-monetary exchange. It gives us the method to realize the designs of E.F. Schumacher and George McRobie. It gives us the modern, in-dividuated and familiarly monetized manner in which to re-create a tribal or village, communitarian economics within our present com-munities, within our present urban realities, and alongside our present economic structures.

On a small scale, practising LETSystems are building such economies, based on the ordinary survival activities that we all under-take daily. The next questions, and the more important ones, are whether those familial economic activities can be expanded in kind, such as for local self-production, and extended in their reach. Can those expanded familial economic activities be extended conceptually and practically to an entire community within our macho-economic world, as they were in a more primitive world? We need to examine how extensive they may already be, in degree and kind, and whether their expansion is necessarily within or parallel to the market economy and its support, or whether it can be partly or wholly out-side.

Can we function with strangers as we function with friends? Can economic life itself become more *real* and less *abstract?* Can we bring something more personal into our exchanges than a snatch of hard coin and an automatic *have a nice day!*? Should we? Do we need a new ethical norm for our economic lives? Could such a new paradigm be both ecologically and socially more equitable? Is this a foundation upon which to build a new and more sustainable economic paradigm?

I think so.

Our local "root" economy has the capacity to recognize and put our own particular local or regional valuation on the *invisible work,* that large range of fundamental home and community activities which we all must do for ourselves and each other, day by day, but which are degraded, devalued, or simply not recognized as *economic* by the *money demand* system of our macho market economy. Properly valued, those undervalued activities can form the active base of productivity for a newly sustainable local economy of fundamental need-fulfillment and ecological sensibility. Our modern information technology has given us a simple and easy method of exchange-facilitation conducive to the co-operative ethic of those activities and their locus. All we need do is put it into practice.

Loosening the Tie that Binds

It is our *universally transferable commodity money* that is the major tie binding us and our communities into the extractive "market" and "capital" economies. Money is the major instrument of the colonialist control and extraction functions which militate against *community*. And entrenching our *universally transferable commodity money* as the principal medium of exchange tends to deny people free and un-mediated access to the direct realization of their own skills, labour, time and resources — their *natural money*. That entrenchment requires that *natural money* to be translated first, through formal employment, into our *universally transferable commodity money*, where it is subject to simple and easy alienation from both individuals and community. *Money supply* is also a device by which economic activity is *regulated* — read *controlled* — in our system, and that by decisions we do not make in our communities, and which are not necessarily made for our benefit. An evolutionary program to re-establish control of our own economic lives, which is the basis for control of our social and political lives, begins with understanding that we must move away from the use of *money as we know it*, and then starting to do that — laying down that binding golden chain.

It is possible to begin to develop a community economic life in an acceptable modern form, connected to community instead of to the world "money-market" economy — by beginning to formally mediate our present informal local *real value* exchanges with a local medium of exchange that we control, and then expanding that local informal economy in both *real-goods* (and services) exchange and *real-goods* (and services) production for our own use, understanding that the economy is a matter of the goods and services produced and exchanged — and is to be accounted and reckoned in those *real goods and services* — rather than a matter of the medium of exchange and its accounting and reckoning.

Recognizing the *real* goods and services we produce, distribute and consume locally, and not accumulations of the exchange medium, as the *real, living wealth* of our community — and of ourselves as individuals — removes us from the realm of economic fantasy and lets us see clearly the real world of our economy, both in terms of the ecosystems that are its foundation and of the people who take part in it. Locally produced, those real goods and services are readily available for local transparent distribution and consumption and (what is their *disadvantage* on a national or world market) they are harder (than money) to move very far. They are, therefore, harder to insinuate into, and do not bind us so fully within, the national and world market economy. So we can create in our various localities a valuable counterpoint and balance to the international "money-market" *cash-mediated* economy, improving our freedom from its vagaries, our security, and our local autonomy.

There is a shift of consciousness involved here, as well as a shift in economic practices. We can accomplish both shifts readily if we recognize that the medium of exchange is pure information and not properly itself a commodity — that wealth is a matter of productive capacity and not a matter of possessing quantities of a medium of exchange, and that this is true on both the individual and collective, or community, levels. There are also other advantages in mediating local exchange with simple information. It makes our *natural money* directly available to us all without artificial shortages interfering, and makes our time, work and resources resistant to manipulation and coercion for purposes that are not our own. And the information our economic activity provides can also be used in additional ways, so as to reveal the gaps and mismatches in our local mutual meeting of needs and resources, for example, to track and inventory resource use and availability, production, supply, distribution and consumption in ways that are useful for sustainable local management, and to keep track of, and manage, our impact upon our local ecosystems.

Easy and efficient direct information mediation of our local economy is available to us through an application of computer technology. Banks are perfectly capable now of keeping track, world wide, of the exchange and flow of *money*, recording that information with computers. But if, as Alan Watts suggests, money is only the *measure* of value — which is to say, *information about* value and not really value at all — then what banks are doing with their computers is recording information about the information about value. One of those steps is redundant. Modern technology permits us now to return to dealing directly in our own individual and collective *natural money* of time, labour, skills and resources. Their representation as *commodity money* is no longer necessary — we have a simpler way now to accomplish tracking their interaction, which is what creates and distributes the living wealth of our communities. With computers and quick, efficient means of communication, it is now *practical* to replace the *mediation of money* with the *mediation of pure information*.

The Information-Mediated Economy

It is now easy for us to keep a local community *needs-production-consumption* data base fresh by constantly updating information. And such a data base should be quite straightforward to manage thereafter. Because the data base is strictly local, reflecting local needs, capacities and resources, it can respond very quickly to the continuous changes impacting upon it, and so remain dynamic and not stagnate. We can easily know who needs what in our local communities, and also who can, or could, supply that locally. There are then only three more problems: whether and how the local ecosystem can afford the resource use, how to produce for those needs from that local ecosystem, if it is not already being done (which may require some business development help) and how to facilitate the distribution of what is produced so as to meet the needs expressed. Only a small extension of the local *needs-resources-production-consumption* data base would then be required to record, as pure information, the patterns and flows of individual *exchange* within the local economy, as well as needs, resources, production and consumption. That *exchange information* — who provided what and who received what, when, how, and perhaps why — also *itself* provides the *facilitation medium* by means of which we can manage and direct the exchange of goods and services produced, as well as the direct information about the distributive equity of our local economy, and possible gaps in its provision of goods and services. We can also quickly know and react to ecosystem degradation, either questions of pollution or of over-production and over-consumption, since we have an intimate and vital connection with our local ecosystem, monitoring it continually. Relying on our local resources as we do, we are less insulated from eco-folly than when we are using someone else's ecosystem to satisfy our needs and wants.

The Communitarian Ethic

Once we have liberated people's capacity to respond to their individual, mutual and collective needs with their own *natural money* of time, labour, skills and personal and community resources, irrespective of the *money demand* system and our artificial commodity money with its endemic problems of scarcity, poverty and inflation, it will also be possible to replace the concept of *money demand* as the arbiter of production and supply with that of *basic need*, and replace the concept of direct, immediate reciprocity, or *payment*, as the chief mode of exchange facilitation, with the morality of *community right* and *the gift*. Local option would permit such a system to be informed and directed by its own ethic and value system, one that assumes, for example, that each community member has a right to sustenance. Other ethics could prevail, but, since the medium of exchange is not structurally scarce and does not structurally enable the development of pockets of power, the local community economy would probably function most easily with the ethic of the *gift* economy and the morality of providing according to need and giving according to capacity.

In a generalized local economy functioning in this way, a few simple rules would be required to balance individual in-put and out-take, production, distribution and exchange. Such rules would need to be or become a local *societal norm* just like those in the money economy which now internalize the morality of *paying your debts* or that *good fences make good neighbours*. They would be rules adapted — not merely adopted — from the primitive ethic which assumes that members of the family, or tribe — in this case, the community — have inalienable rights to basic sustenance. If such rights are not already endemic to the community — as in the case of families or perhaps existing tribal communities — they could be, as with the LETSystem, *defined* by a reciprocal membership commitment or formal contract that is entirely voluntary, since the "market-money" economy is still available for those who choose not to participate.

In a LETS economy, the ratio of consumption and production must balance, generally, over the long run and over the whole community involved, but no individual's consumption and production would necessarily have to balance at any given time, either as a matter of necessity or as a function of the mediation medium or its structure. Perhaps not ever. Some individuals, indeed, such as the very young, the very old or the infirm, might constantly receive more than they give, balanced by others' preponderance of giving over taking. Every individual's reciprocation pattern, however, can be known, and even can be subject to public commentary, but the *system itself* does *not* require immediate individual reciprocal balance. Any such requirement, or lack thereof, is a matter of collective decision-making within each LETS community.

Recognizing everyone's right to sustenance, coupled with the pointlessness of hoarding the medium of exchange, would tend to replicate the principle of reciprocity as it was practised within so-called primitive tribal societies, where it functioned to encourage equal distribution of available resources and to reduce any advantage of hoarding goods, or, in this modern interpretation, profit. Taking our *commodity money* out of the system in favour of freely exercising the innate power of our own *natural money* so that we can replace *demand* response with *needs* response and distribute production according to that need, we may even eliminate *want*, at least that want which results from the stratified inequities of resource access and distribution characteristic of our present economic and social system. To go that far, we probably need a different mundane *faith*, or social mythology, like that invoked by Michael Ignatieff in *The Needs of Strangers*, where he speaks of the *mediated* quality of the relationship, in our modern welfare state, between those who need and those who, like himself, support them: "responsible for each other, but not responsible to each other ..." It is this

> solidarity among strangers, this transformation through the division of labour of needs into rights and rights into care that gives us whatever fragile basis we have for saying we live in a moral community.[2]

The LETSystem does not ensure that shift of *faith*, but it provides a way to move toward re-establishing that *responsibility to* one another without requiring that anyone *necessarily* give over the comfortable distancing of *responsibility for*. It lets us do that without the concomitant loss of human respect and dignity — non-quantifiable needs — which loss, Ignatieff notes, accompanies the administration and delivery of the unearned satisfaction of needs — *rights* — in our welfare states. It offers an answer to Adam Smith's "... ruthless demolition of the illusions of utopian economics ... that a republic could isolate itself from foreign luxury, the international market and the division of labour."[3] It provides a way for a society — an urban society, at least — to become "master of its own needs within an open international economy"[4] by choosing its domain, not as nation or the world, but at the level of community, and subordinating the macro-economics of the world trading system to the micro-economics of local need.

There is no technical barrier to accomplishing this now. Any barriers are ideological: that is, devolving, finally, into questions of faith and *belief*. Just as with money, according to Lewis H. Lapham: "The complex mechanisms of the modern world depend as certainly on faith in money as the structures of the medieval world depended upon faith in God."[5] Moving into the space made technically possible, would, however, make a different faith both possible and practical.

The Immanent Sustainable Economy

A LETS community functioning with a *real-goods* "root" economy that is self-reliant in providing for its own basic needs would live from *immanent production* realized at home. That is, it would not engage in *ex-*

cess production for profit, but produce only enough for its needs, now — and only those things that it needs. This might seem to be dangerous. What if productivity fails, or shortages develop? Our local economic production would have to be based on profound security of resources, which has environmental implications of sustainability. We would need to emulate the so-called primitive adaptive device of living principally within the means of our ecosystem and according to its productivity in its *least productive* years. Immanent use must include prudent production stockpiling of surpluses produced in those years that were more productive than the least. Our local economy ought to be part of a larger regional economy in which several localities balance their local economies with prudent and appropriate inter-community *exchanges* of surplus local production. Security can be approached through diversity, mutual complementarity and open reciprocity, and in caring for the productive capacity of our ecosystems. It need not be a matter of wealth accumulation.

But remember also that our re-constituted "root" economies, as we are presently imagining them, are but strong local partners of the general "market" and "capital" economies, not a total replacement of them. In the case of local or regional shortages, the community could also fall back upon the "market-money" economy as a safety net. Prudence suggests that such a contingency should and could be planned for, and resorting to a cash economy in the event of local failures would be a last, not a first, resort — just the opposite of the present situation.

The Evolved Community Economy

While the first objective of our evolutionary economic program is to re-establish a self-reliant and independent local economy, its goal is to re-balance our economic life between the nurturing, local *Yin* and the aggressive, external *Yang*. So also might we protect ourselves from the problem that Jean Bodin observed in 16th-century France:

> I find that the high prices we see today are due [principal-
> ly to] the abundance of gold and silver ... [as well as] mo-
> nopolies, and scarcity caused partly by export and partly
> by waste, by the pleasure of kings and great lords, and
> the price of money, debased from its former standard ....[6]

Bodin recognized that the prosperity of France in the couple of hundred years previous, before the influx of gold and silver from the

Americas through Spain, had been brought about by France's isolation (because of politics and war) from most of the world and its trade. France had been forced to concentrate on agriculture and other basic subsistence strategies. The result, in a fundamentally fertile land, was a population propelled to prosperity by its own self-generated economic activity. As I have claimed for our modern situation, Bodin believed that fundamental prosperity of France was being threatened by the influx of artificial riches through the new, freer connections with the world, and by the populace turning away from their own subsistence activities, and even from local trade, to become merchants and traders to the world, a much easier, but much more precarious, life.

> It is true that the mechanical arts and merchandise would flourish much more, in my opinion, without being diminished by the traffic in money.[7]

The opening up of France to world trade in the 15th and 16th Centuries hooked the French into the world market-place and the money-market economy, but not to its basic benefit, according to Bodin. And not to the benefit of the majority of its people, according to Fernand Braudel.[8] And, while his economic thinking is unsophisticated, Bodin is not wrong. Attention to the basics, to self-reliance, and a healthy reluctance to rely totally upon the market and its instrument, money, is the road to real wealth and sustainable security in the 21st Century, just as it was before this world market race began over five hundred years ago.

I submit that establishing immanent, parallel economies at the level of our communities or, at the most, on the basis of a relatively homogenous bio-region, *outside* the "market-money" economy, and as independent from it as possible — a straightforward and simple task with the LETSystem, although not organizationally easy — is the *essential step* to be taken to initiate both sustainability and a truly effective Community Economic Development.

Utopia: Smith, Rousseau and Marx

Michael Ignatieff, in his small book *The Needs of Strangers*, writes:

> Political utopias are a form of nostalgia for an imagined past projected onto the future as a wish. Whenever I try to imagine a future other than the one towards which we seem to be hurtling, I find myself dreaming a dream of

the past. It is a vision of the classical *polis* — the city-state of ancient Greece and renaissance Italy — which beckons me backwards, as it were, into the future.

Its human dimensions beckon us still: small enough so that each person would know his neighbour and could play his part in the governance of the city, large enough so that the city could feed itself and defend itself; a place of intimate bonding in which the private sphere of the home and family and the public sphere of civic democracy would be but one easy step apart; a community of equals in which each would have enough and no one would want more than enough; a co-operative venture in which work would be a form of collaboration among equals. Small, co-operative, egalitarian, self-governing and autarkic: these are the conditions of belonging that the dream of the *polis* has bequeathed to us.[9]

He has, of course, described the objectives I have ascribed to Community Economic Development, and the essential characteristics — missing only the environmental aspects — which I have claimed are possible for a community using the LETSystem of exchange facilitation. Is this utopian dream an impossible one? I don't believe so. I believe the LETSystem makes that *utopian dream* a *practical proposition,* and that it is much more than a dream, it is a necessity.

Ignatieff writes further on utopian thinking with reference to Adam Smith, Jean-Jacques Rousseau and Karl Marx. He notes that both Smith and Rousseau shared the philosophy of stoicism, in which human will is the predominant force. Rousseau believed that human will could keep man co-operative in a competitive world, that he could and would *choose* to overcome social and political and economic inequality. Smith believed that the natural result of the free competition of greed would result in the overall efficient provision of material goods, which man would, then, *willingly* find adequate for the first time in history. Smith invoked his stoicism in the unfounded belief that humankind would, once enough was achieved, *choose* to resist excess and enjoy an equality of plenty. His *rational economics* was equally utopian, as we have discovered to our sorrow.

In the end, Smith had to make demands on the virtue of this utopia's participants as austere as Rousseau's. A market society could remain free and virtuous only if all its citizens were capable of stoic self-command. Without this self-command, competition would become a deluded scramble, politics a war of factions, and government a dictatorship of the rich. Smith was optimistic, but it was an optimism based on a stoic hope that the human will would prevail, and each individual would retain the capacity to know the difference between what he wants and what he needs.[10]

Of course, Smith's *stoic hope* was unrealized, and we have the *scramble, war and dictatorship* that he feared. According to Ignatieff, Marx, seeking to address that, essentially tried, equally *stoically,* to reconcile Smith and Rousseau. He relied on the political will of Rousseau *plus* the productionist view of Smith to suggest that if inequality were overcome and the productivity of labour were raised, then "… all men's relative and absolute needs for commodities could be satisfied."[11] But all of these utopias foundered on the limitations of both human behaviours (social factors) and the capacity of the natural world (environmental factors).

Most of us are not stoics, and we are notoriously limited in our ability to distinguish between our needs and our desires, which know no bounds. But the world is also now full of humanity. Its limits of forgiving resilience to our tendency to excess have been reached. The end of history has been proclaimed. The end of human society may be in sight, as we recklessly despoil our world. How, then, do we bring about the profound change that is obviously necessary, without relying — utopically — on human good-will. How do we — constantly wanting — continue to live? How do we limit human desire to human need, and our exploitation of the earth to its finite limitations, not as a matter of *stoic will,* but as a natural concomitant of our social and economic structure?

Anita Gordon and David Suzuki, in *A Matter of Survival* tell us that utopia is, indeed, what we must achieve. "It appears with chilling clarity that for the first time in history, the things that used to be thought of as too utopian or too impractical are the only viable solutions to a global problem."[12] If utopia is necessary, for the first time in history, it may be also practical, although it will not be by dint of any exercise of human will. It is too much to expect that the vast majority of humankind will ever act in anything but its own short-term perceived best interests. It never has. To believe in the possibility of a universal moral enlightenment is "utopic" thinking in the old sense. There is, however, a practical route to utopia which we can take. If we agree that it is the functioning of the market-place through the mediation of commodity money that has alienated us from our communities, and that functions to destroy our communitarian relations and the very biosphere that supports our life on earth, then we can act to dis-engage to a significant extent from the market-place, mend our communities and live within our biospheric means in the various ecosystems we inhabit.

The Re-constructed and Visible Root

I believe that the only possible way we *can* answer the questions above lies in *making the attempt,* and making it in *small units* where production, exchange and consumption are open and transparent to public view and where people avail themselves, fundamentally and primarily of their local resources, and suffer in small the consequences of any over-exploitation of their own environment. I suggest further that the replication of empty growth that is endemic to the *money system* as we know it, and which Smith's disciples place at the centre of our being, must be abandoned as the sole and central ethic upon which we organize our economic life. It is killing us, body, soul and planet. I know that the only way to do that is to move away from that system itself, to insulate ourselves very carefully from it, and re-vitalize, as an alternative to balance against it, our older and more convivial ways. I also know that a practical alternative is readily at hand which — without conflict or revolution — can alter our economic ethic and morality by altering the structure of our economics.

Using the LETSystem, we can certainly make visible and acknowledge the value of the economy of so-called *"women's work"* that Marilyn Waring notes is so invisible at the moment. It is also possible with it to value, subjectively if not objectively (and even idiosyncratically) the monetarily unquantifiable benefits of the natural environment. LETS could safely do that without subjecting either to the objectification and alienation of the patriarchal money system — that is, to the predation of the money bats. Using the LETSystem, or something like it, is the essential "break-through" to moving away from the use of money, at least *money as we know it.*

Having moved away from *money as we know it* and having established an *information-mediated economy* expanded somewhat from the *informal economy* of the family in both kind and extent, a vigorous, consciously devised and re-structured "root" economy, based on a more directly *real* belief system and founded in the relatively familiar *money-*

style but *money-less* exchange medium of the LETSystem, could then begin to reclaim a large part of the "market" economy that is not necessarily, or perhaps even properly, a part of the "market" economy. This "root" economy could reclaim those relations and products, to different degrees, perhaps, but to similar effect, within the urban-rural neighbourhoods of re-countrified cities or in smaller communities, in towns, reserves and villages. If we can then include at least a portion of the trade of existing locally-owned businesses, we can begin to reclaim more of our local manifestations and institutions of trade and commerce into what might actually be a *truly free* market economy that does not, however, bear the money system's imperative of demand, but functions according only to need, and the capacity to fill that need.

The key to any community developing itself according to the way it wants to develop is to begin to produce basic goods and services for its own consumption. The LETSystem can help in that, especially on the consumer side, but also in the production process, by getting around some of the need for money: by enabling the local economy to express some portion of itself in a currency that it creates for that purpose and which is available as needs be. To develop such a local economic structure, parallel to the market-money economy we are familiar with, but separable from it, the community need only start by auditing whatever ordinary skills and goods people, including the poor, already have to exchange with one another, then building up the experience of dealing with one another for things that are needed, and expanding from that the range of things it is possible to exchange — including production of goods that are not present.

The local structure will expand, first by adding the unmediated exchanges going on already between primary producers and final end-users, such as the annual fall *tomato and zucchini* exchange among urban gardeners (a little economy that is already being harvested by imaginative food banks); and then, using familiar community economic development techniques and the system described above, it will build up from there, paying special attention to the *production* of basic goods and services, and their *processing* in value adding small industries. Some cash dollars are going to be needed to get that underway in any significant proportion, but it should be possible at some point to move to using the internal LETS currency to acquire basic material for value-added processing. Making it possible to develop the capacity to do that should be a guide for choosing what value-adding industries to develop, because that represents a third step, in which the internal economy can begin to become more complete and self-perpetuating.

With the LETSystem, it is possible to create nominally *paid* employment in processing those back yard surpluses and serving that *charity* market on a co-ordinated and orderly economic basis. On a slightly larger scale, our present urban structures might permit us to feed ourselves partly from back yard gardens, or from urban-rural alliances of producers and consumers. If we then have the capacity to see self-reliance, not as Braudel's *"prison,"*[13] and not, as Vandana Shiva notes, as a "poverty that is a result of misery and deprivation" but as what she describes as "subsistence economies which satisfy needs through self-provisioning" and which "are not poor in the sense of being deprived,"[14] then that kind of self-reliance will be our local community freedom from money poverty, its lack of choice, value-alienation and debt-enslavement, and from the manipulation of those who control and direct the "market" and "capital" economies.

But we do not need to abandon the "market-money" economy entirely — cannot, in practice, for it alone will provide much of what we want and even some of what we need for a long time — perhaps forever. Our community economic goal is self-reliance, not necessarily a self-sufficiency which is, in our crowded and "developed" world, probably not possible. We need to accustom ourselves to using two economies, and to using them integrally. Value can migrate between the two economies. Money can be exchanged for Barter Credit, for example, or vice-versa. The inclusion of businesses will integrate the two, and value will flow between them when, for example, a new toaster at a hardware store becomes translated, through one or more exchanges, into a frozen meal prepared in the local cashless economy.

Not only can this integration not be stopped, it should be encouraged. The wealth of the local business cycle will be expanded by the migration into it of value created in what was formerly the informal economy to which local business previously had no access. Local business involvement in the local cash-less economy is important to local business for that reason, and it is very important to the local cash-less economy, especially in its early stages, as a means of making the local currency more valuable by virtue of being "spendable" in more places and for more goods and services. And, of course, if we want our local economy to expand seriously, we need the inclusion of local business to as great an extent as possible. It is the venue where most of the "serious" economic activity takes place and will continue to take place, irrespective of how successful our internal "prosumer" self-production becomes.

Careful monitoring of the value flow between the two economies is, however, necessary. Value created in the (formerly) informal economy, which we will have regularized as an information-mediated local economy, should not be permitted to migrate into the "market-money" economy through the participation of local merchants without an equal and opposite flow of value from the "market-money" economy into the local cash-less economy in the form of goods or services provided by merchants situated principally in the "market-money" economy. The two economies must be considered to be separate economies, and value flow between them considered as "foreign-exchange" and "balance of trade" and "balance of payments" problems. They can be dealt with satisfactorily in that mode, but there is no automatic mechanism to regulate the value flow between economies: it must be a matter of conscious policy.

The point is that we can begin, and then work to expand the scope of what we do, until it becomes a comprehensive economy, in the essentials of survival at least. With the LETSystem, it is possible to create nominally paid employment in any function, and even organize resources for any kind of industry, including the resources of cash money supplies, through "foreign exchange" transactions. We can now *begin* to turn away from complete integration and incorporation into the body of the exterior "market-money" economy, with all its negative ethics and destructive effects, by re-building our *real* economy, from our own resources, within our own communities, even in the inner city. We can undertake this Community Economic Development in a simple practical way, starting *now*, by re-building upon our everyday skills and whatever resources can be mustered, the economy of the home-place in which we first flourished. Exactly where that will take us, I cannot predict. But I am convinced of the need to begin and the direction to set out.

The steps toward our evolutionary alternative local economy are few, simple, straightforward, and direct. If you choose to take them, take them gently and make haste slowly, but start taking them now.

1. Establish a system of exchange that does not bear the money system's imperative for a money demand: a LETSystem is a good example;
2. Establish people's familiarity in practice with economic exchanges using that exchange medium: work at developing the convivial community;
3. Identify whatever productive capacity is available locally — people, material, labour, resources, land, and minor cash capitalization: work to expand capacities;

4. Identify whatever needs are required locally, beginning with matters of basic sustenance but also including less vital wants: work to match needs and wants to productive capacity;
5. Organize the major production components required to fill the needs you have identified with the capacities you have identified: work to produce the basics that people in your community need;
6. Using the internal exchange medium, expand that local productivity in both quantity and variety: work to develop a full local economic cycle of production, distribution and consumption;
7. Expand local networks of local evaluation and distribution within which the local moneyless exchange of that local productivity can be accomplished: work to develop community economic structures;
8. Extend those networks, structures and that productivity to support appropriate inter-community trade of prudent surpluses, in order to secure what cannot be had locally: network your local economy to other similar localities;
9. Involve, early or late, as many local businesses as possible in the cash-less economy network, exchanging their market economy goods for value created in the local economy: work toward general community familiarity and acceptance;
10. Establish community-based economic and ecological monitoring and management institutions: work to achieve an equal and sustainable balance of economic activity in your community between the local, pro-sumer economy and the national-world "market" economy.

If we believe that an economic system based on the values and substance of family and community could really be extended outward from home and community (*how far?*), then the project is merely a matter of organization, and the questions about it are those about what kind of economic structures and practices could facilitate those activities — whether those structures and practices would produce the effects that we would like to see such a system bring about (the opposite of those of the "market" economy) and whether those structures would preserve the essential differences that we perceive as desirable.

I know that it is our economic system itself that leads, structurally, to exploitation of people, peoples and our ecosystems. I believe that nothing less than an economic re-structuring will be effective to liberate either — both — us and our environment. I am certain that if we want any fundamental change, we must change our economic structure fundamentally, because it determines all else. What I am advocating as a means for making that fundamental change is largely unproven yet. It is, at this stage, still an experiment. I know the experiment works in small. Many more people — communities — must now take part in expanding and completing the experiment — this evolution to a new economics, a new society and a new world. You are invited to take it up. You are urged to do so, for our survival's sake.

Act now, in your community, to bring your economy home from the market.

COMMUNITY CIRCLE

BUILDING COMMUNITY WITH BARTER CREDIT

Original Cartoons
by Bill Shuttleworth

Additional drawings
and Text
By Ross Dobson

Community Circle, Barter Credit and The LETSystem

THE LOCAL EMPLOYMENT AND TRADING SYSTEM

COMMUNITY CIRCLE

A non-profit corporation providing services to support communication, self-employment, production, and trading among members co-operating in a bounded system.

LETS REGISTERED

The LETSystem originated in 1983 in the Comox Valley on Vancouver Island with Landsman Community Services, Inc., which maintains a world LETS register.

WORLD-WIDE

About 100 LETSystems are now operating in Canada, The U.S.A., Australia, New Zealand, and Great Britain.

GREEN DOLLARS

The LETSystem can be considered to be an alternative or personal money system, its unit of value called the Green Dollar - always equal to $1.00.

BARTER CREDIT

Community Circle views LETS trading as Barter extended by Credit. We focus on production of goods and services, using the LETSystem to facilitate community economic development.

BARRELS
4 - 7

We and our communities are like leaky barrels filling with water.

1

Except it is money running in the top and out the bottom. We can keep more in the barrels either by pouring more in or holding in what is there. A community barrel has a lot of little barrels inside, so - since a dollar counts every time it is spent - there is another way for a community to get richer. By passing the money around the little barrels before it leaks out the big barrel, a community can spend itself rich - as long as its people have the capacity to make what they need, and can trade it around.

BASKETS
8 - 13

When money is scarce, people can't buy, even if things are available. Trading stops and recession sets in.

2

But it is not the money that makes a community rich, it is the products and services it is able to provide and trade. Money only measures the value of those things. Using another measure for value, we can keep passing that value around and around our community without needing money to make it happen. Barter Credit gives us that other measure. It provides us with another basket to put in our big barrel.

WORK
14 - 19

Barter Credit opens up a new way to earn. When formal jobs are scarce, we can employ each other, using whatever skills we have that others can use.

3

Because Barter Credit lets us trade with one another without using money, we can very easily create our own jobs providing some of the goods and services that others in our community need and want. For people not used to working at jobs, that's good practice for formal employment. For the unemployed with job skills, it's a way to keep earning or get new skills.

0

To Find The Chapters In This Pamphlet

LOOK FOR THE NUMBERED GRAY MARKER COLUMN

PEOPLE 20 - 23	PRODUCT 24 - 29	BUSINESS 30 - 35	GROUPS 36 - 41	HOME 42 - 47

PEOPLE 20 - 23

Using Barter Credit relieves some of the restrictions that not having money puts on our lives. Barter Credit can unlock our capacity to realize useable value from what we have and do. We see that our personal value does not depend on having money or a formal job.

4

Doing things for one another, we also make a personal contribution to the lives of other people. And, when we by-pass money, and get some of what we need without it, we get to keep more of the money we do have, either to save or to use for other things.

PRODUCT 24 - 29

As long as we can make or do things that others in our community need, we can always employ each other - and plug some of those leaks in our barrel. But a local economy really begins when people in a community get together to produce goods and services for Barter Credit exchange.

5

Barter Credit can be used to build cash funds for community development as well as a currency we can use to get around money shortages for production, employment and trade.

BUSINESS 30 - 35

We can never run short of Barter Credit because the trading itself creates it as it is needed. Barter Credit customers can always have Barter Credit to spend, so we can increase the cash-flow, volume and book value of any business. Accepting Barter Credit creates a price advantage at no dollar cost. Small and locally owned stores compete better with national chains.

6

Using Barter Credit also reduces the economic drain from any business community. It can never run away with your value like dollars do.

GROUPS 36 - 41

Community groups can recognize volunteer work in a valuable currency without using up scarce grants money. Groups can earn Barter Credit in community projects and trade it for things they need - or for dollars. Charities can issue dollar-value tax receipts for Barter Credit donations. The Income Tax and Sales Tax rules are exactly the same as for dollars.

7

Barter Credit is recognized by Revenue Canada. Just add it to your dollars when reporting at Tax-time.

HOME 42 - 47

Barter Credit is a positive bond in any community. In its interdependent network, contacts expand and our lives grow. We meet and trade with others like ourselves and contribute to others' well being as well as our own. New life for cash-poor communities is created as we make employment for ourselves and our friends and neighbours, and make ourselves and our community more self-reliant.

8

The only limits are a community's own needs and capacities.

Our Community Barrel And How It Leaks

EACH OF US IS LIKE A LEAKY BARREL

OUR BARRELS

Money runs in at the top of our personal barrels, and at the bottom it leaks out holes for food, rent, clothes, taxes - all the costs of living.

We can never plug all those leaks - some are necessary.

FILLING THE BARREL

If we manage to keep the leakage low, and if we're getting enough in-flow from our job to let the barrel start to fill up, then we can get it to run out holes for the luxuries and other good things of life - or hold onto some savings.

COMMUNITY BARRELS

It's the same with communities. But the in-flow taps - the big employers, industries, businesses and "outside investment" that we keep chasing when we want to "develop" our local economies - are also the biggest out-flow taps too.

COMMUNITY LEAKS

Outside investment doesn't come in unless it can get more for its dollars than it can somewhere else.

That "more" comes out of our local work, environment, resources, or (through tax concessions) our pockets.

And the dollars still fly away when other fields look greener.

WITH BARTER CREDIT WE CAN REDUCE OUR DEPENDENCE ON INPUTS..

INPUT MORE THAN OUTFLOW - WE HAVE SOME EXTRA TO ENJOY

IF WE HAVE NO INPUTS, DOES THAT MEAN WE HAVE NO ECONOMY?

OUTFLOW TOO HIGH OR INPUT DRIED UP - WE'VE GOT TROUBLE

Our communities now depend almost entirely on inputs from the national-international "World" economy, and on outputs that flow to that world economy.

Our well-being depends on the world economy staying healthy and on our being able to compete for some special place within it - having some unique resources or skills we can sell for fewer dollars than any other community.

Experience tells us that the world economy does not stay healthy, but suffers periodic seizures. And it also tells us that most of our communities cannot compete successfully in that centralized economy, but are shrinking away as central "World Class" cities grow. Sometimes, in desperation, we sell too much for the dollars we need.

But the measure of any community's economic strength is not only how much money comes into it, but how long it stays and circulates. That is an indication of how much a community does *for itself*.

A poor community is one where a dollar bounces in and then bounces right out again. A community where the dollar bounces six to eight times is counted wealthy in our economic system - it does more *for itself*.

But the "World Class" dollar will eventually leave *every* community, taking with it what it represents of the only true measure of our wealth - our own productivity.

1

The Value We Create Runs Out On Us

COMMUNITIES HAVE ANOTHER OPTION

EVEN IN GOOD
TIMES OUR
DOLLAR LEAVES
EVENTUALLY

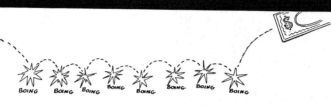

BOING BOING BOING BOING BOING BOING BOING BOING

JOBS TEND TO GO
WHERE THE
MONEY HAS GONE
BEFORE

OUR KIDS FOLLOW
THE MONEY AND
THE JOBS AND
LEAVE TOO

WAY OUT

OUR MONEY COMES TO
US ONLY IN RESPONSE
TO THE GOODS AND
SERVICES WE CAN
OFFER...

AND THEN ONLY FOR
THE ADDED VALUE IT
CAN PICK UP AND
TAKE AWAY TO WHERE
IT CAN GET MORE...

COUNT UP THE
NATIONAL
OPERATIONS IN YOUR
TOWN...

WOULD ANY BE
THERE IF THEY
DIDN'T TAKE OUT
MORE THAN THEY
PUT IN?

173

All Our Barrels Are Inside The Community Barrel

AND WHAT GOES AROUND COMES AROUND

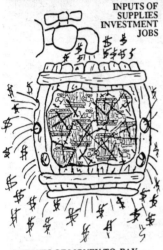

INPUTS OF
SUPPLIES
INVESTMENT
JOBS

OUTPUTS OF MONEY TO PAY
FOR SUPPLIES, INVESTMENT,
JOBS

If the small barrels inside the big barrel are connected more to each other -

Then each one's leaking soon becomes the next one's input.

Even if that seems like a long, difficult uphill job, less will be lost.

After all, even water will run uphill if you start the flow going with a pump.

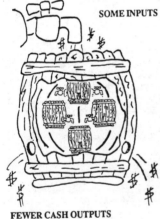

SOME INPUTS

FEWER CASH OUTPUTS

So maybe someday we won't need many inputs from outside, or a pump.

If we don't need to spend our resources on so many inputs from outside...

That translates into independence, empowerment, greater wealth... and freedom.

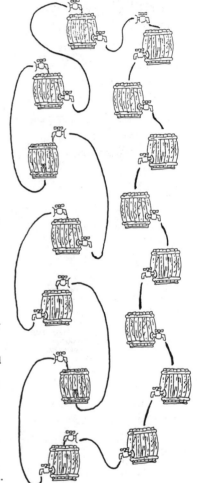

It's Time We Got Back To Home And Community

SO WHAT IS "THE ECONOMY" ANYWAY?

The word "economy" comes from two old Greek words: *OIKOS* (house) and *NOMOS* (steward). Their households produced everything they needed for life. The *OIKONOMOS* - the housekeeper - was responsible for keeping the barrel healthy, plugged and productive. And the work did not have to become money before it could become sustenance.

Making people dependent on central economies once was called empire building and done with armies. Now it is done with money and is called economic development. But it still forces everybody out of their own barrel into one big barrel. And requires us to translate our work into money before we can get our necessities.

Much of history is how production became public, not private, how the home economy became the market economy, and how money became the arbiter of what we can get to live on, and why.

But the old household economy still exists in every family that pools its resources to get by, and in the help we give our friends. Our *OIKONOMOS* is still available to us at the market-money economy's back door.

DAVID SUZUKI

The global market-place generates a terrible dependence that further impoverishes the already destitute and leads rich countries like Canada to sell off energy and forests that should be retained for future generations... all for the immediate benefit of dollars.

ERIC KIERENS

People are looking for institutions where they can put their money and the money will stay within the community to be cycled and re-cycled back again from investments to consumer goods and back again.

Right now we put our money into institutions and it could be down in Argentina tomorrow buying guns because the bottom line says you can get 18 % or 22% down there and only 12% in Canada.

So much of our money haemorrhages right out of our country, out of our communities.

ABRAHAM ROTHSTEIN

People have skills, talents and ability. They want to work. But when the mainstream economy is closed off and there is recession and unemployment, then people are helpless.

We Need Another Basket
For Our Barrel

THE MONEY BASKET TENDS TO RUN OUT OF EGGS

MONEY BELIEF

Money depends on believing a piece of paper issued by an authority is "worth" something. Using money, you don't have to "believe" in the people you deal with.

BARTER

Barter gets around the need for money. If I have what you want and you have what I want, we can barter - but if not, or if they are different in value, we can't.

CREDIT

Barter opens up if you believe the other will keep a promise to give something in return in the future. "Credo" is Latin for "I believe".

BARTER CREDIT

Combining Barter with Credit breaks the barter barrier. You return value, not to your barter partner, but to someone, sometime, in your barter community.

COMMUNITY CREDIT

Others don't lose if you don't balance your give and take - they have your Barter Credit to trade with. But your community loses. And, since all trading records are public, soon no one will deal with you. You lose!

WITH BARTER CREDIT WE CAN REDUCE OUR DEPENDENCE ON MONEY..

DOLLARS HAVE NO VALUE OF THEIR OWN - THEY ONLY MEASURE VALUE

IF WE HAVE NO MONEY, DOES THAT MEAN WE HAVE NO TRADE?

WOULD WE STOP BUILDING BECAUSE WE RAN OUT OF FEET AND INCHES?

In the money system, when you run out of dollars, trading stops, even if goods are available and people need work. If we can't buy things, they don't get produced. But you do not need to have Barter Credit before you trade with it - you can trade from a zero or minus account. In fact, for every plus there *must* be a minus. It's the *trading* that counts - it creates Barter Credit.

With Barter Credit, the only thing that will stop trade is the absence of goods, services, need or real capacity. Real poverty is still possible, but not the artificial poverty that results from failures and manipulations of the money system. It is inflation and depression-proof.

Barter Credit is an upside-down kind of money. You and your trading partners create and back it yourselves, but only when you trade. It has no other use, and itself has no value - it commands no "interest."

Unlike money, Barter Credit cannot ever itself be a commodity. Since there is no such thing as Barter Credit "interest" it has no life of its own, and can't replace real goods and services as an artificial measure of "wealth".

What backs your Barter Credit is your commitment and capacity to both give and receive, and to keep those in balance over time: to keep your plus or minus account balance moving back toward zero. A zero balance, not a plus balance, is "best" in Barter Credit.

176

2

Barter Credit
Opens Another Basket

MAINTAINING A DYNAMIC TRADE BALANCE

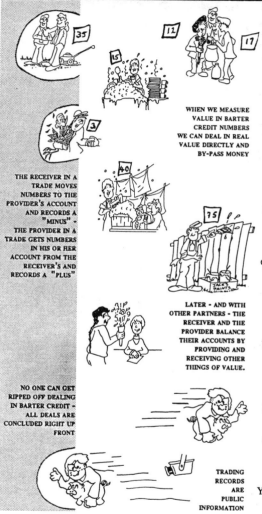

WHEN WE MEASURE
VALUE IN BARTER
CREDIT NUMBERS
WE CAN DEAL IN REAL
VALUE DIRECTLY AND
BY-PASS MONEY

THE RECEIVER IN A
TRADE MOVES
NUMBERS TO THE
PROVIDER'S ACCOUNT
AND RECORDS A
"MINUS" -
THE PROVIDER IN A
TRADE GETS NUMBERS
IN HIS OR HER
ACCOUNT FROM THE
RECEIVER'S AND
RECORDS A "PLUS"

LATER - AND WITH
OTHER PARTNERS - THE
RECEIVER AND THE
PROVIDER BALANCE
THEIR ACCOUNTS BY
PROVIDING AND
RECEIVING OTHER
THINGS OF VALUE.

NO ONE CAN GET
RIPPED OFF DEALING
IN BARTER CREDIT -
ALL DEALS ARE
CONCLUDED RIGHT UP
FRONT

TRADING
RECORDS
ARE
PUBLIC
INFORMATION

Call Community Circle to open an account. Give your name, address, postal code, and phone number. Pick a code name, too - it's like a signature for "telephone cheque-writing."
Say what you would like to do for Barter Credit. That goes beside your name in a membership catalogue.
Place a notice in the bulletin for things you want to offer or receive. Give your name, account number and code-name, and the number of times you want the notice to run. Notices are acknowledged in Barter Credit.
There is a membership cost, which you may pay in cash or acknowledge in Barter Credit. If you use Barter Credit your account opens with that amount of debit. If you pay cash, it is credited with the equivalent Barter Credit.
There is also a "chequing" cost, a Barter Credit acknowledgement for each transaction you have, and one for delivering your bulletins and account statements.
When you want a transaction with someone, you contact them and you agree on terms, and how much of the price will be acknowledged in Barter Credit.
When you have received your goods or services, you call Community Circle and record your name and account number, the name and account number of the person who gave you what you received, the amount of Barter Credit involved, and what you received. You are authorizing the transfer of Barter Credit from your account to the other person's account.
All your transactions and notices show up on your account statement, with your account balance and the total amount of all your transactions. You can check all your activity on one record.

Accounts All Start at Zero
Then Move To Plus or Minus

EVERY ENTRY IS MADE IN TWO ACCOUNTS

This is not what Barter Credit accounts look like...

The real accounts are only blips on computer disks, but these graphs help us visualize them.

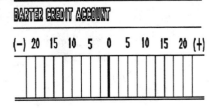

They all start at zero, and each entry moves the account balance either plus or minus.
A minus is not an overdraft, but a normal entry in a Barter Credit account. For every plus there has to be a minus.

Note also that as the numbers in the Barter Credit accounts move around, they always total exactly zero. There's really nothing there!

Unlike a bank, a LETSystem can never go bankrupt!

Little Miss Muffett opened an account....

She paid her $15.00 membership in Barter Credit . She didn't have the cash just then. She can redeem her pledge later, if she wants to, by trading cash for that Barter Credit.

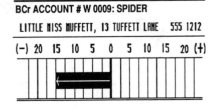

Miss Muffett's account opened at zero, but immediately moved to minus $15BCr, which was her acknowledgement for her membership.

But that entry is only half the story...

The other half of that entry was in the Community Circle administration account, which moved to plus $15BCr.

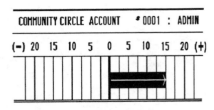

Miss Muffett has "paid" her membership in full - in Barter Credit. We don't call it "payment", though, we call it "acknowledgement". Remember, there's really "nothing" there!

If Miss Muffett had paid cash, her Barter Credit account would immediately return to zero, and so would the administration account.

Incidentally, the membership fee is not necessarily $15BCr. Fees are set by the membership and may vary from time to time.

You Never Put Any Money In
You Never Take Any Out

Then Miss Muffett traded.... even from minus $15BCr....

Gardener Peter Piper gave her five dollars worth of peppers, and she acknowledged him by having five dollars worth of Barter Credit transferred from her account to Peter's.

Miss Muffett's account is now $21BCr negative - her original fifteen acknowledging Community Circle for her membership, five acknowledging Peter Piper, and one more to Community Circle, acknowledging the exchange facilitation service.

The $1BCr. service acknowledgement is like a bank's cheque charge. It is transferred automatically from her account to the Community Circle administration account.

Peter Piper, who was at zero, is now $5BCr positive.

Notice that, with Miss Muffett's acknowledgement of what he provided for her, this trade relationship between Peter and her is closed.

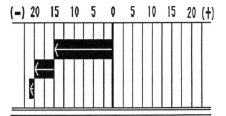

BARTER CREDIT ACCOUNT # W 0009: SPIDER

LITTLE MISS MUFFETT, 13 TUFFETT LANE   555 1212

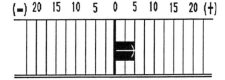

BARTER CREDIT ACCOUNT # W 0007: RED HOT

PETER PIPER, 12 GARDEN GROVE   555 1313

And the Community Circle account...

With the service acknowledgement from Miss Muffet's trade with Peter Piper, the Community Circle administration account is now at $16BCr, positive.

Barter Credit service acknowledgements and memberships provide Community Circle with Barter Credit to acknowledge goods and services that members provide.

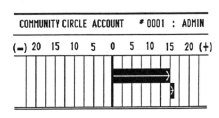

COMMUNITY CIRCLE ACCOUNT   # 0001 : ADMIN

Incidentally, the service acknowledgement is not really $1.00BCr. That just makes the charts simpler. Service acknowledgements are also set by the membership and may vary from time to time.

Trading is the Key - The Accounts Just Follow

THE ACCOUNTS MOVE AS TRADE ROLLS ON

Then Miss Muffett traded again...

Tom Piperson wanted some of Miss Muffett's curds and whey, and he also liked her stuffed spider.

He called her up in Tuffett Lane and they agreed that the combination of Curds and Whey and the stuffed spider together was worth $25.00 in Barter Credit.

It is possible that Tom may have paid more. Miss Muffett may have needed some cash dollars to pay for thread, veterinary medicines for her cows, and maybe some dollars for sales and income taxes - which the government still insists on getting in ITS currency. Or she might simply have needed some cash.

But the Barter Credit Network does not concern itself with the cash portion of its members' transactions - just the Barter Credit.

So Tom acknowledged Miss Mufffet with a transfer of $25BCr, and Community Circle with the $1BCr service acknowledgement.

Miss Muffet's account is now at plus $5BCr and Tom's is at minus $26BCr.

That is - $25BCr to Miss Muffett, and $1BCr to Community Circle, where the administration account is now at plus $17BCr.

And the Gooseville Barter Credit Network is off and trading, its members providing what their neighbours need, confident that their needs will be met in their turn, and on the road to some independence from economic ups and downs.

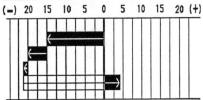

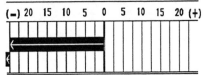

And their trading relationship on this deal is closed.

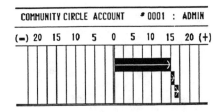

Oh, happy Gooseville Barter Credit Network!

It's As Important To Receive As It Is To Give

Money confers power, but it does not create wealth, only moves it from person to person, place to place. Neither does it make an economy. People working with resources create wealth and economies.

Third world nations were not poor until they hooked into our money economy and started to judge their needs - and their economies - by our wants.

Famine is real: crops fail, and what we produce is not fairly distributed. But most of the failures of our economy are failures of the money system.

The money system requires payment. Unless we can pay for what is wanted in money, nothing can be "demanded" - even if it is needed and available.

But our money system is only a few hundred years old. Before that, whoever could work produced and whoever could not was fed. We produced and consumed for ourselves and according to our "need", not according to a money "demand".

We can be like that again if we can bypass money and concentrate on supplying and exchanging what is needed. It is people producing and exchanging - not money - that creates a healthy economy.

ROSS DOBSON

Barter Credit accounts are like bank accounts in some ways and Barter Credit is a nominal currency, but it is important to try to leave our money thinking behind and concentrate on production and trade of real goods.

KENT GERECKE

Barter Credit accounts are merely the records of transactions - the transfer of value between members of the Barter Credit Network, measured in a different way. It is the transactions that are important, not the measure.

GEOFF SLATER

Barter Credit can be treated like a money, but only so far. It is different because you never have to get yours from somebody else. That's one reason there is no debt. Nobody ever needs the Barter Credit you have - their trading creates their own.

MICHAEL LINTON

What backs Barter Credit over-all is the joint commitment of everyone in the Barter Credit Network to give value for value received, at some future time to someone in the system. That is a community obligation, but it is not a debt.

Barter Credit Works For Employment

EVERYDAY WORK

When we use Barter Credit, the everyday things that we do - done for other people - become a source of value we can trade for other things we need or want. In the Barter Credit Network, our skills, time and work are freed from first having to become money before we can trade them for the things we need.

SELF EMPLOYMENT

We can spend as much or as little time as we have available doing the things we can do. When we do them in exchange for Barter Credit acknowledgement, we are creating employment for ourselves.

OUR OWN JOBS

Some of us might choose to make things to trade for Barter Credit. Others might provide services. Either way we make jobs for ourselves on the basis of whatever skills and time we possess.

JOBS FOR OTHERS

Whenever we use Barter Credit to get something we need, we are providing work for someone else in our community. A vigorous Barter Credit economy can pull itself a long way up by its own bootstraps, and money - or the lack of it - does not have to get in the way!

WITH BARTER CREDIT WE CAN REDUCE OUR DEPENDENCE ON FORMAL JOBS..

MORE AND MORE - GOOD JOBS ARE GETTING REALLY HARD TO FIND

IF WE HAVE NO JOBS DOES THAT MEAN WE HAVE NO VALUE?

MAYBE IT'S TIME WE MADE OUR OWN FOR OURSELVES AND OUR NEIGHBOURS

Most of us grew up expecting to get a job and be independent. Having a job and getting a paycheque has been what being a responsible, independent adult is all about. But it may be that depending on getting a job so we can have money to live on is not independence at all, but dependence - on the money system we don't control.

Getting a job depends on learning to do the things that employers want, then finding an employer who will pay for what we have learned to do. Keeping it depends on being able to do it to that employer's satisfaction for a dollar price the employer is willing to pay. We feel valuable.

When our employers need different things, find machines to do what we were trained for, or find somebody else to do the job for less money, they cut back, lay off, close down or move away. The jobs we are trained for vanish, and so do the paycheque, the independence and our sense of being valuable. We have to find another employer who wants our skills - maybe even leave home to follow the jobs.

Another way to work is to do what we did before there were employers and formal jobs - do things for each other. The Barter Credit Network is a way to advertise our skills to each other. Some of us have formal job skills, some only the ordinary skills we all need. Together, though, we have a lot of what we really need.

3

GAINFUL EMPLOYMENT FROM ORDINARY SKILLS

SUPPOSE WE ALL MADE TWO LISTS...

ONE OF THINGS THAT WE LIKE TO DO...

AND ONE OF WHAT WE HATE BUT MUST DO...

AND THEN SUPPOSE WE TRADED THE LISTS AROUND...

WE COULD PROBABLY EMPLOY EACH OTHER WHEN WE CAN'T FIND FORMAL JOBS

WE MIGHT SURPRISE OURSELVES WITH WHAT WE ARE ABLE TO PROVIDE FOR OURSELVES

ESPECIALLY IF WE CONCENTRATED ON PRODUCING THINGS FROM THE RESOURCES WE HAVE RIGHT NEAR HOME

WE COULD FIND OURSELVES WELL ON OUR WAY TO PROVIDING MOST OF OUR BASIC NEEDS IN OUR OWN COMMUNITY - AND MOST OF OUR OWN JOBS

183

Figure Out What You Can Do For Others

I LIKE TO:

_____

_____

**I COULD TEACH SOME-
ONE TO:**

_____

_____

**TO HELP SOMEONE I
WOULD:**

_____

_____

FOR MY CLUB I:

_____

_____

SOMETIMES I WILL:

_____

_____

I HATE TO:

_____

_____

**PEOPLE HAVE ADMIRED
MY:**

_____

_____

**WHAT I'D REALLY LIKE
TO DO IS:**

_____

_____

MY HOBBIES ARE:

_____

_____

IF I HAD A BUSINESS I'D:

_____

_____

Figure Out What You Can Do For Yourself

SOME STEPS TOWARD SELF-HELP

I COULD:

_____

_____

MY NEIGHBOURHOOD COULD USE A:

_____

_____

WE COULD GET TO-GETHER AND:

_____

_____

I ALWAYS WANTED TO:

_____

_____

SOMEBODY OUGHT TO:

_____

_____

It starts with communication. We have to start talking directly to one another, and let each other know what we have and what we need, what we can do and what we want done.

It continues with commitment. We deal with one another regularly and use Barter Credit as a way of keeping track of what we do and supply for each other.

Just by keeping those records, we can each be recognized for what we do for other people, then hang on to the value of that as we are credited for it, and use that credited value to get other things for ourselves.

That is just like working and getting paid, but without formal jobs - using whatever skills we already have, and getting around the need to translate them into money first.

Next comes imagination. We look around to see what people in our community need and have trouble getting, and then get together to produce those things for Barter Credit. Doing things for others soon turns into doing something for ourselves - providing our own independence - from jobs that keep vanishing - from the market that keeps demanding more and more of our cash - and from the ups and downs of the world market economy.

That much extra independence means we have more freedom - from dependence on money - from dependence on jobs - from dependence on employers - and freedom to be ourselves!

Starting Out Small
We'll Build Our Own Economy

AND THE VALUE GOES 'ROUND AND 'ROUND

Lets design our local economy. The black boxes represent the accounts in the Barter Credit Network. Trade exchanges are represented by the white and patterned arrowhead lines.

The Barter Credit Network Administration account is at the centre of the chart. The other accounts are those of members - at this stage, individuals who are both consumers and producers.

Chart 1 shows how economic exchanges look to the mind that is thinking in terms of money. Payment flows from consumers to producers of goods and services.

But money is not real wealth, remember, it only *measures* wealth. We want to build a cashless, real-goods economy, based on what is really *needed* and on exchange unhindered by money manipulations.

We want to get out of the money bottleneck and concentrate on the production and flow of the goods and services, freed of money "demand".

What is happening in real-goods terms is shown in chart 2. Goods and services flow freely to consumers. This is the part of the exchange that is most important. It *is* "the economy".

But both parties to any trade are contributing equally to the community economy: one by providing goods or services, one by providing that other with an outlet for them - with a job.

So, as we chart our developing economy - as in chart 3 - we will show the relations of trade, which are always two-way and in balance, but not the directions of flow.

1

ADMINISTRATION

MEMBERS AS CONSUMERS

MEMBERS AS PRODUCERS

2

ADMINISTRATION

MEMBERS AS CONSUMERS

MEMBERS AS PRODUCERS

3

ADMINISTRATION

MEMBERS AS CONSUMERS

MEMBERS AS PRODUCERS

CONSUMER EXCHANGES
SYSTEM SERVICE EXCHANGES

ALL BCr ACCOUNTS

Users Can Create Their Own Jobs

THE INFORMAL ECONOMY

What we call "the economy" is the job-money-market economy. We must have jobs to get money to pay for what we need in the market. Everything is geared to having a job to get money to live with.

We try to solve poverty by giving money to people who don't have jobs, but we don't give them enough money to get out of poverty because we think other people would quit their jobs.

We don't try for full employment because corporations say they'd have to pay too much for labour, and governments say too much earning causes inflation.

The problems and restrictions of the "job-money-market" economy have created the "underground" and "informal" economies, where people deal with one another according to their own rules.

In some developed countries now, up to 30% of the actual economic activity is "informal" or "underground". We can build on this "invisible" economic activity to flesh out our own, local economies.

Formal jobs need formal employers. But now we can put ourselves to work in a new way that is not limited by formal employment. Work has a new face.

CHARLES

I am a carpenter by trade, but I have not had much employment in recent years.

But people who couldn't afford to employ me now are glad to do so. They don't have to spend so much in cash when we use Barter Credit.

I have been able to get things I would not have been able to afford otherwise.

BARBARA

My family has found employment that was readily available even when there were no jobs to be had.

And we got things that we could not have had before without money.

People have been able to meet each others' needs regardless of the state of the economy.

The value of this system is actually its separation from the money system.

MARGARET

I had a garage sale, cared for children, made frozen casseroles to order.

Even though the economy is bad, my family is alive and functioning.

I hate to think where we could have been otherwise.

187

Barter Credit Works For People

WE ALL HAVE NATURAL INTRINSIC WORTH

SELF WORTH

Barter Credit is created by our own effort and trading. As long as we have the capacity to do or provide something that other people need, want or can use, we don't need money to experience the satisfaction of acknowledgement for what we do.

EMPOWERMENT

When what we can do is appreciated, we are empowered. Even those who are not able to hold formal jobs in the money system can gain acknowledgement for valuable non-monetary contributions.

VALUATION

The value of a Barter Credit trade is what the traders decide it should be. We can function with our own value-system and value things that the dollar system does not, or value things differently and according to our own beliefs.

FREEDOM

Using Barter Credit frees up our capacity to realize useable value directly from what we do without first having to push it through the money bottle-neck.

And when we can get some of what we need without money, we can save more of the money we do have for the things only money can buy.

WITH BARTER CREDIT WE CAN REDUCE OUR DEPENDENCE ON DOLLARS...

WITH BARTER CREDIT WE CAN MAKE OUR OWN VALUE REAL

IF WE HAVE NO DOLLARS, DOES THAT MEAN WE HAVE NO WORTH?

AND VALUE THE REALITY OF THE THINGS THAT WE CAN DO

The dollar system says a dollar *is* a dollar's worth of value, and it requires us to first turn what we do into money, through employment, before it can be "worth" something to us by getting us things we need.

That causes problems when money is scarce or otherwise with-held from us - real problems that are not necessary. One is that people who do not have any dollars start to feel "worthless".

The Barter Credit system lets us turn the ordinary things we do directly into self-made spending power that lets us "realize"- make real - our own true worth, directly.

We get an uplift when we see that we can make a direct personal contribution to the lives of other people and to our community - that we are "worthy". And the people who receive things from us are always able to acknowledge us with Barter Credit, which feels a lot better than being on the receiving end of charity.

The money system also tends to interpret all values as market values, putting a dollar price on everything. When market values get mixed up with things like love and family, distortions result.

Barter Credit lets us apply our own values to our trading, evaluate what we do by our own standards, and bring our own moral values into the marketplace.

4

Measuring Differently We Realize Our Worth

COMBINING OUR WORTH BUILDS COMMUNITY

WITH BARTER CREDIT WE ARE NEVER IN DEBT TO THE PERSON WE TRADE WITH.

OUR COMMITMENT IS TO THE COMMUNITY TO RETURN VALUE FOR VALUE RECEIVED AND TO KEEP TRADE MOVING

THE BARTER CREDIT ECONOMY IS ONE WE CREATE BY OUR TRADING - AND ONE WE ARE IN CHARGE OF

BIG PLUS ACCOUNTS AND BIG MINUS ACCOUNTS WILL BOTH STOP TRADING

THE VALUE HAS TO KEEP MOVING - ALWAYS BALANCED BETWEEN PLUS AND MINUS

THAT KEEPS THE VALUE CIRCULATING AT HOME - WORKING IN THE COMMUNITY WHERE WE FIRST CREATED IT.

Using Barter Credit we are free to spend the "natural money" of our time, effort and talents without first changing them into dollar money. We do that simply by providing the goods or services to those who need them and accepting Barter Credit acknowledgement in return. Using Barter Credit, the gifts we give expand in value because their value does not die with one exchange but continues to circulate in the community.

And when we receive things from others in return for our Barter Credit numbers, we are creating employment for them.

When we are unemployed we can create earnings for ourselves from the value of everyday tasks by performing them for Barter Credit.

When we are wage earners, we can still help build our local economy, even when we do not have much time to do things for Barter Credit. We can use Barter Credit to get things we need, and then later buy it back from the system with cash.

For people who do that, Barter Credit is like a no-interest credit card. And it helps with the dollar costs of the system's operations.

Just by letting each other know what we need and what we can do, and providing as much as we can for each other, we can actualize our natural buying power and increase our economic security and feelings of self-worth.

189

Communication and Trade Expand Relationships

OUR WORTH GROWS IN A PARALLEL ECONOMY

The foundation of the Community Circle is the membership and their commitment to provide goods and services to one another for Barter Credit acknowledgement.

With only that beginning, Barter Credit exchanges between members can start, and we can start to live in two parallel economies, one free of money restrictions, where we can realize our own self-worth directly.

THAT'S ALSO HOW WE LOCATE OTHER MEMBERS OF THE BARTER CREDIT ECONOMY TO TRADE WITH

We can still use "their" economy for the things we can't produce for ourselves, but we can also start weaving our own community basket.

We can keep Barter Credit records in paper and pencil and post needs and wants on a bulletin board, but a computer does it quicker and simpler, and published want-ads and a membership catalogue circulate more widely.

WHEN WE FIND A TRADE PARTNER WE MAKE OUR DEAL IN DOLLARS - BUT USE BARTER CREDIT FOR ALL OR PART OF THE PRICE

A Barter Credit Network can develop a "gross neighbourhood product" very quickly. Even individuals who start by saying "there's nothing I can do" discover things they can do that their neighbours appreciate.

And, yes, things we do now without thought of payment should be recorded in Barter Credit, because it preserves and circulates the gift to a wider circle of receivers.

WHEN OUR TRADE IS DONE WE CALL IN THE DEAL TO THE NETWORK TRUSTEE WHO MAKES THE ADJUSTMENT IN THE ACCOUNTS

Recording all exchanges shows better where the plugs and leaks are in our community barrel, and a clearer picture develops of the alternate economy our community already has.

The next step is to get together to produce things we need for exchange within the Barter Credit network, and start plugging the leaks.

WE ARE TRADING IN TWO ECONOMIES

ONE IN DOLLARS AND ONE IN BARTER CREDIT

THEY ARE PARALLEL BUT SEPARATE

Users Tell Us
It Makes a Difference

THE DUAL ECONOMY - SUBSISTENCE PLUS

We are starting to see traditional subsistence economies as not necessarily poor in the sense of being deprived. Their people just do not consume what our industrial "money" economy produces.

Traditional economies satisfying basic needs through self-provisioning have been called the original affluent society. We see them as "poor" only compared to our market-driven consumerism.

Poverty ought to be described as true need, and affluence as the availability of the necessities of life.

Papua-New Guinea has two economic circuits. One is urban, fed by mining and timber projects - part of the world "money" economy. The other is the traditional subsistence economy of the rural majority. Papuans live comfortably in both.

It would be a neat trick to use the market economy for the things we can't provide for ourselves, but could do without, and create our own local subsistence economies to give us our basics.

Then we wouldn't have to rely completely on the world market economy, with its cruel ups and downs, or on first turning work into money to buy a living.

JOY

I am a single mother on social assistance with three pre-schoolers. I have been able to get car work and carpentry done without using money. I can fit my time and skills, done in return, around my family's needs.

The children got hand-crafted toys and I got pottery, jewellery and candles for Christmas. We get clothes through the system now, and even some of our food.

PAULETTE

For a month after I joined I did nothing. I was really afraid to commit myself to "spending" without "having" any credit first.

I have two little kids, what could I do? I talked to my neighbours. Gradually I saw that I and my family had all we needed to operate. We had spare time we were wasting and we had spare things going unused.

Once trading began we danced in a class, got family counseling, ate perogies, and traded off a lot of baby equipment. When the kids were in bed I wrote letters for people.

I really can do things that people need!

Barter Credit Works for Production

ARE YOU DEPENDENT ON AN EMPLOYER?

GETTING TOGETHER

When several people combine their skills, time, labour and resources, it becomes possible to produce beyond the capacity of any single individual.

CO-OPS & BUSINESSES

Barter Credit Producer Co-operatives and Businesses can easily be set up on the basis of Community Circle membership, with no additional legal requirements.

AGREEMENTS

Simple agreements are available that let us get started producing for Barter Credit exchange with other members. We go through all the steps - but in miniature.

LOCAL INDUSTRY

Barter Credit Co-ops and Businesses give our local economy a firmer base, and make Barter Credit itself more valuable, with more things available on the basis of time and work rather than money.

HANDS-ON EXPERIENCE

When business starts to grow, Barter Credit business experience helps us know what to do to expand into the general economy, should that become desireable.

WITH BARTER CREDIT WE CAN REDUCE OUR DEPENDENCE ON INDUSTRY...

I CAN DO IT MY OWN SELF

IF WE HAVE NO INDUSTRY DOES THAT MEAN WE HAVE NO PRODUCTION?

BUT IT'S BETTER WITH HELP FROM MY FRIENDS

Whatever we can do or produce for one another for Barter Credit is a source of value we can trade for things we need or want. When we start our own Barter Credit ventures, we can produce even more of what we need.

There are some special features of Barter Credit Business or Co-operative ventures.

Their prime focus is not on making money, but on providing for need.

They are small-scale and expect to be short term. They are prepared from the beginning to dissolve when the need has been met.

The financing of Barter Credit ventures is also unique. Needed cash capital is acknowledged - and dividends realized - with immediate Barter Credit transfers. Investors have immediate returns, and ventures are relieved of debt burdens.

The expertise needed - legal, book-keeping, managerial, entrepreneurial, advertising, marketing and sales advice - even sales outlets - can often be found among the members of the Barter Credit Network.

And there is a ready communication system in place to provide the services to publicize what our ventures produce to a market that has already said it wants it.

It requires a little organization, but Barter Credit Businesses and Producer Co-operatives make good sense.

5

Members Form Small ProductionVentures

DIFFERENT SKILLS AND DIFFERENT RESOURCES MAKE A WHOLE GREATER THAN ITS PARTS

THAT IS ESPECIALLY TRUE OF BARTER CREDIT FINANCING

THE VENTURE GROUP CAN EXCHANGE BARTER CREDIT FOR DOLLARS FROM A NUMBER OF DONORS OR A PRODUCTION DEVELOPMENT FUND TO PROVIDE MATERIALS

MUCH OF WHAT ELSE THEY NEED TO PRODUCE THEY CAN GET WITH BARTER CREDIT

THEY NEED TO RETURN TO THE DONORS OR PRODUCTION DEVELOPMENT FUND ONLY THE DOLLARS THEY ACTUALLY USED

COMMUNITY CIRCLE BARTER CREDIT CO-OPERATIVE PRODUCTION AGREEMENT

The Community Circle members listed in the attached documents agree among themselves and with Community Circle Services, Inc.:

To co-operate in the production of the goods and/or services also listed therein, and

To establish for that purpose, as a creature of Community Circle Services, Inc., a production venture to be known as:

BIRD CITY BUILDERS

They also agree:

That they shall begin, carry out, and cease operations at the times and under the terms and conditions also listed therein;

That they shall organize the venture for the production or provision of the specified goods and services to other members of the Community Circle Barter Credit Network;

That they may exchange Barter Credit from their venture's Barter Credit account for cash dollars from the Community Circle Production Development Fund;

That they shall exchange Barter Credit for such cash dollars only to the amount required for the purchase of resources for production that are not available for Barter Credit;

That, for all other purposes, they shall, in their venture, use Barter Credit transfers and not cash dollar payments;

That they shall use the cash dollars so received in the manner and within the time specified, and according to the budget and schedule also attached, and return an equal amount to the Production Development Fund within the time also specified;

That the dollar portion of the price of their venture's product to Community Circle Members shall be limited to the recovery of cash dollars expended, plus tax liabilities;

That their venture shall otherwise provide its product to Community Circle members for Barter Credit acknowledgement;

That their venture's product may be sold casually to the public, provided it is for cash prices not less than the combined Barter Credit and cash dollar prices required of Community Circle members;

That they may, after one year of operation, incorporate their venture separately from its Community Circle membership;

That, if they do so, they shall do so subject to an additional agreement among themselves and with Community Circle Services, Inc.;

That, in any case, they shall continue to provide the venture's product to Community Circle members for Barter Credit and limited cash, as above.

Signed at **WINNIPEG** on **AUG 3 / 1991**

For Community Circle Services, Inc.

For the listed members

Goods and Services
For Barter Credit Members

A BUSINESS PLAN AND FEASIBILITY STUDY

The Barter Credit Membership which is our market is known to us, but we still need to survey that market and plan carefully.

The Barter Credit approach has a market survey requirement built in - it responds to an expressed need. But it is necessary for us to confirm or better understand that need.

A Barter Credit production co-operative organizes a package of human, capital, and other resources - our own and other people's skills, materials and advice - because its members believe they can re-combine those resources into something more useful than they were as "unorganized" resources.

And also because people in the network have already told them that they want what they can make of that new combination.

After we have checked around and decided that we can produce something that our fellow members have told us they want and need, and after we have found out that there are the right people who can and will work together to produce what we plan to produce, we still have to find out if we can produce it and then get it to the people who want it.

"If" we can produce it involves figuring out what we need so we can actually do the work - space, time, tools, material, and other resources - like keeping records of inventories, payrolls, etc. - and making sure we can finance what we want to do.

Barter Credit financing - really just the organization of people and resources, since the Barter Credit itself is no problem - is freely available, but it takes us only half way.

FIRST WE HAVE TO GET INFORMATION ABOUT OUR MARKET

TALKING WITH OUR FELLOW MEMBERS CAN GET US THE INFORMATION WE NEED

THERE WILL BE MEMBERS WITH BUSINESS EXPERIENCE WHO CAN OFFER HELP FOR BARTER CREDIT ACKNOWLEDGEMENTS...

... AND WE CAN ASK OUR FELLOW MEMBERS DIRECTLY IF THEY WANT WHAT WE'RE THINKING OF PRODUCING

WE HAVE TO FIGURE OUT WHAT RESOURCES WE NEED TO PUT TOGETHER

WE NEED PEOPLE WITH SKILLS, TIME AND A CAPACITY TO WORK AND MATERIALS, TOOLS AND A PLACE TO WORK..

AND WE NEED TO KNOW HOW MUCH WE NEED IN CASH DOLLARS AND HOW MUCH IN BARTER CREDIT - AND FOR WHAT, AND WHEN

194

Ventures Grow Into
New Businesses And Co-ops

A FINANCIAL, PRODUCTION AND MARKETING PLAN

NOW WE'VE GOT TO
WORK OUT
PRODUCTION PLANS

AND THEN BUSINESS
STRATEGY AND A
MARKETING PLAN

AGAIN
WE CAN
FIND HELP
THROUGH THE BARTER
CREDIT NETWORK

AND WE NEED A PLACE TO PRODUCE STORE AND
ADVERTISE OUR PRODUCT AND A WAY TO DELIVER IT TO
OUR CUSTOMERS

WE NEED TO
KNOW HOW
AND WHEN WE
CAN RETURN
THE DOLLARS
WE USED FOR
MATERIALS
AND
PRODUCTION

AND HOW
TO REDEEM
OUR
COMMITMENTS
OF BARTER
CREDIT
WITH SOME
PROFIT
LEFT

Yes, after dumping on dollars for 26 pages, we now admit we are going to need some to get production going, because we can't get everything we need with Barter Credit - yet.

So, our financial plan starts with figuring out how much dollar cash we are going to need.

Some of that we can borrow from the Community Circle Production Development Fund.

We could also go directly to other members, or maybe to some of our aquaintances who might become members to join us.

Our financial plan continues with how we're going to spend that dollar capital - and the other Barter Credit capital that people are providing in time, skills, work-space and labour according to our business plan.

Our production plan is how to actually produce our product, and our marketing plan is how to make it available to our target market and get it into the hands of the people who told us they wanted us to produce it.

Whatever we do is really a co-operative venture of the whole community - co-operation among those who provide the cash and other resources for our product, those who produce it, and those who "need", receive and consume it.

All of these people are going to want their resources back in some form sooner or later - either in Barter Credit or in product.

So we owe it to the community and to ourselves to plan carefully so the "sales" of our product can redeem not only our cash borrowings, but the commitment that our use of Barter Credit in its production entails.

195

Users Start By Producing For Each Other

NEW PRODUCTION AND NEW EMPLOYMENT

Now we have begun producing goods or services for other members of our Community Circle, we have added an important new building block to our local, self-reliant economy - focused, co-operative producers.

We are producing things that people need and want and - since most of our price is Barter Credit - we are making it available to them more readily than the marketplace does with its demand for cash payment. We are breaking the dollar bottleneck.

Chart 4 indicates this valuable new two-way production relationship between members as more formal producers - supplementing what individual members provide for one another - and members as consumers.

We are doing something else valuable too. We, and the people who use what we are producing for them, are providing employment. We are creating additional value which goes into the community economic exchange as wages and profits - chart 5.

Together, we and those in the Community Circle asking us to produce, and using what we produce, are building up the real wealth and combined worth of our community.

The special character of Barter Credit ventures - responding to expressed needs and wants of the community - has a built-in edge of success as well as the built-in benefit to the community of fleshing-out its capacity to take care of its own needs.

And when production rather than profit is the principal aim and purpose of our ventures and decisions about what is produced are community based, productive capacity can respond quickly to changes in its needs.

4

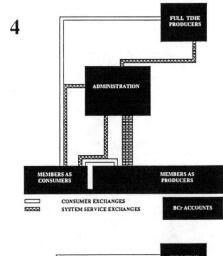

5

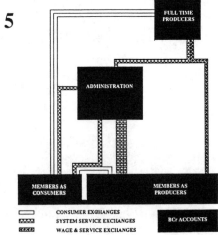

Ultimately They Produce
For The Community

A "personal-private" economy like the old Greek "family" economy still exists in the "production" of home work that we all still do at home, which grows as our families grow and the "production" of home work is co-operatively shared.

It's there also in the help we give friends and neighbours - trading day care, lending tools, raising fences, volunteering for the community club, and in the "zucchini economy" in which we share our backyard abundance.

Using Barter Credit, we can improve our "informal" production and exchange systems and start expanding the range of things we produce "at home" and the people we produce them for.

With Barter Credit, we can safely use the model of the original "household economy" among not only our family, friends and neighbours, but among like-minded strangers as well.

And, getting together to produce things that we need, we can bring much of "our economy" back into our own, friendly, hands and make a healthy new balance with the "job-money-market" economy that is leaving so many of us out.

REV. LINDSAY KING

The problem with the economy now is not supply or need. There is supply and there is need, and there's lots of work to be done that is not being done. What's missing is the grease, the money. And money is just a way of keeping score.

MAGGIE MILLS (UK)

There are plenty of people with skills, energy, time and talent to offer - and no work.

FRANK MCCORMICK (NZ)

More and more things are produced locally. This makes it more feasible.

C.E.D. BULLETIN

Community Economic Development is a process with a purpose... to meet community needs.

The C.E.D. goal is the transformation of the structure and organization of production and the overall quality of community life and well being.

It should be flexible and adaptable enough to suit any economic condition - growth, no-growth or conditions of decline.

197

Barter Credit Works for Business

TIRED OF THE BOOM-BUST ROLLER COASTER?

THE LAST LINK

Any professional doing business with the public is the last link in a long economic chain that he or she can't rattle very much any more. The largest part of the final price for any product or service is already built in somewhere else.

THE FIRST TO GO

Retailers, especially, get squeezed when customers revolt against the prices that have to be charged - or simply can't afford to pay them any more. The last links in the chain are the first to feel the pinch of recession.

TAKING CHARGE

Barter Credit can help a business take charge of its business again, in a small way by improving cash flow, competitive position and secure custom, and in a larger way - once local production for Barter Credit is established - by creating an independent local market which community forces are in charge of.

BUSINESS SELF-HELP

Business and professionals can help themselves by expanding the places where Barter Credit is accepted. Services become available to them for kind, not cash, and scarce dollars stretch farther.

WITH BARTER CREDIT WE CAN REDUCE OUR DEPENDENCE ON WORLD TRADE...

STORES CAN TAKE PART OF THEIR PRICES IN BARTER CREDIT

IF WE HAVE NO WORLD TRADE DOES THAT MEAN WE HAVE NO BUSINESS?

BUSINESS CONTINUES EVEN WHEN JOBS ARE SCARCE AND PEOPLE ARE OUT OF WORK

For a business, Barter Credit acts like a coupon redeemable for any other goods or services available from any person or business in the system. Any business can safely accept it because it can be exchanged for things the business needs. The Barter Credit "coupon" is not a "cost".

Accepting Barter Credit as part payment, a local business can gain a dollar-price advantage over larger outside operations. And part of its custom is safe from economic downturns - Barter Credit traders do not rely totally on formal jobs or the fickle money economy for spending power.

Barter Credit users realize a stable currency from the value of putting our everyday skills and our formal training to work for our fellow-members as they are needed. The currency to acknowledge that work is always available because it is generated by the work itself.

Barter Credit customers will always be able to shop with a Barter Credit business because they will always have Barter Credit to exchange. Nobody can ever "run out" of Barter Credit.

6

The Benefits And The Costs

WHAT DOES A BUSINESS GET WITH BARTER CREDIT?

Increased cash-flow with increased business book value.
Secure repeat customers who have more spending power.
Listings in a community catalogue at no additional cost.
Cashless access to goods and services from other merchants and professionals.
Improved marketing control with computer verified records.
Dollar credit accounts secured against write-offs and credit defaults.
Automatic credit customer accounting.

WHAT WILL BARTER CREDIT COST A BUSINESS?

Barter Credit can cost a business virtually nothing.
Internal charges are in self-generated Barter Credit.
Barter Credit business expenses are tax deductible.
Charitable donations of Barter Credit are tax-deductible for dollar tax credits.

HOW DOES A BUSINESS PREPARE FOR BARTER CREDIT?

Decide what percentage of prices the business can accept in Barter Credit.
All dollar costs and taxes must be received in dollars.
Part of the rest of prices can be accepted in Barter Credit.
Barter Credit can be a constant averaged percentage of prices.
More or less Barter Credit can be accepted for each item.
Barter Credit can be accepted at certain times or on certain days.
The percentage of Barter Credit accepted should be substantial.
The more valuable a business makes Barter Credit the more customers it attracts.

HOW IS BARTER CREDIT HANDLED AT THE CASH REGISTER?

The customer presents a Barter Credit Identification.
Payment is accepted in Barter Credit for the percentage of prices advertised.
The class of goods and the Barter Credit price are entered on the Record-Check.
The customer signs the Record-Check like a credit card receipt.
A copy of the Record Check is sent regularly to Community Circle.
The business's account is credited with the customer's transfer of Barter Credit.
The business receives an account statement listing each customer's purchases.
The account statement is reconciled with the business's Record-Check copy.

HOW CAN BARTER CREDIT CONTROL CREDIT ACCOUNTS?

Current credit customers are transferred to Barter Credit use.
Full payment for all purchases from those customers is accepted in Barter Credit.
The customer pays cash periodically for the amount of their BCr purchases.
That amount of BCr is then transferred back to the customer's account.
The business will always have full value in BCr if not in dollars - no write-offs!
The business doesn't have to keep the accounts - Community Circle does it.

199

Secure Customers
Create Convivial Trade

DOUBLE SECURITY WITH ID AND BARTER-CHECK

COMMUNITY CIRCLE
ACCT# 0009
THE BARTER CREDIT NETWORK

CUSTOMERS PRESENT A BARTER CREDIT IDENTIFICATION

THE BUSINESS KEEPS A SIGNED SALES RECORD

FOR SECURITY...

MAIL

THE BUSINESS SENDS A
COPY OF THE RECORD
CHECK TO COMMUNITY
CIRCLE

BARTER CREDIT RECORD-CHECK FOR
ACCT # 301 PERIOD ENDING 04/91

BUSINESS NAME TOM'S GROCERY

ADDRESS 12 LARDER LN. PHONE 555-1212

DATE	CUSTOMER NAME	ID#	GOODS OR SERVICES SUPPLIED	$ PRICE	BCr	SIGNATURE
4/12	DOBSON	11	CANNED GOODS	12.95	5	*(signed)*
4/13	GREEN	31	MEATS, PRODUCE	26.	4	*(signed)*
4/15	GOODWYN	45	HARDWARE	37	10	*(signed)*

The Barter Credit Record-check is your business's record of Barter Credit sales.
It also verifies for you and Community Circle that the correct Barter Credit transfers are properly made by your customers.
At the cash register it is handled like a credit card receipt, except that it is a common receipt for all your Barter Credit customers.
At the end of the period you send a copy to Community Circle for processing.

BARTER CREDIT MAKES SALES SAFER - ALL SALES
ARE PAID IN FULL UP FRONT AT TIME OF SALE

Revenue Canada Rules Barter Credit Acceptable

TREAT BARTER CREDIT JUST LIKE DOLLARS

INTERPRETATION **BULLETIN** D'INTERPRÉTATION

SUBJECT INCOME TAX ACT
Barter Transactions

OBJET LOI DE L'IMPÔT SUR LE REVENU
Troc

NO IT-490   DATE July 5, 1982
REFERENCE Section 3 (also sections 9 and 69)

Nº IT-490   DATE le 5 juillet 1982
RENVOI Article 3 (également les articles 9 et 69)

Canadä

1. The purpose of this bulletin is to outline the Department's views on the income tax implications arising from bartering.

2. In its simplest form, bartering consists of trading by exchanging one commodity for another. Recently, however, the practice of bartering for goods and services has evolved into a sophisticated computer-controlled system of commerce proliferated by franchised, member-only barter clubs, where credit units possessing a notional monetary unit value have become a medium of exchange.

3. A barter transaction is effected when any two persons agree to a reciprocal exchange of goods or services and carry out that exchange usually without using money. In a barter transaction between persons who are dealing with each other at arm's length, it is a fundamental principle that each of those persons considers that the value of whatever is received is at least equal to the value of whatever is given up in exchange therefor.

Income Tax Implications

4. The Department takes the view that barter transactions are within the purview of the Income Tax Act. Such transactions can therefore result in income or expense as contemplated by sections 3 and 9 thereof or can result in the acquisition or disposition of capital property, eligible capital property, personal-use property or inventory, depending upon the circumstances of the persons who are bartering and the nature of that which is bartered, on the same basis as if cash was the consideration.

5. In the case of services bartered by a taxpayer for either goods or services, the value of those services must be brought into the taxpayer's income where they are of the kind generally provided by him in the course of earning income from, or are related to, a business or a profession carried on by him. Examples are a dentist or the owner of a plumbing business who agrees to fix someone's teeth or drains (respectively) in return for services or property provided by the other party. Where the taxpayer is an employee, e.g. a mechanic, occasional help given to a friend or neighbour in exchange for something would not be taxable unless the taxpayer made a regular habit of providing such services for cash or barter.

6. In the case of goods bartered by a taxpayer for either goods or services, the value of those goods must similarly be brought into the taxpayer's income if they are business-related. For example, the value of groceries given by a grocer to someone in exchange for something else must be brought into the grocer's income. In addition, other goods bartered may give rise to a capital gain. Such would be the case if capital property in the form of a valuable painting, a sailboat or land is bartered for goods or services.

7. In arm's length transactions, where an amount must be brought into income or treated as proceeds of disposition of capital property, that amount is the price which the taxpayer would normally have charged a stranger for his services or would normally have sold his goods or property to a stranger. The cost of the services, goods or property received by him is the same amount as the total value of the goods, property or services given up, plus any cash given as part of the barter, and minus any cash received as part of the barter. The same rules would apply in non-arm's length transactions, subject to the provisions of section 69 which would override them where appropriate, e.g. by restricting the cost of goods received to their fair market value.

8. Where the goods or services given up cannot readily be valued but the goods or services received can, the Department will normally accept the value of the latter as being the price at which the transaction took place if the parties were dealing at arm's length.

Revenue Canada
Taxation

Revenu Canada
Impôt

EXPENSES PAID IN BARTER CREDIT ARE TAX-DEDUCTIBLE IN DOLLAR AMOUNTS

Put Your Block Back
In The Local Economy

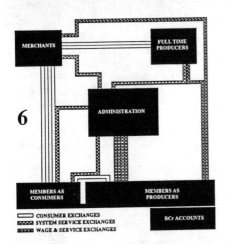

6

BARTER CREDIT CAN RESTORE THE LOCAL MERCHANT

When you join your business to the Barter Credit Network, you are replacing what used to be one of the pillars of every community economy - the local merchant.

Almost extinct in this age of national chain stores owned by international business conglomerates, the local merchant is an irreplaceable building block in any local economy.

Using Barter Credit can restore the position of the local merchant, along with the local producer and the locally-buying consumer.

OUR LOCAL BARTER CREDIT ECONOMY IS NEARLY COMPLETE

Whether you think of our local economy as Barter Credit flowing in purchasing power, wages and profits, or think of it as goods and services flowing in the other direction, the circle always comes back on itself because value stays within the Barter Credit community. But more than a trade balance of inputs and outflows is achieved.

When consumers consume from far-distant sources, they are exporting both the value they have produced, re-presented as dollars, and the value that went into their primary family and community support which contributed to their being able to make those purchases - what they received from the invisible work of the home, and from the community services and natural amenities that are not counted in our dollar economy.

When producers produce for far-distant markets, they are exporting the value which the local community has put into their primary family support, and the value of their community amenities, right along with whatever they produce. That primary support is not counted into the dollar trade balance, either.

When local producers serve a market of local consumers through local merchants, local value stays at home. That portion of your business value which you invest in your local Barter Credit Network will re-circulate back to you over and over again, and not be lost. Neither will your family and community value.

The Community Circle connects the community's primary producers, by means of the community's merchants, with the community's consumers, and all of them to the other community necessities - its family life, its community life, and its culture. To stay healthy, any community needs such a re-circulating flow of production and exchange and caring and culture, together, in a seamless whole.

Barter Credit Users
Preserve Their Buying Power

COMMUNITY AND THE BUSINESS ECONOMY

Competition is healthy when competitors are about equal. Small businesses can't go head-to-head with big ones. Locally owned businesses can't compete with national and international chains.

Local economies are the same. There may be such a thing as healthy competition among the communities in any region, but satellite communities tend to lose in competition with the central community. Which is why it is central. And there will always be some among the satellites who lose out also to other satellites, and wither.

Developing a community economically within the money system goes against what drives that system. No national or international chain outlet in any community will be there for long if it does not take out more value than it puts in.

Any national or international merchandising chain store or franchise operation is not an outlet, it is an intake.

The local economy needs prosperous, locally-owned, locally-oriented businesses. And local businesses need a strong local economy driven by value exchanges that cannot run away. You can build that local economy with Barter Credit.

JIM (GROCER)

I can get advertising for Barter Credit, painting and carpentry, cleaning and landscaping. And I give my staff bonuses with it!

GALE (APPAREL)

I have very little overhead, creating personalized knitwear for women and children, so I can take a large part of my prices in Barter Credit.

But I can use my Barter Credit to get other things I need, so the dollars are there when I need to buy my wool.

WILLIE (DRY GOODS)

When we were setting up, we got our books done for Barter Credit, which really helped because we had almost no cashflow!

PETER (DENTIST)

When I get cancellations, or on slow days, I accept up to 75% of my fees in Barter Credit.

I do five hundred or a thousand dollars a month now on Barter Credit.

That's business I would not otherwise have - and I'd probably have closed last winter without it.

Barter Credit Works
for Non-profit Organizations

PROGRAM MONEY RUNNING OUT?

COMMUNITY GIFTS

Non-profit organizations are like community gifts. They rely on the good will and volunteer effort of people who care. The giving and receiving in non-profit community organizations are rarely in balance. Most of the rewards are in the effect of our work.

PROFESSIONAL GIVERS

There are those of us who find full, paying careers doing community gifting through our non-profit organizations. It does not diminish the value of the gift because we get paid in dollars for the work we do. It just makes it possible for us to give more and give regularly.

NOT FOR MONEY'S SAKE

But the dollar economy doesn't handle gifting very well. Money and gifts are like oil and water . They can mix - but not naturally. Barter Credit and Gifting are more compatible.

SHARING THE GIFT

Combining Barter Credit for the Gifting with the money that all non-profits need to operate, more of us who give of ourselves in community work can be recognized and acknowledged more adequately.

WITH BARTER CREDIT WE CAN REDUCE OUR DEPENDENCE ON GRANTS..

COMMUNITY GIFTS SHOULD HAVE COMMUNITY RECOGNITION

IF WE HAVE NO GRANTS DOES THAT MEAN WE HAVE NO PROGRAMS?

START THE GIFTING CIRCLE WITH YOUR GROUP

Barter Credit is backed by commitment value not cash value. Volunteer organizations have a high commitment value and are ideal users of Barter Credit.

We can acknowledge volunteers with Barter Credit to start the gifting circle. With such tangible acknowledgement we can attract additional volunteers to do more of the routine maintenance tasks. More staff time and grants money can then be dedicated to program delivery.

Then we can expand beyond the volunteer sector and provide services to clients for Barter Credit. Agencies can use Barter Credit to connect more organically to the community, providing employment, receiving donations and raising cash funds through Barter Credit.

A whole community economy can be based on the volunteerism of community agencies - an economy that responds to a community's own special capacities and needs and depends less on outside circumstances, and one in which we can also define our values in terms we choose.

7

Expand Your Group's People Capacity

GRANTS CRUMBLE WHEN
MONEY GETS SCARCE

BARTER CREDIT CAN
QUICKLY GIVE YOU
TEMPORARY SUPPORT

THE THIRD PILLAR OF SERVICE SUPPORT

Most community service organizations are used to working with two main pillars of support: money from grants and donations and the unpaid work of dedicated volunteers.

Most organizations choose to put scarce dollars to work on programs and delivering service to the community. Volunteers know that and are generous with their time and effort. Staff knows it too and willingly work for wages that are often low.

But funding is never as generous nor as secure as we would wish and experienced volunteers burn out and new volunteers need training. Barter Credit can make changes in the bust and burn-out cycle. It offers a third pillar to support community work.

Organizing our everyday maintenance tasks within a Barter Credit acknowledgement system can attract more volunteers and relieve pressure on dollar budgets.

Adding Barter Credit acknowledgements to what we pay our staff remunerates our staff better. We can stretch our cash, our volunteers and our staff farther using Barter Credit.

205

Barter Credit Donations Become Cash At Tax Time

GIVING WAS NEVER EASIER

DOLLAR TAX RECEIPTS FOR BARTER CREDIT

Barter Credit is not hard for organizations to receive. People can afford to be more generous with Barter Credit than with scarce money. Charities can receive regular donations from members and clients who are also in The Community Circle. They can receive donations from other sources in the Community.

Revenue Canada recognizes Barter Credit as a "nominal currency" and has agreed that charitable organizations can give official receipts in dollar amounts for donations of Barter Credit. Donations of Barter Credit then become tax credits for the donors under present Income Tax Legislation.

Barter Credit is also not hard for organizations to earn. We can hold Barter Credit garage sales or donation drives. We can volunteer community services on behalf of our organizations for Barter Credit acknowledgement. Eventually organizations could charge in Barter Credit for some of the services they offer.

Our organizations can use Barter Credit directly to acquire goods and services offered within the Barter Credit network. Or they can translate it into cash in exchanges with dollar donors.

206

Revenue Canada Revenu Canada
Taxation Impôt

R.V. Dobson
1607 - 77 University Crescent
Winnipeg, Manitoba
R3T 3N8

May 1, 1987

Dear Mr. Dobson:

Re: Letswin Green Dollar Trading Network

Please excuse the delay in replying to your letter we received on February 17, 1987. However, as you are aware we referred your letter to Head Office for an opinion. The following two questions were addressed and opinions provided as follows:

1. the value of goods and services received by members within LETS is considered to be taxable as income, and

2. should members of LETS transfer their Green Dollar credits to a charitable organization these amounts would qualify as charitable donations for purposes of paragraph 110(1)(a).

In response to the first point, it is our view that it would involve a finding of fact in each case as to whether the value of goods and services received would be considered to be taxable income. In this regard the guidelines set out in IT-490 should be reviewed. With respect to the second item, it is our opinion that the Green Dollar value of the accounts, transferred to a registered charity would be deductible in computing a taxpayer's taxable income under paragraph 110(1)(a) assuming, of course, that the transfer meets the basic requirements, set out in paragraph 3 of IT-110R2, namely:

a) some property is transferred by a donor to a registered charity.

b) the transfer is voluntary, and

c) the transfer is made without expectation of return.

There is, however, one aspect of this arrangement that concerns us, and that is the fact that the Green Dollars may only be used to acquire goods and services from members of LETS. As a result, the registered charity could wind up buying goods and services in return from a particular donor. If that were to occur, pursuant to a pre-arranged agreement, the donor would have received consideration in return for his donation, and the Green Dollars transferred to the registered charity would not have been paid gratuitously by the donor.

This would not preclude your members from claiming donations, however, in any subsequent audit by us we would obviously consider this point in deciding whether the claim should be allowed to to the donor.

Yours truly,

K.E. Mannion
Chief of Audit
Winnipeg District Office

KEM/hgv

Tel. (204)   Tél. (204)
391 York Avenue   391, av. York
Winnipeg, Man.   Winnipeg (Man.)
R3C 0P5   R3C 0P5

Canada

Arts and Culture Can Be Themselves

CULTURE DOES NOT HAVE TO DIE FOR LACK OF SUPPORT

OR SELL ITSELF TO CORPORATE SPONSORS IN ORDER TO STAY VIABLE

ARTISTS SHOULD BE DOING THEIR ART AND NOT HAVE TO SPEND TIME OUT CHASING GRANTS

BECAUSE PEOPLE CAN BE MORE GENEROUS WITH BARTER CREDIT ARTISTS ARE MORE READILY ACKNOWLEDGED FOR THEIR WORK IN A BARTER CREDIT COMMUNITY

ARTS, CULTURE AND COMMUNITY LIFE

Art and culture are high value-added activities. Most of their value comes from the artist's input. But the work of artists tends to be undervalued in our dollar economy.

In order to get financial support in the dollar economy, Arts and Cultural Groups usually have to become advertising and public relations vehicles for corporate sponsors or demonstrate to governments that they are significant businesses that provide employment and generate cash-flow.

In either case arts and cultural groups have to spend time marketing themselves to prospective supporters and the buying public instead of doing their art or engaging in their culture-supporting activities.

In a Barter Credit economy, culture and the arts can become again what they once were - the necessary spiritual aspects of community life, valued, not as a business or economic generator, but for their own proper place in community life, unshackled from dollar restrictions.

207

The Non-profit Block
Fills Out The Local Economy

VOLUNTEERS' INVISIBLE WORK RECOGNIZED

7

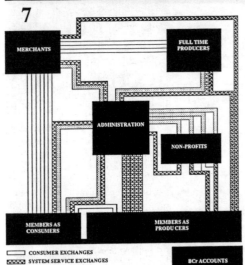

MERCHANTS

FULL TIME
PRODUCERS

ADMINISTRATION

NON-PROFITS

MEMBERS AS
CONSUMERS

MEMBERS AS
PRODUCERS

☐ CONSUMER EXCHANGES
▨ SYSTEM SERVICE EXCHANGES
▨ WAGE & SERVICE EXCHANGES
▨ CHARITABLE TITHING EXCHANGES

BCr ACCOUNTS

LIVEABLE
COMMUNITIES
ARE THE ONES
WHERE
PEOPLE
CO-OPERATE

IT'S OFTEN
THE UNPAID
WORK OF
VOLUNTEERS
THAT MAKES
COMMUNITIES
LIVEABLE

WHAT TO DO WHEN THE CASH FLOW DRIES UP

First, start making Barter Credit payments to supplement your staff incomes. Not in place of dollar wages, but in addition to them.

Second, begin rewarding your volunteers with Barter Credit transfers in an organized way. It says "thank you" and becomes tangible as they realize its value in exchanges for goods and services.

Third, address the need to create Barter Credit inflow to match the outflow you have established. This can be through donations or in acknowledgement for the services you offer. This is the opposite of what you would do with money, where you would cut back services. But Barter Credit is a currency created by your trading exchanges themselves. The more activity you engage in, the more there is. Between your commitment to provide services and your volunteers' commitment to what you do, generating service and value exchanges is no problem.

Barter Credit is based on your commitment to return value to your community - and that is what you are all about, isn't it?

Celebrate Community By Passing On The Gift

THE GIFT ECONOMY

The economy of the gift validates community. Gifts are not earned or paid for. The value they represent is not passed back, as in buying and selling, it is passed on. Given without regard for the ability to pay-back, they affirm our rights as members of a community. Gifts are not hoarded, either. They do return - but only along the circle that goes around the whole community. They affirm relationship and celebrate community.

None of us, even the affluent, ever leaves the gift economy. We all give and receive non-monetary resources daily in this largely overlooked economy, within our families and our neighbourhoods and among our network of friends, associates and colleagues. They sustain us.

This is the economy that people live in when they fall through the floor of the "market-job-money" economy and it still acts as the essential base for the whole "market-money-job" economy as it waxes and wanes. It is the ultimate socio-economic safety net that is fundamentally necessary to keep home and hearth together, maintaining ourselves and our families and our communities.

JANINE

Non-profits can't pay for all they need just to stay in existence. Volunteers are absolutely necessary.

Barter Credit can help expand volunteering, and make life a bit better for the ones you have.

LAURA

I don't think of Barter Credit as "getting paid." I get acknowledged for what I do, and that's important.

And I can use that to get cleaning and yard work and free more volunteer time!

SHEILA

Using Barter Credit we can do a lot internally and with other non-profits - or with professionals for their services - without using up program money.

RUTH

None of us can renovate an office. But we can find people who can and pass on Barter Credit we earn doing what we can do.

So we turn some counseling or shopping for the elderly into a new floor- without using up our scarce program money.

Barter Credit Works
For The Whole Community

REBALANCING LOCAL MATERIAL LIFE

ORDINARY LIFE

Throughout most of the world and most of history ordinary life has been a seamless fabric of culture and commerce. The compartmentalization of life into separate realms of family and business life, personal and community life, economic and spiritual life belongs only to the modern "developed" world.

INVISIBLE SUPPORT

Even in developed nations today, however, the ordinary material life of families and communities has gone on invisibly supporting the whole structure of economic life, largely ignored by the apologists of development.

DEVELOPED LIVES

Barter Credit provides us with a modern way to put our lives back together again and regain control of our time, our work, our productivity - and our communities.

COMMUNITY IS HOME

Barter Credit gives us the opportunity to make the invisible supports of our material life visible once again by centreing our material life about the mundane work that has always kept home and family and community functioning.
Welcome Home!

WITH BARTER CREDIT WE CAN REDUCE OUR DEPENDENCE ON CONSUMERISM

IF WE HAVE NO CONSUMERISM DOES THAT MEAN WE HAVE NO COMMERCE?

HOME IS WHERE THE HEART IS

AND ALSO WHERE YOU CAN HANG YOUR WORK HAT

Barter Credit re-integrates community life. It is no longer necessary to divide commerce from communion, charity from trade, work from pleasure, need from demand, business and work from home and family, or bottom-line necessity from top-drawer quality of life.

Barter Credit provides a new way for people to realize their natural value, free from the bottleneck of money control. It is a new way to organize work in the old way - aligned to our personal time-tables - and it gives us a convenient way to match our productivity with our real needs.

Barter Credit provides a way for local business to regain its place in a convivial community economy and enhances our capacity to make our gifts of time and effort freely to community need and to our spiritual and cultural requirements.

Barter Credit provides us with a way to come home again to a holistic and sustainable life-style fitted to our locality and region and its special qualities and needs - safe from the colonization of "World Class" commerce based on money values.

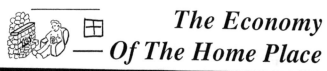

The Economy Of The Home Place

YOU CAN DO MORE WITH BARTER CREDIT

FIND OR CREATE AN ACTIVE GROUP THAT WILL TAKE THE LEAD IN CREATING A LOCAL ECONOMY

DISCOVER THE ALTERNATIVES THAT CAN BE DEVELOPED IN YOUR TOWN TO REPLACE COMMODIFIED INDUSTRIAL WORK

USING BARTER CREDIT WE CAN BUILD A NEW LOCAL ECONOMIC STRUCTURE ON THE INVISIBLE WORK OF HOME AND COMMUNITY

STARTING WITH PRODUCING AT HOME AND EXCHANGING FOR NEED WE CAN MAKE A SELF RELIANT LIVING MAKING COMMUNITY WORK

A MATTER OF CHOICE

New Economist Hazel Henderson says an economy is simply a set of rules devised by a culture to promote its cultural norms - what that culture thinks is valuable. The greatest error of our market-money apologists is the belief that the market can fulfill all human needs. But if we wish to function according to a different ethic, morality and set of values, we must function in a different economy.

We cannot operate in the hard world of the marketplace with the open morality of the family and the home. We cannot healthily operate the dynamics of home and family - or of community - with the commodified values of the market-place.

What keeps home, hearth and community together is a whole range of activities that are economic in nature but also familial and convivial.

In a Barter Credit economy we can evaluate what we do and produce in our own terms.

We can recapture those activities and those values into a holistic local economy that re-invents our ordinary material life. We need to begin writing the economic theory of the home-place. Barter Credit is the beginning.

The Community Circle
Is Now Complete

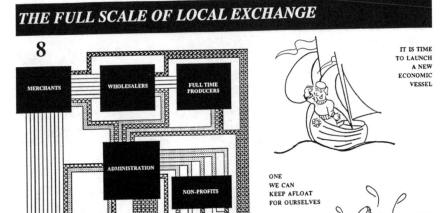

8

MERCHANTS | WHOLESALERS | FULL TIME PRODUCERS

ADMINISTRATION

NON-PROFITS

MEMBERS AS CONSUMERS | MEMBERS AS PRODUCERS

CONSUMER EXCHANGES
SYSTEM SERVICE EXCHANGES
WAGE & SERVICE EXCHANGES
CHARITABLE TITHING EXCHANGES

BCr ACCOUNTS

IT IS TIME
TO LAUNCH
A NEW
ECONOMIC
VESSEL

ONE
WE CAN
KEEP AFLOAT
FOR OURSELVES

IT'S ALWAYS WISE
TO HAVE A SPARE

DE-LINKED FROM MACRO-ECONOMICS
RE-LINKED TO LOCAL PRODUCTIVITY

The economy is really the activity of people dealing with one another in carrying on the necessary interactions of ordinary life - material and cultural, public and private. With modern computer technology, it is no longer necessary to measure and mediate this activity using a centrally-issued currency.

Banks today keep information about money electronically. If money is just a measure of value, then they are keeping information about the information about value. The money step is redundant. What we need to do is pay attention to the reality of value, not its measure.

Barter Credit is a way of keeping information directly about our exchanges with one another, and in doing that simple thing, we open up the possibility of a new way to function economically at the community level. Need, productivity, exchange and consumption can all be measured directly, giving us a true picture of our community economy, and the tools to manage it for ourselves.

The Choice Between Money and Barter Credit

THE MORALITY OF THE HUNT OR OF THE HOME

THE TRUTH ABOUT MONEY

IT IS OUT OF OUR CONTROL

Money is created by central authority
The control of the supply is external
We lose control of our economic life

POVERTY IS BUILT INTO MONEY

Money itself is traded as a commodity
Scarce money must be competed for
The price is always too great for some

MONEY IS INFLATIONARY

Money increase is the greatest good
Money increase itself is opted for
Money increase drives resource depletion

MONEY ALIENATES WEALTH

Our money comes to us only in response to
what we can offer, and then only for the added
value it can pick up and carry away: all other
results are secondary or accidental.

THE BARTER CREDIT DIFFERENCE

WE ARE IN CONTROL

Barter Credit is created by our exchanges
It is never scarce or in short supply
We have control of our economic life

NO MONEY POVERTY

Barter Credit is not tradeable
It is always available to all as needed
Only lack of resources can create poverty

IT IS INFLATION PROOF

Production for need is the greatest good
Only goods availability affects value
Resources are not depleted for profit

OUR WEALTH STAYS AT HOME

The value produced in our communities remains
at home as a currency which continuously circulates locally, preserving and passing on to its
members their own created wealth.

---

*Any government - band, village, town, or city - could organize the interior economy of its
jurisdiction to use Barter Credit instead of money. Doing so would free it from the restrictions
of the money economy and alter the dynamics of its community life to more traditional values
of family, community and home. It would unfetter the real capacity of its people from the
artificial restraints of money scarcity, and empower them to create their own wealth from their
own resources and community life. And keep that wealth under their own jurisdiction.*

213

The Choice
Is Available Now

COMPETITION OR CO-OPERATION

THE
BARTER CREDIT
ECONOMY

local not general

circular not reciprocal

sustainable not consumptive

fills needs not demands

produces for use not profit

cooperative not competitive

inclusive not exclusive

fosters community not isolation

creates belonging not alienation

functions by choice not coercion

contributary not extractive

conservationist not exploitative

rewards function not power

based on giving not taking

focuses on usership not ownership

relies on gifting not selling

honours home values not market values

internalizes family values not vendor values

214

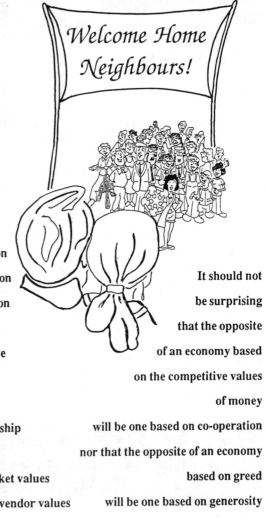

Welcome Home Neighbours!

It should not
be surprising
that the opposite
of an economy based
on the competitive values
of money
will be one based on co-operation
nor that the opposite of an economy
based on greed
will be one based on generosity

Local Sustainability And World Economics

THE COMMUNITY ECONOMY

The economies of our villages, towns and cities together create the economy of our nation, not the other way around. There is really no such thing as a national economy, and pretending that there is bases our economic life on misleading assumptions and false information.

The measure of the health of any so-called national economy is in the health of its community economies, and the health of those community economies is not measured in dollars but in the amount and extent of local production, local exchange, local consumption of local productivity, and locally focused community life.

Any community - to be a community - must produce for itself. Not everything, necessarily, but enough of its basic needs to be fundamentally self reliant. And the primary need it has is to produce its own employment and exchange.

To be counted a real community, it cannot rely on parachuted-in incomes and industries and parachuted-out consumer exchanges. Those that do are only partial or artificial communities, dependent on events elsewhere.

Real wealth grows at home.

JANE JACOBS

Macro-economics is the... theory and practice of... national and international economies. It is a shambles.

Never has a ... supposed science been so generously indulged, and never have experiments left in their wake more wreckage...

HAZEL HENDERSON

The new economic theories are going to grow out of what's happening now in every country... a resurgence of local level initiatives and... self-employment, small business, the growth of co-ops, and the growth of alternative limited purpose currencies to make up for the deficit when the national currency is not available to a local community to complete the trades they need to make with each other.

JOHN FRIEDMANN

To... transform themselves into politically active, producing units, families (ed: and communities) must selectively de-link from the system that keeps them in servitude.

(They) must learn to be more self-reliant in the production of life and do for themselves what they used to obtain from the market.

Appendix II

The LETSystem Described

Definition

A LETSystem, Local Exchange Trading System (also known as Local Employment and Trading System) is a self-regulating economic network which allows its account holders to issue and manage their own money supply within a bounded system.

Essential Characteristics

1. The agency maintains a system of accounts in a quasi-currency, the unit being related to the prevalent legal tender as 1/1.
2. All accounts start at zero, no money is deposited or issued.
3. The agency acts only on the authority of an account holder in making a credit transfer from that account to another.
4. While there is a general obligation to trade, there is never any obligation to trade at any specific time or with any particular person.
5. An account holder may know the balance and turnover of any other.
6. No interest is charged or paid on balances.
7. Administrative costs are recovered, in internal currency, from accounts on a cost-of-service basis.

Account Holders' Agreements

1. The LETSystem is a not-for-profit organization whose rights and authority are vested in a Trustee who acts as an agent for the account holders who are principals. The LETSystem provides an information exchange and recording service through which users can maintain such accounts of their trading as they require.
2. Account holders shall be willing to trade in the internal currency.

3. The trustee will transfer amounts of the internal currency from one account to another only on the authority of the account holder making payment.
4. The trustee may decline to record an acknowledgement considered inappropriate.
5. A unit of the internal currency shall be considered to represent a unit of value equal to the major unit of the national currency.
6. An account holder may know the balance and turnover of any other.
7. Accountability for taxes incurred by account holders as a result of their trading activity is the obligation of those involved in an exchange.
8. The LETSystem undertakes no obligation to report to taxation authorities or to collect taxes on their behalf.
9. The LETSystem makes no warranty or undertaking as to value, condition, or quality of the goods or services exchanged.
10. The trustee is authorized to levy charges on user accounts in the internal currency at rates assessed from time to time by the trustee in liaison with a board of advisors.

All the above elements are essential to qualify an organization as a LETSystem.

Landsman Community Services, Ltd., September 3, 1989
Community Circle Services, Inc., March 23, 1993

Appendix III

Some Published Accounts of LETSystems

Bonnie Bridge, "No Money Required," *Winnipeg Free Press Sunday Supplement*, May 14, 1989.

Ken McQueen, "No Money Down," *Ottawa Citizen*, Oct. 1, 1989.

Ben Garrison, "Everson Man Wants To Barter," *The Herald*, Bellingham, WA, 1989.

Judith Belton, "Do Not Pass Go, Do Not Collect $200...," *Times Colonist*, Victoria, B.C., June 8, 1986.

Marta Fritz, "Byta grejer ger nya vanner," *Alternativet*, Stockholm, Sweden, Nov. 1990.

"Community Development and Hillhurst/Sunnyside," *The Voice*, Calgary, Nov., 1987.

Brendan Weston, "Barter Late Than Never," *Montreal Mirror*, Jan. 24-31, 1991.

Donna Allen, "The Traders Who Throw Cash Away," *The Mail*, London, U.K., Jan. 6, 1991.

Bob Bater, "A Green-backed Community," date and provenance unknown, Bristol, U.K.

Alan Kershaw, "The Bartered Bride," *Future Shox, The Bulletin*, Melbourne, Australia, Jan. 9, 1991.

Christine Langlois, "Is Bartering Back?," *Canadian Living*, April, 1988.

Yolande Mennie, "Ottawa's (Cash) Free Market," date and provenance uncertain: probably the local paper in Wakefield, Québec.

Bert Hill, "Bucking The System," *Ottawa Citizen*, April 8, 1991.

Lesley Simpson, "Bartering Makes a Comeback," *Toronto Star*, January 5, 1991.

Helen Brown, "Back To Barter," *Sunday Focus*, New Zealand.

NOTES

Chapter One

1. John Friedmann, *Planning in the Public Domain: From Knowledge to Action*, Princeton University Press, 1987, Princeton, New Jersey, p. 358.
2. Adam Smith, *An Inquiry Into the Nature and Causes of the Wealth of Nations*, Edwin Canaan, ed., The University of Chicago Press, 1976, p. 18.
3. Lewis H. Lapham, *Money and Class in America: Notes and Observations on the Civil Religion*, Ballantine Books, New York, 1988.
4. George Woodcock, *Anarchism: A History of Libertarian Ideas and Movements*, Penguin Books, New York, 1986, p. 170. He is quoting Kropotkin in this passage, but does not attribute his quotation.
5. *Our Common Future, The Report of The World Commission on Environment and Development*, Oxford University Press, 1987.
6. This report of Keynes is made, without detailed reference, in *Small Is Beautiful: Economics as if People Mattered*, E.F. Schumacher, Harper and Rowe, New York, in 1975, p. 24. Italics added.
7. *Our Common Future*, op. cit., p. 44.
8. Alvin Toffler, *The Third Wave*, Bantam Books, Toronto, 1981.

Chapter Two

1. Braudel's work is in three volumes, Sian Reynolds, tr.: Volume I, *The Structures of Everyday Life;* Volume II, *The Wheels of Commerce;* Volume III, *The Perspective Of The World;* Fontana Press, 1985 (William Collins Sons & Co., Ltd., London, and Harper and Rowe, Publishers, Inc., New York, 1984). They are referred to hereinafter as Braudel, Vols. I, II, & III.
2. Braudel, Vol. I, p. 23.
3. Ibid. Italics added.
4. Braudel, Vol. I, pp. 23-24.
5. John Kenneth Galbraith, *Money: Whence it Came, Where it Went*, Houghton Mifflin Co., Boston, 1975, p. 5. (Italics added.)
6. Braudel, Vol. I, p. 24.
7. Bottomore, Tom, ed., *A Dictionary of Marxist Thought*, Harvard University Press, Cambridge, Mass., 1983, pp. 9-15; and *Karl Marx, Early Writings*, McGraw Hill, N.Y., 1963. See also Richard Schact, *Alienation*, pp. 73-122.
8. Braudel, Vol. I, pp. 23-24.
9. Toffler, op. cit., pp. 266-267.
10. Braudel, *After thoughts on Material Civilization and Capitalism*, The Johns Hopkins University Press, Baltimore, Md., 1977, pp. 5-6.
11. McRobie, *Small is Possible*, Sphere Books Ltd., London, 1982, p. 188.
12. Braudel, Vol. I, p. 24.
13. Braudel, Vol. III, p. 630.

Chapter Three

1. Michael Ignatieff, *The Needs of Strangers: An Essay on Privacy, Solidarity and the Politics of Being Human*, Penguin Books, New York, 1985, pp. 10-14.
2. Braudel, Vol. II, p. 64.
3. Bottomore, op. cit., pp. 9-15.
4. Braudel, Vol. I, p. 28, and Vol. III, pp. 628-632.
5. Braudel, Vol. I, p. 134.
6. Ibid, pp. 436-437.
7. Braudel, Vol. II, p. 59.
8. Ibid, p. 59.
9. See Chapter Ten, the section titled "Schumpeter's Equation." See also Braudel, Vol. II, p. 21.
10. Joyce Nelson, *Sultans of Sleaze: Public Relations and the Media*, Between the Lines, Toronto, 1989, p. 106.
11. Braudel, Vol. I, pp. 436-437.
12. Howard Adams, *Prison of Grass: Canada From a Native Point of View*, Fifth House Publishers, Saskatoon, Saskatchewan, 1987, p. 7.
13. Ibid, p. 26.
14. HKL & Associates, Ltd., *The Economics of Community Development*, a report prepared for the Native Economic Development Program, Province of Manitoba, January, 1986. One of the authors was John Loxley, current Chairperson, Department of Economics, University of Manitoba.
15. Peter B. Meyer, "Bio-regions as Econo-regions," *Raise the Stakes: The Planet Drum Review*, No. 11, Summer, 1986.
16. The example is Red Sucker Lake in Northern Ontario: the source of the statistics, private conversation with workers for the Mennonite Central Committee in Winnipeg.
17. Advertisement for Manufacturer's Life Insurance Company, *McLeans's Magazine*, Toronto, April 11, 1988, p. 20.
18. Laurier LaPierre, "Global Economics is Driving Us Into This Crazy Situation," *If You Love This Country*, David Suzuki, ed., McLelland and Stewart, Toronto, 1987, p. 66.
19. Dianne Maley, "New Wave Economics Good News," *The Winnipeg Free Press*, April 28, 1988.
20. Eric Kierans, former Canadian Minister of Finance, on the CBC-TV business series *Venture*, April, 1986, in a documentary about the LETSystem then functioning in Courtenay, B.C.

Chapter Four

1. Braudel, Vol. III, p. 27.
2. Barker, Penney & Seccombe, *Highrise and Superprofits*, Dumont Press Graphix, Kitchener, Ontario, 1973, p. 3.
3. Jane Jacobs, *The Economy of Cities*, Random House, New York, 1970, p. 131.
4. Jane Jacobs, *Cities and the Wealth of Nations*, Random Hose, New York, 1984, pp. 182-203.
5. Braudel, Vol. I, pp. 525-528.
6. Ibid.
7. Ibid, pp. 528-53.

8. Ibid, pp. 489-490.
9. Ibid, pp. 532-533.
10. Ibid, pp. 533.
11. Braudel, Vol. II, p. 64, or see Chapter Two, "Money and Power."
12. George McRobie, op. cit., p. 188.
13. Ibid, p. 185.
14. R.G. Collingwood, *The Principles of Art*, Oxford University Press, 1979, p. 101.
15. David Morris, *The New City States*, The Institute for Self Reliance, Washington, 1981, p. 5. Descriptions of Morris's work are also published in *Self-Reliant Cities:Energy and the Transformation of Urban America*, Sierra Club Books, San Francisco, 1982.
16. *Golem* is a Hebrew word meaning an artificially created life-form, made by man, not God, from lifeless matter.The creation usually runs amok, in cautionary tales, bringing grief to its maker. Frankenstein's monster, although made of human parts not clay, is a *golem*. Mary Shelley was criticizing the *hubris* of science. The same criticism is apt, I think, for the *hubris* of the apologists for rational economic man. So did, I believe, J.R.R. Tolkien, the author of *The Lord of the Rings*. He used a transliteration of the word as the name for his greed-imprisoned cave-creature, *Golum*.
17. Peter Berg, Beryl Magilavy and Seth Zuckerman, *A Green Cities Program for San Francisco Bay Area Cities and Towns*,Planet Drum Books, San Francisco, 1989, p. xii.
18. Ross Dobson, "Sustainable City, Sustainable Country," *City Magazine*, Polis Publishers, Winnipeg, Vol. 10, No. 3, Winter, 1988.
19. "Amish Economics," published in *The New Catalyst*, Lillooet, British Columbia, Fall, 1987 (a shortened version of an account that previously appeared in *Whole Earth Review*, as "Not Man Apart" and in *Fourth World Review*).
20. Murray Bookchin, "Radical Politics in an Era of Advanced Capitalism," *City Magazine*, Polis Publishing, Winnipeg, Vol. 11, No. 2, first quarter, 1990 (reprinted from *Green Perspectives*, The Green Program Project, Burlington, Vermont, No. 18, Nov., 1989), pp. 29-35.
21. Toffler, op. cit., pp. 266-267.

Chapter Five

1. Riane Eisler, *The Chalice and The Blade*, Harper and Rowe, San Francisco, 1987.
2. Howard Adams, op. cit., p. 22.
3. Lewis Hyde, "A Theory of Gifts," *The Gift: Imagination and the Erotic Life of Property*, Vintage Books, Random House, New York, 1979, p. 9.
4. Ibid.
5. Jacobs, *Cities and the Wealth of Nations*, op. cit., p. 218.
6. Daley, Herman E., and John B. Cobb, Jr., *For The Common Good: Redirecting the Economy Toward Community and the Environment and a Sustainable Future*, Beacon Press, Boston, 1989, p. 138.
7. David Cayley, ed., "Citizens at the Summit: Part III," *Ideas*, Canadian Broadcasting Corporation (Radio), Toronto, 1988.
8. Ibid.
9. E.F. Schumacher, *Small is Beautiful: Economics as if People Mattered*, Harper and Rowe, New York, 1975, p. 79.
10. Marilyn Waring, *If Women Counted: A New Feminist Economics*, Harper San Francisco, San Francisco, 1988, pp. 1-3.

11. Braudel, Vol. II, p. 21.
12. Vandana Shiva, "Development, Ecology and Women," *Healing The Wounds*, Judith Plant, ed., Between The Lines, Toronto, 1989, pp. 88-89.
13. "The Role and Limitations of Community-based Economic Development in Canada's North," *Alternatives*, Vol. 14, No. 1, Feb. 1987, pp. 31-34.
14. Robert J. Gordon, "Papua-New Guinea: Nation in the Making," *National Geographic Magazine*, Vol. 162, No. 2, August, 1982, pp. 147-148.
15. "Computerized Barter Clubs Eliminate Cash Deals," *The Globe and Mail*, Toronto, Jan. 20, 1992.
16. Braudel, Vol. II, p. 21. Or see Chapter Ten, the sections entitled *The LETS Money* and *Schumpeter's Equation*, and also footnote 1 of that chapter.
17. Schumacher, op. cit., p. 74.
18. "Building the Economy of Enough From Within," *Catalyst*, Citizens for Public Justice, Calgary and Toronto, Sept., 1983, Vol. 6, No. 8.
19. See Chapter Ten, the sections entitled *The LETSMoney* and *Schumpeter's Equation*, and also footnote 1 of that chapter. See also Braudel, Vol. II, p. 21.
20. Sam Dolgoff, *The Anarchist Collectives: Workers' Self-Management in the Spanish Revolution*, 1936-1939, Black Rose Books, Montreal-New York, 1990.
21. Friedmann, op. cit., p. 359.

Chapter Six

1. A videotape copy of the documentary, and a subsequent similar documentary done in 1991 by the CBC program *Marketplace*, describing the Ottawa LETSystem, are available (for viewing only) from Community Circle, Inc., 511 Newman St., Winnipeg, Manitoba, R3G 2V6.
2. Jacobs, *Cities and the Wealth of Nations*.
3. A videotape of the seminar with the class is available, for viewing only, from Community Circle, Inc., 511 Newman St., Winnipeg, Manitoba, Canada, R3G 2V6.
4. See Appendix II for a formal definition of the essential characteristics of a LETSystem.
5. For a description of how a LETSystem functions generally, please refer to Appendix II. For a detailed description please refer to Appendix I, the pamphlet *Building Community With Barter*.
6. The LETS computer program is written in Microsoft's dBase by Michael Linton. It is available in Freeware supplied by Landsman Community Services, Inc., of Courtenay, B.C. Later versions are now available that are free-standing and do not require the user to have a copy of dBase.

Chapter Seven

1. Jacobs, *Cities and the Wealth of Nations*, op. cit., pp. 38-44, and p. 110.

Chapter Eight

1. David Pell and Susan Wismer, op. cit.
2. Jane Jacobs, in an interview with Peter Gzowski, CBC-Radio *Morningside*, first hour, September 5, 1991.

Chapter Nine

1. The programs are available from Community Circle Services, Inc.
2. See Appendix I, the handbook *Building Community With Barter Credit.*

Chapter Ten

1. Braudel, Vol. I, Chapter 7, "Money," pp. 475-476. Braudel describes this as *"Schumpeter's Equation."* J.A. Schumpeter (1883-1950) was an Austrian economist who became a Harvard University professor after emigration to the U.S.A. in 1932. He is known for his theory that the entrepreneur is the dynamic factor in the business cycle, and for a theory of the economic development of capitalism, Braudel's principal focus. Source: *The Concise Columbia Encyclopedia,* Avon Books, New York, 1983, p. 756.

   The equating referred to, which took a long time to evolve and was only understood in the 18th Century (and not fully accepted until the 19th) moves toward money being considered *real:* getting it to that point was the *telic purpose* of the exercise, according to Braudel, and it is with this assumption that our money system now operates. But, as Braudel, and Schumpeter himself, point out, the equation also works in reverse: money is nothing but credit, a *note* denoting or representing a certain level of value, or, as Linton says, *a ticket of entitlement.*
2. Braudel, Vol. I, pp. 475-476.
3. Several LETSystems are operating in British Columbia. There are operative LETSystems in Ottawa, Toronto and Kitchener-Waterloo, Ontario. In the United States there are LETSystems in San Francisco, Los Angeles, Hawaii, and in New England. LETSystems are fast growing in New Zealand and Australia. There is a LETSystem in London, U.K., Wales, and in Stockholm, Sweden.

   Because LETSystems are self-replicating, it has proven impossible to maintain a comprehensive listing of them.

Chapter Eleven

1. Braudel, Vol III, p. 632.
2. Michael Ignatieff, op. cit., p. 10.
3. Ibid.
4. Ibid.
5. Lewis H. Lapham, op. cit.
6. Jean Bodin, "The Dearness of Things," *The Portable Renaissance Reader,* James Bruce Ross and Mary Martin McLaughlin, eds., Penguin Books, 1977, p. 202.
7. Ibid, p. 207.
8. Braudel, Vol. I, p. 24.
9. Michael Ignatieff, op. cit., p. 107.
10. Ibid, pp. 124 & 125.
11. Ibid, p. 126.
12. Anita Gordon and David Suzuki, *A Matter of Survival,* Stoddard Publishing, Ltd., Toronto, 1990, p. 148.
13. Braudel, Vol. II, p. 21.
14. Vandana Shiva, op. cit., pp. 87-89.

BIBLIOGRAPHY

Economics

Daley, Herman E., *Steady State Economics: The Economics of Biophysical Equilibrium and Moral Growth*, W.H. Freeman and Company, New York, 1977.

_____ and John B. Cobb, Jr., *For The Common Good: Redirecting the Economy Toward Community and the Environment and a Sustainable Future*, Beacon Press, Boston, 1989.

Dauncey, Guy, *After the Crash*, Green Print, The Merlin Press, Ltd., London, 1988.

Galbraith, J. K., *Money: Whence it Came, Where it Went*, Houghton Mifflin Co., Boston, 1975.

Hawken, Paul, *The Next Economy*, Holt, Reinhart and Winston, New York, 1983.

Hayek, F. A., *Choice of Currency and Denationalization of Currency*, Institute of Economic Affairs, London, 1976.

Heilbroner, Robert L., *The Worldly Philosophers*, Touchstone Books, Simon and Schuster, N.Y., 1980.

Henderson, Hazel, *The Politics of the Solar Age: Alternatives to Economics*, Anchor Books, Anchor Press/Doubleday, Garden City, New Jersey, 1981.

H.K.L. and Associates, Ltd., *The Economics of Community Development*: A Report prepared for the Native Economic Development Program, Province of Manitoba, January, 1986.

Jacobs, Michael, *The Green Economy: Environment, Sustainable Development, and the Politics of the Future*, Pluto Press, London, 1991.

Lapham, Lewis, *Money and Class in America: Notes and Comments on the Civil Religion*, Ballantine Books, New York, 1988.

Simon, Julian, *The Ultimate Resource*, Princeton University Press, Princeton, N.J., 1981

Smith, Adam, *An Inquiry Into the Nature and Causes of The Wealth of Nations*, Edwin Canaan, ed., The University of Chicago Press, 1976.

Waring, Marilyn, *If Women Counted: A New Feminist Economics*, Harper San Francisco, San Francisco, 1988.

White, A. D., *Fiat Money Inflation in France*, Private Publication by John McKay & Co., Toronto, 1914.

History

Adams, Howard, *Prison of Grass: Canada From a Native Point of View,* Fifth House Publishers, Saskatoon, Saskatchewan, 1989.

Braudel, Fernand, *Civilization and Capitalism, 15th to 18th Century,* Vol. 1, *The Structures of Everyday Life;* Vol II, *The Wheels of Commerce;* Vol. III *The Perspective of The World,* Sian Reynolds, tr., William Collins Sons & Co., London, 1984, Fontana Press, 1985.

———, *Afterthougths on Material Civilization and Capitalism,* Patricia M., Panum, tr., Johns Hopkins University Press, Baltimore and London, 1977.

Crowly, Terry, ed., *Clio's Craft: A Primer of Historical Methods,* Copp Clark, Toronto, 1988.

Darnton, Robert, *The Great Cat Massacre and Other Episodes in French Cultural History,* Vintage Books, Random House, New York, 1985.

Dolgoff, Sam, *The Anarchist Collectives: Workers' Self-Management in the Spanish Revolution,* 1936-1939, Black Rose Books, Montreal, 1990.

Ginsburg, Carlo, *The Cheese and The Worms:* The Cosmos of a Sixteenth Century Miller, John and Anne Tedeschi, tr., Penguin Books, 1982.

Hostetler, John A. and Gertrude Enders Huntington, *The Hutterites in North America,* Holt, Reinhart and Winston, New York, 1967.

Johnson, Paul, *A History of Christianity,* Penguin Books, 1984.

Jean Bodin, "The Dearness of Things," *The Portable Renaissance Reader,* Ross, James Bruce and Mary Martin McLaughlin, eds., Penguin Books, 1977, pp. 202-207.

Stanford, Michael, *The Nature of Historical Knowledge,* Basil Blackwell, Ltd., Oxford, 1986.

Tuchman, Barbara W., *A Distant Mirror: The Calamitous 14th Century,* Ballantine Books, New York, 1978.

Woodcock, George, *Anarchism: A History of Libertarian Ideas and Movements,* Penguin Books, New York, 1986.

Planning and Development

Blumenfeld, Hans, *The Modern Metropolis,* Paul D. Spreiregen, ed., M.I.T. Press, Cambridge, Mass., 1972.

Bowles, Ray T., *Social Impact Assessment in Small Communities,* Butterworth's, Toronto, 1985.

Campbell, Tom, *Seven Theories of Human Society,* Clarendon Press, Oxford, 1981.

Dobson, Ross, "Sustainable City, Sustainable Country," *City Magazine,* Winnipeg, Vol. 10, No.3, Winter, 1988, pp. 10-18.

Freidmann, John, *Planning in The Public Domain: From Knowledge to Action,* Princeton University Press, New Jersey, 1987.

Gordon, David, ed., *Green Cities: Ecologically Sound Approaches to Urban Space*, Black Rose Books, Montreal, 1990.

H.K.L. and Associates, Ltd., *The Economics of Community Development*; A Report prepared for the Native Economic Development Program, Province of Manitoba, January, 1986.

Jacobs, Jane, *The Death and Life of Great American Cities*, Random House, New York, 1961;

_____ , *The Economy of Cities*, Random House, New York, 1969;

_____ , *Cities and the Wealth of Nations*, Random House, New York, 1984.

Morris, David, *Self-reliant Cities: Energy and the Transformation of Urban America*, Sierra Club Books, San Francisco, 1982.

Nelson, Joyce, *The Sultans of Sleaze: Public Relations and The Media*, Between The Lines, Toronto, 1989.

Pell, David and Susan Wismer, "The Role and Limitations of Community-based Economic Development in Canada's North," *Alternatives*, Vol. 14, No. 1, Feb. 1987.

Smith, Michael P., *The City and Social Theory*, St. Martin's Press, New York, 1979.

Alternatives, Vol. 14, No. 1, Feb. 1987, pp. 31-34.

Other References

Baruchello, Gianfranco and Henry Martin, *How to Imagine: A Narrative on Art, Agriculture and Creativity*, Oxford University Press, 1979.

Bodley, John H., *Anthropology and Contemporary Human Problems* (Second Edition), Masyfield Publishing Company, Mountain View, California, 1985.

Brundtland, Gro Harlem, The Brundtland Report, *Our Common Future, The Report of The World Commission on Environment and Development*, Oxford University Press, 1987.

Hyde, Lewis, *The Gift: Imagination and The Erotic Life of Property*, Vintage Books, Random House, New York, 1983.

Ignatieff, Michael, *The Needs of Strangers*, Penguin Books, New York, 1984.

Gordon, Anita and David Suzuki, *A Matter of Survival*, Stoddard Publishing, Ltd., Toronto, 1990.

Gorz, Andre, *Ecology as Politics*, Patsy Vigderman and Jonathan Cloud, tr., Black Rose Books, Montreal, 1980.

Linton, Michael, *The LETSystem*, texts concerning the LETSystem published on computer disks by Landsman Community Services, Inc., Courtenay, B.C., 1983 - 1987.

Planet Drum Review, Planet Drum Foundation, San Francisco.

National Geographic Magazine, Vol. 162, No. 2, August, 1982.

INDEX

SUBJECT INDEX

CRITICAL PERSPECTIVES ON HISTORIC ISSUES

This series presents work from the Karl Polanyi Institute of Political Economy at Concordia University in Montréal. Karl Polanyi is justly famous for his book, The Great Transformation (1944), an original and penetrating analysis of the socio-political implications of a market economy and the disruption caused by attempts in the early 19th century to implement it. Polanyi emphasized the novelty of the "market system" as a potent cause of turmoil, although he also knew that previous societies had contained markets. How and why did the market shift from simply being one among many economic institutions to dominating the world system? To answer these questions, Polanyi initiated an ambitious interdisciplinary research project following World War II at Columbia University, and in the last decade, it has become evident that another generation of students is carrying on the project.

ISSN: 1195-1869

THE ANTHROPOLOGY OF POLITICAL ECONOMY: SITUATING ECONOMIC LIFE IN PAST SOCIETIES
Colin A.M. Duncan and David W. Tandy, editors

The papers in this collection are linked by their common origin in the set of profound questions forwarded by Polanyi's great post-war research programme. Each article both raises theoretical questions and presents historical material.

Colin Duncan is currently with the History Department at Queen's University, Kingston; David Tandy, the Classics Department of the University of Tennessee, Knoxville.

200 pages $19.95
Paperback ISBN: 1-895431-88-3 $38.95
Hardcover ISBN: 1-895431-89-1

HUMANITY, SOCIETY, AND COMMITMENT: ON KARL POLANYI
Kenneth McRobbie, editor

Karl Polanyi's lesser-known writings, his correspondence, teaching, and views on the future of socialism are brought together for the first time in this exciting and timely collection.

Kenneth McRobbie teaches cultural studies and intellectual history at the University of British Columbia. He is a poet and a translator of contemporary Hungarian verse.

210 pages $19.95
Paperback ISBN: 1-895431-84-0 $38.95
Hardcover ISBN: 1-895431-85-9

EUROPE: CENTRAL AND EAST
Marguerite Mendell and Klaus Nielsen, editors

This book examines the impact of the recent changes in Eastern Europe and the former Soviet Union from socio-economic, political, and cultural perspectives. It speaks of a new ideology which values markets over people, and raises the issue of the role of local communities — can these now be mobilized to form the basis for alternative community-based strategies, or will they more likely turn inward and become protective, suspicious and fearful of the future?

Marguerite Mendell holds a Ph.D. in economics and is principal at the School of Community and Public Affairs, Concordia University, where she also teaches political economy. Klaus Nielsen is Associate Professor at Roskilda University in Denmark.

200 pages $19.95
Paperback ISBN: 1-895431-90-5 $38.95
Hardcover ISBN: 1-895431-91-3

ARTFUL PRACTICES: THE POLITICAL ECONOMY OF EVERYDAY LIFE
Henri Lustiger-Thaler and Daniel Salée, editors

Behind the transformation of our post-war social, economic and political institutions, a larger drama is being played out as broad segments of the population are increasingly marginalized and left alone to face the tyranny of ever-triumphant market forces. This book examines the artful practices of citizens coping with these massive changes and points to a new political economy of everyday life.

Henri Lustiger-Thaler is with the Department of Sociology and Anthropology at Concordia University. His most recent publication is *Political Arrangements*. Daniel Salée is with the School of Community and Public Affairs at Concordia University.

200 pages
Paperback ISBN: 1-895431-92-1
Hardcover ISBN: 1-895431-93-X

$19.95
$38.95

THE LIFE AND WORK OF KARL POLANYI
Kari Polanyi-Levitt, editor

Polanyi's insights into the social and political impact of the market-driven economy were both timely and prescient, and have guaranteed him a place among the great thinkers of the twentieth century...a good starting place for those wanting to know more about Polanyi, and a useful source for anyone seeking to understand our "interesting" times.
Canadian Book Review Annual

264 pages, photographs
Paperback ISBN: 0-921689-80-2
Hardcover ISBN: 0-921689-81-0

$19.95
$38.95

* * *

FROM THE GROUND UP: ESSAYS ON GRASSROOTS AND WORKPLACE DEMOCRACY
C. George Benello

Len Krimerman, Frank Lindenfeld, Carol Korty and Julian Benello, editors
Foreword by Dimitrios Roussopoulos

George Benello argues that modern social movements need to rise to the challenge of spearheading a radical reorganization of society based on the principles of decentralization, community control, and participatory democracy.

Where the utopian confronts the practical, Benello is perhaps most creative...a valuable contribution to creating a new politics.
Z Magazine

251 pages, index
Paperback ISBN: 1-895431-32-8
Hardcover ISBN: 1-895431-33-6

$19.95
$38.95

DISSIDENCE: ESSAYS AGAINST THE MAINSTREAM
Dimitrios Roussopoulos

Dissidence is a collection of writings by Dimitrios Roussopoulos from the journal he founded, *Our Generation*. The best of the Montréal Left always stood apart from that of the Canadian and North American Left. These writings reflect the unique politico-cultural cauldron this city created from the sixties to the eighties. The contribution of Dimitrios Roussopoulos is often that of a dissenter, not only from mainstream society, but also from within the Left.

240 pages
Paperback ISBN: 1-895431-40-9
Hardcover ISBN: 1-895431-41-7

$19.95
$38.95